CW01496197

VIC KEEGAN'S LOST LONDON

IGNATIUS SANCHO

First published in 2020
by Shakespearesmonkey
174 Ashley Gardens
London SW1P 1PD

ISBN: 978-0-9540762-7-6

Cover illustration Christopher Keegan
www.chriskeegan.co.uk

Formatting and Compilation by The Amethyst Angel

Victor Keegan's blogs:
OnLondon.co.uk (Lost London section)
LondonMyLondon.co.uk
victorkeegan.com
Instagram - vickeegan
Flickr - Flickr.com/shakespearesmonkey
Twitter: @vickeegan
@BritishWino
@LonStreetwalker
@ShakespearesLon

victor.keegan@gmail.com

First Edition

CONTENTS

1: WESTMINSTER'S PRISON GATE

2: THE HIDDEN HOTEL CECIL

3: THREE MYTHS ABOUT CLEOPATRA'S NEEDLE

4: THE REMAINS OF THE WHITE FRIARS' HOME

5: THE SWAN THEATRE

6: THE SPITALFIELDS CHARNEL HOUSE

7: THE MILLBANK PENITENTIARY

8: HIDDEN HISTORY OF HOLBORN VIADUCT

9: THE WESTMINSTER OPERA HOUSE THAT NEVER WAS

10: THE GRAVE OF ALEXANDER DAVIES

11: CHARLES I VERSUS OLIVER CROMWELL

12: SAINT PANCRAS OLD CHURCH

13: MESOLITHIC VAUXHALL

14: THE SOUTH BANK COADE STONE LION

15: THE BAR AT BERMONDSEY ABBEY

16: THE REMAINS OF THE MARSHALSEA

17: THE CANTERBURY MUSIC HALL

18: ALL HALLOWS-BY-THE-TOWER

19: THE OAK ROOF OF WESTMINSTER HALL

20: PINEAPPLES

21: ST MARY ALDERMANBURY

22: THE GARDEN OF WESTMINSTER ABBEY

23: THE MONUMENT

24: THE JERUSALEM CHAMBER

25: THE CLEARY VINEYARD

26: ST MARY WOOLNOTH

27: THE MIRACLE OF THE WANDLE

28: MARX, LENIN AND THE SECRET OF MARX HOUSE

29: TRACES OF IGNATIUS SANCHO

30: ELIZABETH I AT ST DUNSTAN-IN-THE-WEST

31: THE WHITECHAPEL BELL FOUNDRY

32: THE REMAINS OF THOMAS CROMWELL'S GARDEN

33: SHAKESPEARE'S NEWINGTON BUTTS

34: THE MEDIEVAL JEWEL TOWER

35: THE TEXAS EMBASSY

36: THE MIDDLE TEMPLE HALL

37: QUEENHITHE DOCK

38: STAINED GLASS AT ST MARGARET'S CHURCH

39: THE GARDEN MUSEUM

40: THE INVISIBLE BAYNARD CASTLE

41: FINDING LONDON WALL

42: THE STATUES OF VAUXHALL BRIDGE

43: THE REMAINS OF THE FIRST SOMERSET HOUSE

44: THE HAUNTINGLY BEAUTIFUL TEMPLE CHURCH

45: THE THAMES WATERMEN'S SEAT OF POWER

46: THE GRAY'S INN TIME WARP

47: BEDLAM'S PROGRESS

48: THE FISHMONGERS' HALL

49: THE THAMES FORESHORE

50: THE RING OF FORTS

51: THE WORLD'S FIRST CIRCUS

52: THE DEVIL'S ACRE

53: CARDINAL WOLSEY'S WINE CELLAR

54: THE ORIGIN OF PARLIAMENT

55: TRACES OF THE GREAT EXHIBITON

56: LONDON'S FIRST SHOPPING MALL

57: FLEET PRISON

58: QUEEN ANNE'S MANSIONS 'MONSTER BLOCKS'

59: THE BROADWOOD PIANO FACTORY

60: HOW ELECTRICITY FLOWED FROM MAYFAIR ART

61: PENAL FOUNDATIONS OF WESTMINSTER CATHEDRAL

62: THE AGELESS BEAUTY OF THE BLEWCOAT SCHOOL

63: THE ROYAL AQUARIUM

64: THE NOTORIOUS NEWGATE PRISON

65: THE GREAT EASTERN STEAMSHIP

66: THE STATUE THAT WAS TOO BIG FOR ITS BOOTS

67: THE SPARKLING DUCK ISLAND

68: THE WESTMINSTER ABBEY ANCHORAGE

69: THE DUKE OF YORK'S COLUMN

70: ALBION MILLS

71: CHELSEA PHYSIC GARDEN

72: LONDON ROOTS OF HARVARD, SMITHSONIAN & YALE

73: PRINCE ALBERT'S MANSIONS FOR THE POOR

74: THE DISAPPEARING RIVER TYBURN

75: SHAKESPEARE'S BOAR'S HEAD

76: KENNINGTON PALACE

77: THE MOVING STATUES OF TRAFALGAR SQUARE

78: MAPPING THE SLAVE TRADERS' HOMES

79: THE CHURCH OF ST MAGNUS THE MARTRYR

80: THE LAMBETH ROOTS OF ROYAL DOULTON

81: BLACKFRIARS MONASTERY

82: SHAKESPEARE'S BLACKFRIARS THEATRE

83: THE PERFIDIOUS ROGUE OF DOWNING STREET

84: THE MEDIEVAL TOWER OF LAMBETH

85: QUEEN MARY'S STEPS

86: THE HUGE NORTHUMBERLAND HOUSE

87: THE ROYAL UNITED SERVICES MUSEUM

88: THE THREE TUNS PUB

89: ELEANOR'S CROSSES

90: THE COCKPIT STEPS

91: THE DEEP ROOTS OF THE LONDON PLANE TREE

92: ST GILES AND GIN LANE

93: EAST INDIA COMPANY'S LEADENHALL STREET HOME

94: RAGGED SCHOOLS

95: THE GATEHOUSE PRISON

96: THE OTHER CRYSTAL PALACE

97: A MEETING AT THE COLONIAL OFFICE

98: PAVLOVA ON THE PALACE

99: THE PIMLICO ROOTS OF WIMBLEDON

100: WHERE TO LOOK FOR LONDON BRIDGE

101: ST ETHELDREDA'S CHURCH

102: THE SOCIETY FOR THE DIFFUSION OF USEFUL KNOWLEDGE

103: THORNEY ISLAND

104: SHIPBUILDING ON THE THAMES

105: THE LION BREWERY OF WATERLOO

106: THE TOMB OF THE BARE-KNUCKLE FIGHTER

107: EDWARD III'S THAMES-SIDE MANOR HOUSE

108: JACOB'S ISLAND

109: THE GREAT DUST HEAP

110: IN SEARCH OF POCAHONTAS

111: ELIZABETH WOODVILLE'S WESTMINSTER ABBEY SANCTUARY

112: JAMES I'S MULBERRY TREE MISTAKE

113: THE LITERARY HISTORY OF ST JOHN'S GATE

114: THE HORRIBLE HOCKLEY-IN-THE-HOLE

115: GEORGE TRAIN'S VICTORIA STREET TRAM

116: EROTIC ABANDON AT RANELAGH GARDENS

117: SHAKESPEARE IN PALL MALL

118: THE LINCOLN'S INN FIELDS THEATRE

119: GEORGE WILKINS — BROTHEL-KEEPER, PLAYWRIGHT, THUG

120: FLEET STREET'S DAILY COURANT

121: ELEPHANT & CASTLE'S LEISURE SPECTACULARS

122: PALMER'S VILLAGE —
WESTMINSTER'S PIECE OF MERRIE ENGLAND

123: CLERKENWELL HOUSE OF DETENTION

124: VICTORIAN TEA SHOP, STRAND

125: THE DEVIL TAVERN

126: THE BLACKFRIARS ROTUNDA

127: HOLLAND'S LEAGUER, THE LUXURY THAMESIDE
HOUSE OF ILL REPUTE

128: THE REMAINS OF COLONEL BLOOD

129: BRUNEL THE ELDER'S WONDROUS TUNNEL

130: THE ABBEY UNDER THE MINT

131: SHAKESPEARE'S UNDERGROUND LODGINGS

132: WATER TROUGHS OF A HORSE-DRAWN PAST

133: THE FIRST CURRY HOUSE IN TOWN

134: GREAT GARAGES OF MAYFAIR AND ST JAMES'S

135: THE ORIGINAL HUNGERFORD FOOTBRIDGE

136: THE WALLACE COLLECTION

137: THE EXPLODING TEMPLE OF GREEN PARK

138: THE ORIGINAL WATERLOO BRIDGE

139: THE GREAT ROYAL JEWELS HEIST OF 1303

140: THE GOTHIC FOREIGN OFFICE THAT NEVER WAS

141: THE 'HIDEOUS' MORLEY'S HOTEL

142: VICTORIA'S SHORT-LIVED TURKISH BATHS

143: THE GRAND EXTRAVAGANCE OF CARLTON HOUSE

144: THE UNMARKED HOME OF 'REAL TENNIS'

145: THE HOUSE OF JUDGE JEFFREYS

146: FORGOTTEN FACADES OF BUCKINGHAM PALACE

147: THE ADMIRALTY'S HIDDEN CITADEL

148: THE STAR & GARTER'S SPORTING PAST

149: THE GREEN-FINGERED TRADESCANTS OF LAMBETH

150: THE AMAZING ST MARGARET'S

151: THE OTHER GREAT EXHIBITION

152: THE 10TH CENTURY ORIGINS OF SCOTLAND YARD

153: THE COWS OF ST JAMES'S PARK

154: THE ORIGINAL WESTMINSTER BRIDGE

155: PALACES OF THE STRAND

156: MONTAGU HOUSE —
ORIGINAL HOME OF THE BRITISH MUSEUM

157: THE HERO AND THE VILLAIN OF KING CHARLES STREET

158: THE HOUSE WHERE WILLIAM BLAKE LIVED

159: THE MEDIEVAL CITY OF VINEYARDS

160: THE MONUMENTAL LEGACY OF ELEANOR COADE

LOST LONDON MAP

Numbers are placed in approximate places. Those on the very edge indicate locations off the map. To view the map online visit LondonMyLondon.co.uk

POETRY BOOKS BY VICTOR KEEGAN

Crossing the Why

Big Bang

Remember to Forget

Alchemy of Age

London my London

Selective Memories

Duelling Poets (with Michelle Gordon)

INTRODUCTION

My London epiphany happened when I discovered that beneath the road where we lived in Victoria were the remains of a large prison which I had been ignorant of throughout the many decades I had lived there. Around a couple of corners, it turned out, the biggest piano manufacturing factory in the world - beloved by Beethoven - had been located of which no traces remain. On the other side of the road was The Gas, Light and Coke Company the first company in the world to supply public gas and which installed the first public gaslights of which hundreds still exist in central London. Today we know it as British Gas.

Once retirement beckoned this prompted me to exploit a latent curiosity about the rest of London stimulated by looking at old books, old maps and, of course, Internet searches. I started putting them up on a new website LondonMyLondon.co.uk (now largely given over to poems) but soon found that, deprived of the deadlines which made my previous career in journalism so interesting, I soon found that my posts were getting less and less frequent.

Then along came Dave Hill, a former colleague at the Guardian. His regular column on the politics of London had ended and he had set up his own website onlondon.co.uk to cover politics, economics and culture and other happenings across London which the Evening Standard does not adequately cover.

We soon came around to the idea of me trying a weekly column on Lost London. There was no question of being paid because it was a start-up with very little money – but for me the attraction was a weekly deadline with Dave doing all the marketing for it which I am no good at. I told him that it was unlikely that I would be able to unearth 100 items. At the time of writing I have reached 160 and finding it more difficult to find places that may be of general interest. I have no idea whether I will reach 200 which is the reason for publishing this not-for-profit book containing what I have done so far

I am not short of other things to do but researching for the column fulfils several useful goals. In retirement it is vital to have something interesting to do which this certainly is. I also like walking (one of my Twitter feeds is called LonStreetWalker) so I always walk to places I am researching in order to examine them and take photos. It is much better to walk with a purpose rather than solely for exercise.

Above all, it is revealing to me, week by week, the astonishing buried history of this amazing capital and its river, the Thames, without which it would never have existed in the first place.

Vic Keegan

1: WESTMINSTER'S PRISON GATE

The Supreme Court, Britain's highest court of appeal, looks boldly out over Parliament Square. But if you go around the back to a little used road called Little Sanctuary (so called because prisoners in medieval times used to be able to seek sanctuary there) you will see a stone-framed doorway 5ft 10 inches tall that looks like the tradesmen's entrance.

In fact it is the actual entrance to the long-demolished Tothill Fields Bridewell prison, dating back to 1618. It started off as a "House of Correction" enforcing employment on indolent poor people but was eventually enlarged to become a full-blown prison. It was situated next door to the Greencoat School (roughly where the Greencoat pub is today in Greencoat Place, Victoria).

In 1834 the Bridewell was replaced by a larger prison nearby in Francis Street where Westminster Cathedral now stands. It turned out to be much better for some than living outside. Almost half of inmates were recommittals compared with a national average of 25%.

It is not clear how the original entrance made its journey to the Supreme Court, but history has its own serendipity. Some prisoners who pass through prison doors end up with their cases being decided in the Supreme Court. Maybe we should view it more as an artwork or installation.

2: THE HIDDEN HOTEL CECIL

Most people pass by 80 The Strand without a second glance. There is no sign that this is the Strand entrance to what used to be called Shell Mex House, with its dramatic frontage on to the Thames, until the oil industry moved out in the 1990s. The reason for that is that the entire front of the building on the Strand side, not just the facade, hosts the remains of the 1,000 room Hotel Cecil, once the biggest and most sumptuous in Europe and quite possibly the world. Its three dining rooms could serve over 1,000 customers and it was a hugely popular in the Roaring Twenties, especially with tourists from the United States.

Often known colloquially as the Cecil Hotel (rather than the other way round), it covered a three-and-a-half acre site down to the bank of the river. Its builder, the notorious Victorian fraudster Jabez Balfour MP (whose biography has been written by David McKie), went bankrupt and fled to South America before the hotel was finally completed by the liquidator in 1896. It was called the Hotel Cecil because the site had been sold by the Marquess of Salisbury, head of the historic Cecil family, whose ancestors had built a vast palace called Cecil House on the same stretch of land.

3: THREE MYTHS ABOUT CLEOPATRA'S NEEDLE

There are three things you need to know about Cleopatra's Needle. First, it has nothing to do with Cleopatra. Second, it's not a needle. Third, it was never intended to be on the Embankment, where it is now.

It is an obelisk dedicated to the Sun God made during the reign of Thutmose III, a Pharaoh who lived over 1,000 years before Cleopatra. It was intended to be located in Parliament Square, where a full size wooden replica was erected to gauge what it would look like there. But that plan fell through when the builders of the District Line demanded that the government take out insurance in case it collapsed on to the railway beneath.

At 3,500 years old, Cleopatra's Needle is easily the most ancient visible monument in London. It is one of two granite obelisks, both 68 feet high. Its "twin" stands in Central Park, New York and a third, unrelated to the other two, is in the Place de la Concorde in Paris.

It was presented to the UK in 1819 by the ruler of Egypt and Sudan, Muhammad Ali, to commemorate the victories of Sir Ralph Abercromby at the Battle of Alexandria in 1801 and Sir Horatio Nelson at the Battle of the Nile in 1798. Maybe it should have been called Nelson's Column.

4: THE REMAINS OF THE WHITE FRIARS' HOME

The photo shows all that remains of a priory run by Carmelite friars, who became known as the White Friars for on occasion wearing white mantles over their brown habits. It can trace its origins back to 1253 after the friars arrived in London, having been expelled by Saracens from the Holy Land, where their order was founded.

For centuries the church with its buildings and gardens occupied all the space on a large site between Fleet Street and the Thames. It was thus well positioned on the road between the City of London (enclosed by a wall in those days) and the government in Whitehall, though the area itself was insalubrious and many friars died because of the unsanitary conditions.

The priory survived the Peasants' Revolt of 1381, which destroyed surrounding buildings, but not Henry VIII's dissolution of the monasteries in the mid-16th century, when most of the lands were given to Henry's doctor, Sir William Butts, who allowed them to fall into disrepair.

However, in 1608 the dining hall was converted into the Whitefriars Theatre by shareholders including Michael Drayton, one of the most distinguished poets of the age. He, according to gossip in Stratford-upon-Avon, had a drinking session with Ben Jonson and William Shakespeare which resulted in Shakespeare becoming ill and dying.

The remains of the old priory can be approached through the narrow Magpie Alley off Bouverie Street. They are down some stairs at the end of the alley, which also depicts the history of printing including a new journal "The Artful Dodger" launched in 1840.

5: THE SWAN THEATRE

Of all London's lost memories this must be one of the lostest. As you come out of the wonderful new Blackfriars station on the southern side of the river, you will see on your right a big office block. (Which has been demolished since this photo was taken.) You can see the other side of it as you emerge from the Tate Modern.

There is no plaque there, but this was the site of the Swan Theatre, the biggest of Elizabethan times. Opened in 1574, it had room for up to 3,000 people, more than any dedicated theatre in London today and larger than the more famous Globe and Rose theatres 500 or so yards away along the riverbank. As London's population was barely 200,000 during that period, this means that a large proportion of Londoners would have been regular theatre customers.

It is because of the Swan that we have the only sketch of what an Elizabethan theatre actually looked like. It was drawn by a visiting Dutchman, Claes Visscher, and has become the template for thinking about how other contemporary theatres looked.

The Swan was situated in an ancient estate called Paris Garden which was a "liberty" and therefore outside the jurisdiction of the City. It was a seedy place situated close to Holland's Leaguer, the most notorious brothel in the country. It had its own drawbridge, which was pulled up when occasion demanded.

Nothing remains of the Swan because the office block was built before archaeological surveys were made compulsory. Paris Garden, once owned by Jane Seymour, Henry VIII's third wife, has also disappeared – except for a street named after it.

In 1597 the Isle of Dogs, a play by Ben Jonson and Thomas Nashe, was put on at the Swan, leading to their arrest for staging seditious material. No record of the text exists today. Shakespeare must have lived nearby, because in 1596 a restraining order was served on him and others by someone who feared that "gentle" Shakespeare might be putting his life at risk.

THE SWAN PLAYHOUSE
(From Visscher's *View of London*, 1616).

6: THE SPITALFIELDS CHARNEL HOUSE

The charnel house in Spitalfields is the only medieval building still to be found in the whole of Tower Hamlets. Yet you could easily live near it without knowing it is there. Unless you look downwards through a glass pavement (see photo) at 1 Bishops Square as you walk across it, or turn a sharp left and go down some stone stairs to a subterranean level, you will miss it completely.

There, behind thick glass that makes it look like a medieval aquarium, you can stare at what remains, along with a recently added sculpture (pictured) which adds to the sense of the macabre.

The charnel house started its life as a chapel, but for most of its existence it served as a place where the large and ancient Priory of Saint Mary Spital – "spital" is short for hospital – kept the bones of the deceased so that prayers could be said for the rigrepose of their souls.

It dates from the early 1300s, though the hospital – a word deriving its name from the word "hospitality" – was founded in the late 12th century, probably on the site of an earlier Roman cemetery.

The charnel house only came to light 20 years ago when builders constructing the new Norman Foster office block on the site came across remains which had previously not been known about. Goodness knows how many more were lost before the government changed the regulations to require archaeological surveys on sites believed to contain them.

7: THE MILLBANK PENITENTIARY

Across the road from the Morpeth Arms pub, which stands between Vauxhall and Lambeth bridges on the north bank of the Thames, you will see a large stone post. It is an original, and marks the spot where prisoners were taken from the vast 18-acre Millbank Prison, where Tate Britain now stands, to be transported to Australia. It is said that the word "Pom" – as in Prisoner of Millbank – originated here. It is as good an explanation as any.

The octagonal prison, originally conceived as a national penitentiary, opened in 1816. It was devised by Jeremy Bentham to be run on liberal principles (though it didn't work out quite that way in practice) and could hold up to 1,000 men and women. Charles Dickens said the discipline here was "rather severe". It closed in 1890.

The Morpeth Arms, a carefully restored Grade 11 listed building purchased by Youngs in 1984, is situated across the road from the post at the western end of the former jail. Turn right as you come out of the main entrance to the Tate.

In its basement you can still see some of the cells (pictured) and the blocked up entrance to the tunnel that prisoners passed through to reach a waiting boat on the river. If the bar staff are not busy, and you are a customer, ask nicely as they might, just might, even take you down there.

8: HIDDEN HISTORY OF HOLBORN VIADUCT

Amazon's swanky new London office at 60 Holborn Viaduct is built adjacent to the site of the world's first coal-fired power station and also on the site of the oldest pub in London, The Three Tuns, the remains of which are still buried underneath it.

The power station, which began operating in January 1882, was built at Number 57 by the indomitable Thomas Edison as a trial run for his later projects in New York. It had a Babcock and Wilcox boiler and was able to supply electricity for lighting along Newgate Street from the City Temple and the Old Bailey to the General Post Office.

This was thanks initially to the existence of underground culverts built as part the Viaduct's construction, itself one of the great feats of Victorian engineering, which required the demolition of over 4,000 mainly slum homes. This enabled Edison to cock a snook at the gas companies which enjoyed a monopoly on digging up roads for underground cable laying at that time.

Although the experiment was ended after two years, mainly because of cut-throat competition from gas, it paved the way for Edison's triumph in New York and for the mistaken view of many Americans that the first public coal-fired power station was built in the Big Apple rather than London.

However, to beer drinkers the more interesting discovery was the unearthing by Museum of London archaeologists a few years ago of the extensive remains – including walls 2.5 metres high – of a the pub beneath Number 60. This dates back to medieval times, though it was enlarged in the 16th century and later. The pub buildings, which included a brewery and a taproom, straddled Snow Hill, which was then part of the main road from Newgate to the west.

The discovery added a new dimension to the thorny problem of deciding which is London's oldest pub. This is the oldest whose original walls still exist, but there are others that claim to have existed for just as long, but whose structures have since been completely rebuilt.

9: THE WESTMINSTER OPERA HOUSE THAT NEVER WAS

Pictured here is what would have been Europe's, and maybe the world's, grandest opera house, on a site between the Embankment and Whitehall, close to Westminster Underground station. You think I'm kidding? It was very nearly completed. Construction began during the 1870s and proceeded to roof level, using over five million bricks, before the impresario behind it, James Mapleson, ran out of money. Instead of becoming a 2,000-seat National or Grand Opera House as planned, it lay derelict for several years before being demolished, a tragedy no opera could match.

Except not all of it was pulled down. The foundations, which went deeper than the adjoining District Line, were so strong that they were retained and remain to this day. New Scotland Yard, the second HQ of the Metropolitan Police, was erected on them and opened in 1890, prompting the Mapleson family to complain that rooms intended for opera stars were now occupied by prisoners. (In 1967, when the Met moved again, the offices were renamed as one of the Norman Shaw Buildings, after their distinguished architect. They now augment the Palace of Westminster).

The opera house was conceived on a grand scale, with subterranean passages both to the Houses of Parliament – so members could get back in time for the division bell – and to Westminster Tube. They are still there. The site was so large that Mapleson had arranged for the Lyric Club to occupy one corner and the Royal Academy of Music another. It would also have contained a new concert room, together with a large gallery for pictures not accepted by the hanging committee of the Royal Academy to be called "Rejected Gallery", quite possibly modelled on the earlier Salon Des Refusés in Paris.

Mapleson even built a small steamer to tug a large houseboat conveying members of opera companies down the river for rehearsals or recreation. Of all the lost buildings in London, this is surely the saddest.

10: THE GRAVE OF ALEXANDER DAVIES

St Margaret's Church yard in Parliament Square is not short of famous dead bodies, being the resting place of William Caxton, Sir Walter Raleigh, Wenceslaus Hollar, the brilliant engraver of London, and the largest number of regicides you'll find anywhere.

Yet, curiously, there is only one tomb that is above ground. It is near the road and completely ignored by passers-by. And it is the source of the greatest property wealth this country has ever known.

Here lies Alexander Davies, a scrivener, who died of the plague, heavily in debt, in July 1665, leaving a seven-month-old daughter, Mary. She eventually inherited 500 acres of worthless pasture land in what we know today as Belgravia, Pimlico, Buckingham Palace and Mayfair.

To cut a long story short, Mary was married at age 12 to a little known baronet in the north, Sir Thomas Grosvenor, who at the time was busy building his family seat, Eaton Hall. By all accounts they had a happy 20 years together before Mary became mentally ill around 1697.

A few years later Sir Thomas died, leaving behind what became Britain's richest estate and which has remained almost entirely within the Grosvenor family – now headed by the Duke of Westminster – ever since.

11: CHARLES I VERSUS OLIVER CROMWELL

You have to know that it is there. Situated rather high up the wall on the eastern side of Saint Margaret's Church, opposite Westminster Hall, is a lead bust of King Charles I, found in a Fulham junk yard in around 1945 by Hedley Hope-Nicholson, secretary of the Society of King Charles the Martyr. Yes, they want to make Charles a saint.

Hope-Nicholson donated the sculpture to the church in the 1950s. It is poignantly positioned because on the other (western) side of the church, most of the regicides who signed his death warrant are buried under the lawn between St Margaret's and Westminster Abbey.

Look behind you in the direction of Westminster Hall and see that Charles is staring across the road at a statue of none other than Oliver Cromwell, his executioner, erected much earlier, in 1899, at a cost of £500 in the face of furious opposition from Irish MPs.

Another bust of Charles found in the same place at the same time – one account says there were three in that Fulham junkyard altogether – is located nearby in Whitehall at the Banqueting House, where Charles was executed in 1649. And further on, at Charing Cross, is another likeness of Charles, this one a statue of him on a horse, probably cast in 1633 and the oldest equestrian statue in London.

And so, centuries after his death, Charles is taking a long look at Cromwell and at the place of his demise. Civil wars never end, they just change their tactics.

12: SAINT PANCRAS OLD CHURCH

Saint Pancras old church – not to be confused with its Johnny-come-lately namesake on the Euston Road – deserves to have a book written about it. The original building goes back to the fourth century, pre-dating Saint Peter's in Rome and making it one of the oldest churches in Christendom. But that is not what attracts people to this icon on the former bank of the River Fleet, a short walk from Saint Pancras station along the Camden Road.

Pride of place is the Thomas Hardy tree, whose enveloping roots seem to grip the gravestones, not wanting to let go. They were positioned there in the 1865, when the future novelist and poet was working as an assistant architect on the expansion of the Midland Railway. This entailed the young Hardy moving the gravestones and the remains beneath them from their original locations. Some became affixed to the tree. Very Hardyesque.

A few yards away is a mausoleum for the family of Sir John Soane, the architect of the Bank of England and many other buildings. This is one of only two Grade I listed tombs in London, the other being that of someone called Marx in Highgate Cemetery. The sculptural features of the tomb are immediately recognisable as the shape of the world famous K2 red telephone box (and subsequent variations), which inspired its designer Sir Giles Gilbert Scott.

Nearby is the grave of Mary Wollstonecraft (1759 to 1797), the early advocate of women's rights. It is where the poet Percy Shelley, who lived nearby, first set eyes on his future bride Mary Wollstonecraft Godwin, praying at the grave of her mother. She, as Mary Shelley, became the author of Frankenstein.

At the end of the churchyard is Saint Pancras Coroners Court where, in 1943, the coroner, in strict secrecy, authorised the use of one of the corpses in his care as a decoy, which floated ashore on a Spanish coastline with documents suggesting the Allied landing against Germany would be off the Greek coast and not in Sicily, as planned. The ruse worked and the story was later made into a film – The Man Who Never Was.

13: MESOLITHIC VAUXHALL

If you are looking for the oldest part of built London you can forget the Tower of London and the Roman Amphitheatre. Look instead at the foreshore in front of the MI6 building by Vauxhall Bridge. There lies London's biggest buried secret. It is where recorded history began for the capital and you can see it only at extremely low tides, if you are lucky.

Under the water – and preserved by it – are half a dozen posts which date back to the Mesolithic period. They are a staggering 6,000 to 7,000 years old – far older than Stonehenge. Some can be seen in the foreground of a photo (below) I took during a wintery low tide, though it was not low enough to capture most of them.

Why they were built is something of a mystery. Archaeologists think they could be part of a platform associated with the River Effra, which, though underground these days, still empties itself into the Thames nearby. The posts could have been leading to a small island or fishing structure.

It is likely that the people of the Mesolithic period – when humans learned to hunt in groups and to fish, but not yet to farm – may have been more sophisticated than has been realised. Vauxhall, clearly, must be taken extremely seriously as a staging post of history.

A little further upstream archaeologists excavating the site of the new United States embassy discovered something even older, a flint tool dating to the Palaeolithic period around 7,000 to 10,000 BC.

On the upstream side of Vauxhall Bridge, a short distance beyond the Thames Clipper jetty, there is another group of piles sticking out of the water, again only at low tide, dating back to the Late Bronze Age more than 3,500 years ago. Though Johnny-come-latelies compared with what is on the other side of the bridge, they are still pretty amazing. They are best viewed from the riverside walkway as the mud on the shore can be dangerous.

14: THE SOUTH BANK COADE STONE LION

This proud lion on a stone base on the Southwark side of Westminster Bridge by County Hall is not lost, even though it looks as though it belongs in Trafalgar Square. What is lost is a bit of its history. It is one of triplets manufactured in 1837 a few hundred yards away on the site of what is now the Festival Hall by sculptor William Woodington from Coade stone, a ceramic stoneware popular at the time whose manufacture was perfected by businesswoman Eleanor Coade (1733-1821). One of the mill stones from the Coade manufactory once resided outside the Festival Hall, but the curators of our culture have hidden it away somewhere.

More durable than real stone, Coade stone's formula was guarded as secretly as that of Coca Cola. It was made from a ceramic compound of ball clay that had to be fired in a kiln for several days. Its staying power is proved by this lion and hundreds of other artefacts made from Coade stone that still exist all over the country, including in parts of Buckingham Palace and the tomb of Captain Bligh (of Mutiny on the Bounty fame) in St Mary's churchyard, next to Lambeth Palace. The tallest example is a statue of Battle of Waterloo hero Rowland Hill in Shrewsbury, which stands on a column higher than Nelson's.

One of the other triplet lions has disappeared without trace, but the third was given by the Greater London Council to Twickenham rugby stadium (British Lion, geddit!) where it still graces the ground in painted gold splendour. Which is more than can be said for its South Bank sibling, which once adorned the Red Lion Brewery by Hungerford Bridge. It was later painted red by British Rail when it stood outside Waterloo station before it was stripped and moved to its present position. Here it still looks in pristine condition, as indeed it is, except that on the way it lost its manhood. But that's another story.

15: THE BAR AT BERMONDSEY ABBEY

There is nothing particularly unusual about Lokma, a Turkish grill on the edge of Bermondsey Square except that it is built over the remains of Bermondsey Abbey, once a formidable institution that was home to two English queens. What most customers don't realise is that what's left of it can be seen under the glass floor of the cocktail bar. It is not obvious, as there is no light and many of the glass floor panels are opaque. But look closely you can see the excavated remains of the south-western tower of the abbey's church.

That is all that is visible from the extensive archaeological excavations which took place a few years ago, although two or three remnants of the monastery can still be seen in the walls of neighbouring streets such as Grange Walk (look at numbers 5, 6 and 7) and in the adjacent church of Saint Mary Magdalene. The abbey was built on the site of an earlier late Saxon building. The Domesday book records that a Norman church was built there later.

In the 12th century, a monastery was established run by monks from Cluny in France. Later, Catherine Valois lived there after the death of her husband Henry V and Elizabeth, wife of Edward IV, died there in 1492, having experienced the trauma of her two sons (the famous Princes in the tower) being whisked off to the Tower of London by Richard III and to die there in very mysterious circumstances.

Bermondsey Abbey

16: THE REMAINS OF THE MARSHALSEA

The most notorious of five dreadful prisons in Southwark, the Marshalsea was exposed in all its depravity by Charles Dickens, whose father was incarcerated there for a minor debt to a baker. He described it vividly in several of his novels, including Little Dorrit.

The original prison was built in 1373 on what is now Borough High Street and lasted until replaced by a second one (1811-1842) on a different site nearby, the southern wall of which, complete with entrance gates, can still be seen from the small park behind the church of St George the Martyr. It is easily recognisable from the BBC's Little Dorrit TV series.

Wikipedia aptly says the privately run institution "looked like an Oxbridge college and functioned as an extortion racket".

Although it housed intellectuals – Ben Jonson the playwright was incarcerated there in 1597 for sedition – and sexual deviants, it was as a debtors' prison that it achieved notoriety.

Putting debtors in jail made it even less likely that they would repay what they owed, not least because prison fees were added to their liabilities unless they could bribe their way into being released during the day as richer inmates did. Conditions were so atrocious that in 1729 an official government report stated that 300 inmates were known to have starved to death in a period of three months. Hard Times.

17: THE CANTERBURY MUSIC HALL

If you stand at the end of Upper Marsh in Lambeth opposite St Thomas's Hospital and look towards the Waterloo station exit, you will be staring at the seedbed of a revolution in entertainment – though there is nothing there to show it. The only clue is that the block of flats in front of you is marked Canterbury House (see photo below).

Here stood the Canterbury Music Hall. It was Britain's – and maybe the world's – first large venue of its kind and spawned hundreds of imitators, from which can be traced the historical roots of today's stand-up comedians. At its zenith, the palatial building stretched right back to Westminster Bridge Road.

Originally called simply the Canterbury Hall, it was opened in 1852 by entertainment entrepreneur Charles Morton, who had it built at the rear of a pub, the Canterbury Arms, he had purchased with his brother-in-law three years earlier. The area was full of gin palaces, ragged children and inebriated blokes.

In 1856, the hall was replaced by a grandiose larger one,

able to accommodate 1,500 people. It was built around the walls of the older version, which was then demolished, reportedly in a single weekend.

Performers there included Charlie Chaplin's father Charles Chaplin Snr and numerous others including, at one stage, the younger Chaplin himself. Charles Blondin did his famous tight-rope act there. By then, the music hall had a large entrance in Westminster Bridge Road. It also exhibited paintings and was dubbed "The Royal Academy Over the Water".

The hall was reconstructed in 1890 by the redoubtable theatre architect Frank Matcham as the Canterbury Theatre of Varieties, seating 3,000 people, which is as large as the biggest West End theatre today. It lasted until 1942, when it was bombed beyond restoration.

In 1955, the building was demolished and there is little sign of it today. London has so much history, yet much of it goes ignored. At a time when Britain's entertainment industry is doing so well, it is sad that the institutions that started it all are not better remembered.

18: ALL HALLOWS-BY-THE-TOWER

This church – All Hallows-by-the-Tower in Byward Street EC3, founded in 675 on Roman remains – helped shape America. One United States President, John Quincy Adams, was married there (to a local lass) and another, even more distinguished, man was baptised and schooled there. He was the extraordinary William Penn, who sailed to what is now America in 1682 to found the colony of Pennsylvania – named after him – with land provided by Charles II, who owed his dad buckets.

Penn also established the city of Philadelphia and drafted a constitution for Pennsylvania that became a blueprint for that of the future USA. In the new colony he espoused freedom of conscience and equal rights for women, becoming one of the true champions of liberty in the new continent.

But before that Penn managed to be imprisoned both in the Tower of London and in the notorious Fleet debtors' prison for his Quakerism. He railed against other religions calling the Catholic Church "the Whore of Babylon" and Puritans "hypocrites". This made him no friends in the establishment and he was arrested several times for his religious tracts.

In a celebrated case of 1670, when the jury had found Penn not guilty of illegal assembly by preaching in the streets, the judge in the case – who happened to be Lord Mayor of the City as well – threw both Penn and the jury into gaol until the latter relented. In the end, the jury won the right to be free from the control of judges. This ruling helped to shape the subsequent course of American justice.

All Hallows has also played a part in major London historical events: Samuel Pepys watched the Great Fire of London in 1666 from its tower; the Catholic martyr John Fisher was buried there after after being beheaded in the Tower; and the "Hanging Judge" Jeffreys was married there.

Interestingly, William Penn banned capital punishment in Pennsylvania for everything except murder and treason at a time when hundreds of petty crimes carried that punishment in England. Judge Jeffreys would not have approved.

All Hallows Church

The oldest part of the church

19: THE OAK ROOF OF WESTMINSTER HALL

The roof of Westminster Hall was added to the existing building in 1393 by Richard II and remains the largest hammer-beam roof in the world. It has survived the Gunpowder Plot, two world wars and the Great Fire of 1834, which destroyed nearly all the rest of the parliamentary buildings.

But not all the oak beams are the originals. In 1904, Parliament decided that some of them needed replacing. Ireland and Australia offered to help, but MPs wanted English wood to be used.

Eventually George Courthope, whose Wadhurst family estate in Sussex had supplied the original oak 600 years earlier, offered to provide the replacements from the same source as the originals. That is wonder enough. But later, in 1938 Courthope – by then Sir George and an MP – revealed another fascinating fact during a debate on the Forest Commission.

He said: "It may interest honourable members to know that a number of the oak trees which I felled for the restoration of Westminster Hall had over 600 annual rings – that is, they were over 600 years old. And it is safe to assume that the great beams which they were replacing in Westminster Hall must have been at least of a similar age".

Wow! The replacement oaks were already growing near the original ones that had been felled over 600 years earlier. Only in England...

20: PINEAPPLES

Pineapples, ever since Christopher Columbus came across them in Guadeloupe in 1493, have been a symbol of hospitality and wealth. Nobles were prepared to pay the equivalent of £5,000 apiece for them to impress guests at their dinner tables. This might help to explain why they have become hidden symbols of London as a welcoming city – well, until recently .

Once you spot one you start seeing them everywhere. The first I came across were on the top of the obelisks at either end of Lambeth Bridge. I thought they were a one-off tribute to John Tradescant and his son of the same name, 17th century gardeners and botanists often credited with introducing pineapples to England. They are buried a few yards away in St Mary's churchyard, now home to the Garden Museum (which has reportedly maintained that they aren't pineapples at all, but pine cones).

But look around in Central London and find you are seldom far from a stone one. A few hundred yards from Lambeth Bridge, in Smith Square, the church of St John the Evangelist sports a number of them on its spires. If you look up at the two towers on the western side of St Paul's, you won't see a cross or a statue but a pineapple. There is also something

that looks a bit like a pineapple on top of the dome itself. (Pineapple fanatics point out that Norman Foster's iconic office block overlooking St Paul's actually looks more like a pineapple than a gherkin. They have been campaigning for a change of name).

Christopher Wren seems to have been very partial to them, as he also put them on his (war-bombed) Christ Church in Newgate Street (bottom photo) where they are currently adorning the ground like discarded sculptures – perhaps a reminder that London is becoming a less welcoming place to strangers than it once was.

One of my favourites is in the churchyard of St Pancras Old Church. Architect Sir John Soane had one plonked on top of the tomb he designed for himself and which became the inspiration for Giles Gilbert Scott's iconic – though pineapple-free – red telephone box.

Pineapples were often sculpted on to railings as a welcoming sign. There are literally dozens of them in the roads around Devonshire Street north of Broadcasting House, some painted gold, some silver and some black. Others are in Soho Square, the old Greater London Council building, Great Russell Street (top photo), Royal Hospital Road, Whitehall, Mayfair, the Inns of Court, Queen's Gate Lodge, Westminster Abbey's garden, and even at the top of the National Gallery.

21: ST MARY ALDERMANBURY

Here stands Sir Christopher Wren's church of St Mary Aldermanbury – or at least it once did. It has since been exported to America, leaving only its foundations. The church was first built in around 1181, but it was re-designed by Wren after the Great Fire of 1666.

It was bombed during World War II and eventually demolished in 1966 and transported – all 7,000 stones of it – to Fulton, Missouri in the United States where it now graces the campus of Westminster College as a memorial to Sir Winston Churchill, who made his celebrated "Iron Curtain" speech in the gymnasium there in 1946.

The site of the original church is close to the Guildhall off a road named Love Lane. It has a Grade II listing and is now a public space with trees and bushes, but it also hosts a memorial to two men to whom history owes a big debt.

The actors Henry Condell and John Heminges were friends of William Shakespeare and part of his acting troupe. It was they who gathered together all the known manuscripts of his plays to produce the First Folio. Without this, many of Shakespeare's plays would have been lost forever.

Where the church used to be

The church rebuilt in America

Condell and Heminges were buried in this churchyard as was, less salubriously, the notorious "hanging judge" Judge Jeffreys. He was re-interred there by friends in 1694, a few years after his body had been first buried in the Tower of London.

If you are wondering how the church got its name, wonder no longer. It was named after a local benefactor called…. Alderman Bury.

22: THE GARDEN OF WESTMINSTER ABBEY

The Abbey Garden

If this doesn't count as hidden I don't know what does. Only yards from Parliament Square, it is surrounded by a high wall that no one can see over and has no obvious entry point. Welcome to the garden of Westminster Abbey, claimed to be the oldest in the country. It has been in continuous cultivation since the Middle Ages. And it is open to the public…

Fashioned by the monks of the Abbey, the Infirmary Garden as it is known is not only old but is the same size as it was in the 11th century, apart from a parcel of land at the north-eastern end which was confiscated by Edward III in 1365 to build the Jewel Tower (which is also still there). We know this because the medieval walls along the eastern and southern sides are still intact, as is the boundary wall on the other side.

The garden is an oasis of calm at the heart of a busy city just over the road from the cacophony of the Houses of Parliament. It remains calm partly because so few people know about it. Even those who do have to find out how to get in (from the north-eastern end of Dean's Yard) and then negotiate their way past a red-robed official who is there to stop tourists gaining a back door entrance to the main part of the Abbey, thereby avoiding the entrance fee which is now a staggering £22 at the door.

The justification for charging so much for entry into the house of the Lord is that the Abbey is self-supporting with no government funds, and as 95% of the visitors are from overseas maybe it doesn't matter. Local residents can get in free with the appropriate card. The garden itself is free to all and also gives access to the cloisters and Chapter House, though only on three days a week (usually Tuesday to Thursday).

Once inside the garden, it is easy to go back in time to conjure up what it once contained: an orchard, a herbarium dating to 1306 (the main reason for the garden's creation), a dovecote, a cider mill, ponds, fruit and vegetables and even a vineyard. There was also a channel leading to a mill at the southern edge of the garden, from which the word Millbank is derived.

If you were to dig in the garden you would soon come to some of the deposits which formed Thorney Island, the eyot between the Thames and the River Tyburn on which the Abbey was built.

Today's garden has a fig tree, plane trees that were planted in 1850, and two handsome mulberry trees (one black, one white) at each end of the garden. Either side of the stone gateway leading to Little Dean's Yard (part of Westminster School) there are two stone angels, (though at the time of writing were being repaired) reputably made by Grinling Gibbons and Arnold Quellin, which once graced the Queen's Chapel at the other end of Whitehall Palace where the Ministry of Defence building now is.

The temporarily removed sculptures

23: THE MONUMENT

This is not a lost gem but it is definitely a hidden one. Despite its (disputed) claim to be the biggest free-standing stone column in the world, you can't see it until you turn the final corner round one of the large office blocks enclosing it. My photo shows the top of it peeking out, with the Gherkin and the Walkie Talkie behind it to either side.

The Monument is one of the most fascinating structures in the city, yet effectively invisible to most Londoners most of the time. Inside its Doric body is a spiral stone staircase with 311 steps to the top. It is 61.57 metres tall, exactly the distance between it and Thomas Farriner's – or Farynor's – bakery in Pudding Lane, where the Great Fire of London started in 1666, and which the Monument commemorates.

The fire itself was extraordinary. It raged for three days, razing the homes of seven eighths of the City's 80,000 citizens and dozens of churches, yet only half a dozen people were officially reported dead. Another who died as a result of the fire was watchmaker Robert Hubert from Rouen, reportedly afflicted by mental illness, who falsely confessed to starting it, was found guilty and hung at Tyburn amid a climate of xenophobia in the country at that time. His innocence was only recognised later.

The Monument is also a tribute to the two people associated with it who were largely responsible for rebuilding the city after the fire: Sir Christopher Wren and Robert Hooke. Wren gets most of the credit for the Monument, but Hooke was mainly responsible for its construction.

Hooke was a scientist by profession with many inventions to his credit, including the pedometer. Never one to miss an opportunity, he constructed the Monument not just as a memorial but as a scientific instrument as well. He saw it as a tube as well as a stone structure and designed it to double as a zenith telescope for studying gravity and pendulum movements.

Today, the original laboratory can still be entered below the ticket kiosk and Hooke's hinged lid in the flaming urn at the top of the structure can still open to give uninterrupted views of the sky. It used to be the tallest scientific instrument in the world, the Hadron Collider of its day.

24: THE JERUSALEM CHAMBER

Most of the outside walls of Westminster Abbey are not as old as they look. Practically all of the stonework has been replaced over the centuries. But not that of the building which peeps cautiously up above the Abbey shop near the western entrance. This is the Jerusalem Chamber where in real life – as well as in a Shakespeare play – Henry IV was taken, unconscious, to sit by the fire after he had fallen ill praying in the Abbey at the shrine of Edward the Confessor. He was en route to Jerusalem, where he was planning to atone for his sins.

Much of the original stonework inside the Chamber is still there, much as it was when Henry lay there dying. So is the ceiling above and the walls behind the added Victorian panelling. When he recovered consciousness, the king asked where he was and was told: "The Jerusalem Chamber." He concluded then that his life was about to end. A prophecy in Holinshed's Chronicles said that he would die in a place called Jerusalem, but it had become apparent that it wasn't the Jerusalem Henry had assumed. As he says in Henry IV, Part I:

> It hath been prophesied to me many years, I should not die but in Jerusalem,
> Which vainly I suppos'd the Holy Land. But bear me to that chamber, there I'll lie,
> In that Jerusalem shall Harry die.

Shakespeare took the story further. He allowed Prince Henry – the future Henry V – to slip into the Chamber and, believing his father to be dead, to try on the crown, only for his father to wake up in anger. They were, however, reconciled and history moved on.

The Jerusalem Chamber is also the place where the committee overlooking the creation of the beautifully written King James Bible – one of the most influential books ever written – met regularly and where many celebrated people, such as Isaac Newton, were laid out before being buried in the Abbey. Today, it is one of the private rooms of the Deanery and cannot be visited except on open days or when a public lecture is held there. Few such small rooms can boast such a wealth of living history.

25: THE CLEARY VINEYARD

If you were asked in a pub quiz where the nearest vineyard to Saint Paul's is, you might not have the answer. But it is actually only a few hundred yards from the cathedral towards the Thames in a lovely oasis of calm called Cleary Garden. The vines are not huge but are impressively productive, a gift from the Loire Valley to remind us that the space used to be a wine trading area too.

But that is not the main point of interest. If you sit on a bench in the vineyard you are at the top edge of what is surely the biggest hidden gem in London – Huggin Hill Roman Baths. They were saved and excavated in the 1960s amid considerable publicity and controversy, but have since faded from public consciousness and almost entirely from public vision.

Most of the extensive remains of the bath house are buried under office blocks at either side of Huggin Hill at the bottom of the slope. They have been preserved, but only after being filled in. Some of the walls were three metres high. There is no public access. Had they been discovered today, maybe the Bloomberg factor would have meant new buildings being constructed to allow the remains to be on public view.

On the way down the hill, within Cleary Garden itself, there is a remnant of an old Roman wall – part of the north retaining wall of the bath house – and the only sign above ground of the large Roman remains which lie underneath.

The bath complex was constructed in the latter part of the first century AD and is likely to have extended for 75 metres along the front of the river. Public baths were a huge part of Roman life. This one was so big – one of the most important bath houses in the country – it might have been part of a large building or even a palace.

The Huggin Hill remains have not yet been fully excavated, but they are clearly extensive. They embrace seven rooms at the southern end, including a hot plunge room (or caldarium), a cold room (or frigidarium) and a changing room.

The upper part of the terracing, where Cleary Garden now is, would have contained the tanks and reservoirs that fed the baths with spring water that flowed down the slopes to the Thames. If you want to sit in a tranquil space and contemplate what London used to be, then this is the place to do it.

26: ST MARY WOOLNOTH

This Nicholas Hawksmoor masterpiece has God on its side. St Mary Woolnoth was the only City church to survive the Second World War unscathed and has escaped demolition on several occasions, most recently in 1897 when the City and South London Railway was given permission to demolish it to make space for Bank Underground station.

Yes, demolish a Hawksmoor! It was only after a public outcry that a compromise with Mammon was reached. Much of the crypt was sold to the railway company to accommodate a lift shaft. You can still see bits of its ceiling above the station lift beneath the entrance by the church. The rest of the building was underpinned with steel girders, which actually made it stronger.

The other (western) side of the church hosts a Starbucks coffee shop – yes, a Hawksmoor Starbucks! – as a means to raise money. Centuries earlier, the then churchyard was sold to the City authorities and the Mansion House, the Lord Mayor's official residence, was built there.

If you feel such survival could not have happened without the gift of grace, you would not be far wrong, for John Newton, a former slave ship captain who renounced his evil ways to become a pastor, was incumbent at this church from 1780 to 1807. Among other things, Newton wrote the words of Amazing Grace, probably the most internationally popular hymn ever written.

Designed in Hawksmoor's borderline gothic style, St Mary Woolnoth has been a site for worship for over 2,000 years. Traces of Roman and pagan religious structures have been found under its foundations. After the Great Fire of London in 1666, it was repaired by Sir Christopher Wren, Hawksmoor's mentor and collaborator, though it had to be rebuilt by

Hawksmoor as it turned out to be unsafe.

Others associated with the church included Thomas Kyd, author of The Spanish Tragedy, which was more popular in its time than most of Shakespeare's plays. Kyd was baptised there and William Wilberforce, the anti-slavery campaigner, worshipped there. The church has a walk-on part in T S Eliot's The Waste Land – St Mary Woolnoth "kept the hours" – and until

recently the space in the tower above the bells was being used by an architect as an office.

The church itself has charisma bordering on the sublime. Outside, it looks like a Greek temple sitting on a sculptural base with angular parallel lines that wouldn't look out of place at Tate Modern. At the top there are two archways which look like eyes watching over the City – balm to Hawksmoor's psycho-geographic disciples, who read mystical interpretations into practically anything he has built.

Inside, you are struck by four sets of Corinthian columns laid out as triplets in what Ian Nairn described as "a square within a square…where space is made so tangible that you can experience for the price of a bus ticket to the City, the super-reality of the mystics".

The church is built on an impossibly small triangle of land between two City streets with brutalist skyscrapers blocking what must once have been a magnificent setting. But when you push open its formidable doors, you are into a different world that hasn't changed for hundreds of years. Mammon is nowhere to be seen.

27: THE MIRACLE OF THE WANDLE

"No clearer or diviner waters ever sang with constant lips of the land which giveth rain from heaven," wrote John Ruskin of the River Wandle. In his day it was known as one of the finest chalk streams in the country, the one on which Lord Nelson cast a fly as it flowed near his home in Merton shortly before voyaging to Trafalgar.

Then something happened. The Wandle went to Hell and back as the new industrialists realised that its fast-flowing waters were ideal for turning water wheels with which to power factories. There were eventually almost a hundred of them, making the Wandle one of the most intensively utilised rivers for its size in the world. It was also one of the most polluted as manufacturers of paper, snuff, leather and goodness knows what else emptied their chemicals and effluent into this innocent river, killing all the fish and making it seemingly irretrievably polluted. As a child when daring to go near its banks I never thought it would be other than permanently toxic.

But miracles do happen. Thanks to de-industrialisation, higher standards, a strategic plan and an army of volunteers, trout and other fish such as barbel have returned and the Wandle is now one of the cleanest rivers in the land. It is worth walking the Wandle Trail to Wandsworth, where it empties itself into the Thames – almost the only London tributary that hasn't been covered over – and back into deepest Surrey, where it rises, a journey on which you hardly see any roads. The Wandle was lost but now it has been found, an inspiration for any other river thought to be beyond hope.

28: MARX, LENIN AND THE SECRET OF MARX HOUSE

Clerkenwell Green has been a cauldron of radicalism ever since the Peasants Revolt was extinguished there in 1381. A reminder of its revolutionary history is the Marx Memorial Library. The building is where in 1902-03 Lenin edited and published several editions of his Iskra journal, which was smuggled into Tsarist Russia to stir revolutionary fervour. It is said that in 1905 in a nearby pub, the Crown Tavern, Lenin had a drink with Joseph Stalin, on a visit to London on party business in 1903, though this has never been confirmed.

But the Marx Library is sitting on a deeper secret. The building which commemorates the author of the slogan "Religion is the opium of the people" actually stands on the site of a medieval religious building

(Photo courtesy of the Marx Memorial Library.)

– Saint Mary's Nunnery, which dates back to the 12th century. In the basement of the library are the remarkably well preserved remains of a crypt or cellar which looks as though it extends much farther

The nunnery was situated on the opposite side of Clerkenwell Green from Clerkenwell Priory, home of the Monastic Order of the Knights Hospitaller of St John of Jerusalem – warrior monks who protected pilgrims on their way to Jerusalem. The gatehouse of the monastery is still very visible as is the well preserved Norman crypt underneath the ground.

Following the dissolution of the monasteries, much of the stone from the priory was hijacked by the dreadful Lord Protector Somerset to build his palace on the Strand, Somerset House. Justice took its revenge. He was executed before the palace was completed.

29: TRACES OF IGNATIUS SANCHO

If you are walking along King Charles Street in Whitehall, close to the entrance to the grandly classical Foreign Office, it is easy to miss a plaque fixed high up on the wall. I missed it for decades.

The plaque tells us that at number 19 Charles Street – as it was then called – a grocery shop was run by Ignatius Sancho (1729-1780), who had escaped slavery to become a well regarded writer, a playwright, a composer and a London celebrity.

Sancho was feted by Dr Johnson, painted by Gainsborough and a correspondent of Laurence Sterne, author of Tristram Shandy, whom he actively encouraged to campaign against slavery. When a book of his letters was published on a subscription basis – today we would call it crowdfunding – the subscribers read like pages from Debrett's.

The path between Victoria Street and Caxton Street where Sancho is buried

It was fashionable in those days for some aristocrats to have a black butler. Sancho was employed by the enlightened Lord Montagu, who encouraged him to educate himself, which he did with enthusiasm. When the onset of gout prevented Sancho from performing his household duties, Montagu helped him to set up his grocery shop where he also sold sugar and tobacco – ironically, products of slavery.

Charles James Fox (1749-1806), the radical Whig politician, was a prominent visitor to the shop and Sancho apparently voted for him in the 1780 election, which he was able to do thanks to his property rights as a Westminster shopkeeper. He was almost certainly the first black person to vote in Britain.

Sancho, who must have acquired his forename Ignatius from an early encounter with Jesuits, is buried in Victoria Street at Christchurch Gardens, a patch of greenery situated near the Albert pub.

30: ELIZABETH I AT ST DUNSTAN-IN-THE-WEST

It is worth coming to St Dunstan-in-the-West, a mini museum of a church on Fleet Street, just to see the statue of Elizabeth I, though there is plenty more to enjoy. The statue is the only one in London of Elizabeth that was carved during her reign (in around 1586). She is also the only kept woman among London statues, as Millicent Fawcett, the suffragette, left £700 in her will for her upkeep, currently managed by the Society for the Protection of Ancient buildings.

Elizabeth looks perfectly serene and queen-like, but she was never intended to be there. She used to grace the west side of Ludgate, one of the official entrances to the City of London, which was situated around the corner on Ludgate Hill. When Ludgate was demolished in 1760 to widen the street, Elizabeth was removed to St Dunstan along with several other ghostly statues, which can be seen in the entrance beneath her.

They are King Lud and his sons, who would frighten any unsuspecting burglars daring to enter the church at night. If you believe Geoffrey of Monmouth's history – and most people don't – Lud was the pre-Roman founder of London and buried at Ludgate.

But who needs him when there are the spirits of real celebrities

at hand? This was where John Donne preached, where Samuel Pepys worshipped and where Izaac Walton published his classic The Compleat Angler. It is also where Lord Baltimore, who founded the US state of Maryland (though didn't actually go there), was buried in 1632.

St Dunstan also has a celebrity clock, built in 1671 for an earlier version of the church. It was the first public clock in London to have a minute hand. In 1828, when the original church was demolished, it was saved and eventually returned to its present position in 1935, where it still chimes helped by two figures either side of a pair of bells.

The church managed to escape the 1666 Great Fire of London thanks to the Dean of Westminster rousing 40 slumbering Westminster School boys in the middle of the night to throw buckets of water over it. It is still very much a functioning church and, unusually, is shared by the Anglican community and the Romanian Orthodox church in London. An altar screen inside was brought from a monastery in Bucharest in 1966.

31: THE WHITECHAPEL BELL FOUNDRY

This East London company, astonishingly, has been making bells continuously since 1570 during the reign of Elizabeth I and quite possibly from as early as 1420, when Henry V married Catherine of Valois to become heir to the kingdom of France.

While the rest of UK manufacturing has come and gone, the Whitechapel Bell Foundry at 32-34 Whitechapel Road has seen them all off, making church bells, ships' bells and hand bells for customers all over the world. It is the oldest manufacturer in the country and quite possibly the world.

Or was. Sadly, tragically, it had to close its doors in 2017 as the realities of financial life crept up on it and it was forced to join the memories of Lost London. Its most famous product is the 13.5 ton monster known as Big Ben, housed in the clock tower of the Houses of Parliament. It is the biggest bell the Foundry ever manufactured and the gauge used to make the mould was still hanging on the wall at the end.

However, although the foundry is lost to London, Big Ben will chime on, maybe for centuries, once the present renovations are over – as will the nearby 15th century bells in Westminster Abbey, a regular reminder of the longevity of the Foundry's output. One of its exports, cast in 1752 for the State House in Philadelphia and known as the Liberty Bell, became an icon of US freedom and is still on public view in its home city.

On a recent visit to the Foundry, which I shall never forget, I saw a bell on the shop floor that had come in for its 600 year service. Wow! I wonder how many of the current surge of digital products will last even a tiny fraction of that time. The Foundry building is Grade II listed and so hopefully will be preserved.

32: THE REMAINS OF THOMAS CROMWELL'S GARDEN

The photo below shows all that remains of Thomas Cromwell's garden, part of a two acre site he developed when Henry VIII's chief of staff moved into one of the grandest private residences in London. Initially, he took a 99 year lease on part of a property owned by the monks of Austin Friars in the City of London, before expanding it by means of purchases and enforced acquisitions from a 14 room house into a 50 room urban mansion, where he could conduct his business and entertain the king, should the occasion arise.

One of the people dispossessed by Cromwell was the father of John Stow, author of A Survey of London, first published in 1598. Stow saw his father's garden "encroached for the making of Thomas Cromwell's pleasure-grounds".

It was quite usual, and very canny, for monasteries to rent out properties to dignitaries as it gave them much needed income and also influence at court. Among other Austin Friars tenants were ambassadors from France and the Holy Roman Empire, and Erasmus, who apparently left without paying his bill.

In 1543, after Cromwell's execution and the dissolution of the monasteries, the site was purchased from Henry VIII by the Drapers livery company for £1,200. They still own the hall on Throgmorton Street and what remains of the garden, complete with (recent) mulberry trees.

The garden can be seen through a window in the Drapers Hall, or on one of the few days during the year when it is open to the public, or from the road called Austin Friars at the back. Cromwell was beheaded at the Tower of London, where his remains are buried in the chapel of Saint Peter ad Vincula.

33: SHAKESPEARE'S NEWINGTON BUTTS

The words "Shakespeare" and "Elephant and Castle" are not normally found in the same sentence. That is a pity because one of the very earliest theatres of Shakespeare's time, in which his plays were put on and where he himself performed, was the Newington Butts Theatre. This was located under where the Elephant and Castle shopping centre and adjacent roundabout are today. Sadly, there are no remains.

The theatre is believed to have been constructed in 1575 or early 1576 according to archaeologist Julian Bowsher in his authoritative book Shakespeare's London Theatreland. This would make it slightly earlier than either The Theatre or the Curtain Theatre, both in Shoreditch, where many of Shakespeare's early plays were put on. The only purpose-built theatre that predates Newington Butts was the Red Lion in Whitechapel, about which little is known but which definitely did not stage any Shakespeare plays.

The Newington theatre was a good mile from the Southwark theatres – The Rose, The Globe and The Swan – which meant it distanced itself from outbreaks of plague and from the Puritan-run City of London, which strongly disapproved of plays. But its distance from the Thames eventually proved its undoing, being unpopular with players and playgoers alike.

It is on record that in June, 1594 the Lord Chamberlain's Men – the company of actors for which Shakespeare wrote – gave their earliest performances of Titus Andronicus and The Taming of the Shrew at Newington Butts, as well an early version of Hamlet which Shakespeare almost certainly didn't write. Bowsher says: "It is probable that Shakespeare acted there, possibly in 1593 and almost certainly in 1594."

Elephant and Castle

34: THE MEDIEVAL JEWEL TOWER

The Jewel Tower, built in 1365, is one of only two buildings from the medieval Palace of Westminster – seat of kings and parliament – which have remained intact. The other is a near neighbour, Westminster Hall. The Tower's full glory has only recently been revealed because from the 17th Century until the 1960s it had buildings around it on three sides blocking it from general public view (see photo below). There were fears during the 19th century that it would be demolished.

As writer and raconteur Augustus J Hare (1834-1903) observed: "It will scarcely be credited by those who visit it that the destruction of this interesting building is occasionally in contemplation and that the present century, for the sake of making a regular street, will perhaps bear the stigma of having destroyed one of the most precious buildings in Westminster which, if the houses around it were cleared away and it were preserved as a museum of Westminster antiquities, would be the greatest possible addition to the group of historic buildings to which it belongs."

Jewel Tower

Survive the Tower did and – in keeping with Hare's dream – the buildings round it were demolished. It started life under Edward III (1312-1377) as a repository for the royal jewels and later as storage place for official documents. When that function was transferred to the newly built Victoria Tower in 1869 the Jewel Tower became the place where official weights, measures and volumes for the whole of the British Empire were tested – including the volume of a pint of beer. This lasted until the arrival of the motor car and the construction of Lambeth Bridge, when the resulting vibrations proved too much for such a delicate operation.

The lawn in front of today's Tower is roughly where the king's garden was in the private section of the Palace. Not that Edward was there very often. He had other homes to go to at Windsor, Eltham and Sheen. Only the Norman kings stayed regularly at Westminster so they could make a quick getaway down the Thames if the going got rough.

In more recent times, the space to the left of the Jewel Tower – between the Tower and the old Abbey wall – was where Prime Ministers parked their cars.

If you enter the Tower's ground floor room to pay your admission fee today and have a cup of coffee in the café – for which there is no admission charge – it would be easy to miss the beautifully constructed vaulted ceiling, which wouldn't look out of place in a cathedral. The first floor has another vaulted ceiling, a stone one installed in the 1750s as a fire precaution. The second floor looks much as it did in medieval times with a 14th century door, though its wooden ceiling was installed in 1949.

The rectangularly framed windows in the turret on the north (Abbey) side were probably designed by Nicholas Hawksmoor. He was Clerk of Works at Westminster, where he designed the western entrance to the Abbey. He lived in nearby Millbank.

Looking at the Tower from the road you can see the remains of a moat once used as a fishpond, beside which the drain from the Abbey ran to the river, and what is left of the old fortification wall protruding.

35: THE TEXAS EMBASSY

Between 1836 and 1845 Texas was a country in its own right, a republic with an embassy, or legation, in London, the site of which can still be observed in an alley off St James's Street called Pickering Place.

Texas established its London legation, and another in Paris, partly to gather support to prevent an expected invasion from Mexico and partly as a manoeuvre to make the United States worry about the prospect of England and France having troops in their back yard.

At one stage Britain offered to guarantee the Texas borders against both the US and Mexico. But an independent Texas was never going to be an economic success and when it joined the US in 1845 the overseas offices were closed.

The London legation was housed in what had once been a brothel and gambling den in the same building as its landlords, the venerable wine merchants Berry Bros, who have been there since 1730. In 1963 the Anglo-Texan society erected a plaque which reads: "In this building was the location for the ministers from the Republic of Texas to the court of Saint James 1842 to 1845."

When the Texans left they forgot to pay a £160 rent arrears bill. That debt was eventually paid, over 150 tears later, by a party of Texan visitors.

PS: Little known fact – Graham Greene was a founder member of the Anglo-Texan Society.

36: THE MIDDLE TEMPLE HALL

The wonderful Middle Temple (nearest station, Temple) is not lost, just difficult to get into except when events are held there or there is an open day – or if you happen to be a lawyer. It is worth the wait to go inside, because it has survived the Great Fire of London in 1666 and both world wars and is more or less as it was in Shakespeare's time. He must have known it well.

In Henry VI, Part I – written around 1591 – the Earl of Suffolk leads Richard Plantagenet from the Hall of the Middle Temple, where they had been speaking "too loud", into the Temple Garden where the future contestants of the Wars of the Roses plucked red and white roses as the emblems of the future conflict between the houses of York and Lancaster.

The Earl of Warwick later says:

"Will I upon thy party wear this rose.
And here I prophesy, the brawl to-day
Grown to this faction, in the Temple Gardens,
Shall send, between the red rose and the white,
A thousand souls to death and deadly night."

That was an imagined scene, though the garden still exists today in the same place.

A few years later on February 2, 1602 in the same hall, real history took place when the first performance of Twelfth Night, almost certainly with Shakespeare in the cast, took place in the presence of Queen Elizabeth I. It opened with the line: "If music be the food of love, play on".

The Middle Temple Hall is one of the few large medieval buildings in London to survive intact, despite partial reconstruction because of bomb damage or decay. What you are looking at is what Shakespeare saw. The Hall contains a dazzling oak double hammer beam roof and a notable oak screen dating back to 1571. The 29ft long Bench Table, made from a single oak tree, is believed to have been given to the Inn by the monarch herself.

The Hall was constructed between 1562 and 1573 on the site of an earlier one with the same bricks. Today could easily be 400 years ago because hardly anything has changed. You are sheltered by overhanging mulberry trees from which lawyers get the material of their craft when they "take silk". Behind you is Fountain Court, named after the fountain where Ruth Pinch in Charles Dickens's Martin Chuzzlewit came to meet her brother and later her lover John Westlock. To your right are the stairs to Fountain Court where Pip, the hero of Great Expectations, had an unexpected visit from Magwitch, a convict who was his anonymous benefactor. Oh, and a lot of law happens within these precincts too.

37: QUEENHITHE DOCK

Queenhithe Dock is not much to look at, surrounded as it is on three sides by office blocks, and the wonder is that it is there at all. On a bad day it could be mistaken for a refuge for flotsam from the river.

The reason no-one has built on it is because they can't. It is a scheduled ancient monument – quite likely the last Anglo-Saxon dock in the world and the last surviving inlet on the Thames in Central London. It was once a busy port, set up in 899 – the final year of King Alfred's reign – and dealt with trade from places upstream of the Thames while Billingsgate (downstream) dealt with international trade.

The dock is one of the few secular memories of medieval London that is still much as it was in olden days. It is situated on the north bank of the Thames, east of the Millennium Bridge opposite Tate Modern and the Globe Theatre. Archaeologists have uncovered revetments (retaining walls) dating back to 1146 in Bull Wharf next door, which Queenhithe once extended into.

The "queen" in Queenhithe was Matilda of Scotland who, amazingly, was given the revenues from taxes at Queenhithe by her husband Henry I. It was originally called Ethelred's Hythe. A handsome timeline of the dock's history runs alongside.

38: STAINED GLASS AT ST MARGARET'S CHURCH

London has lots of hidden gems but there are few more curious than a large stained glass window in St Margaret's Church, a few yards from Parliament Square. It is a beautiful work of Flemish artistry and looks like a beacon of tranquility in a splintering world.

Its inception can best be described as ill timed. The work was commissioned around 1526 by the magistrates of Dort in Holland to celebrate the marriage of Henry VIII to Catherine of Aragon. But by the time it had been finished – guess what? – Henry had become besotted with Anne Boleyn.

The king is depicted in saintly contemplation in the panel at the bottom left of the window, while on its right hand side, Catherine, against a similar background, is also deep in prayer. Both appear to be looking at the crucifixion scene in the central panel of the window. A perfect couple uniting the warring nations of England and Spain in matrimonial harmony – or it could have been had Henry not secured an annulment of the marriage in 1533, which meant the window had to be disposed of.

It is not known for certain where it was originally intended to be moved to, but it was soon dispatched on a medieval version of pass the parcel among the dignitaries of Essex. First, it was sent to the ancient religious house of Waltham Abbey in Essex, where Henry occasionally stayed to be out of sight and out of mind. It remained until the dissolution of the monasteries when it became a double embarrassment, as its association with a doomed royal marriage was combined with the imagery of a discarded Roman Catholic religion.

Somehow, the window survived and was transferred to a private chapel at New Hall, also in Essex, where its Catholic symbolism would be less noticed. In the ensuing decades the window passed into the possession of the Earl of Wiltshire (Anne Boleyn's dad), the Earl of Sussex and the Duke of Buckingham before landing in the ownership of General Monk, a Royalist who, curiously, served under Oliver Cromwell. He buried it to keep it hidden from the prying eyes of Puritans, who would have been enraged by its Popish symbolism.

The work was subsequently purchased by Edward Conyers of Copped Hall – another Essex location, where Mary Tudor was imprisoned and where Shakespeare's A Midsummer Night's Dream was first performed. Its Cook's Tour then brought it to London in 1758, when Conyer's son sold it to the inhabitants of St Margaret's for 400 guineas.

After that, the story becomes even more complicated. Dean and Chapter of Westminster also regarded the window as Popish and started a lawsuit seeking its removal. The dispute lasted seven years. It was the religious equivalent of Charles Dickens' perpetual legal proceedings in Bleak House, Jarndyce v Jarndyce. Fortunately for us all, the action failed and the window can now be enjoyed by all, hopefully in perpetuity – never forgetting its history.

39: THE GARDEN MUSEUM

If you are having lunch – and why not? – at the delightful Garden Museum in Lambeth, very close to Lambeth Palace, you can peer through its large glass window at two majestic tombs in the architect-designed garden.

One, quite properly, contains the Tradescant family, which was hugely important in the development of English gardens. The other is of someone else who lived locally but to whom history has been less kind: William Bligh.

Bligh will forever be known for the mutiny on the Bounty, the ship he commanded, when a minority of the crew, led by Fletcher Christian, cast him and a band of supporters adrift in the Bounty's launch so those remaining could be left to savour the rumoured delights of Tahiti.

Bligh and 18 crewmen with precious little food were crammed into a craft barely 23 feet long but managed to navigate the boat an astonishing 3,600 miles to Timor, the nearest European settlement, in what was surely one of the great journeys in history.

For a man who served with distinction under Captain Cook and Lord Nelson and who, when later appointed Governor of New South Wales (1806-1809), set about curbing the rampant corruption in Sydney, Bligh deserves a major reappraisal. This has already happen in Australia where in 1987 a statue was erected in his honour to "restore the proper image of a much maligned and gallant man".

It is a wonder the Garden Museum doesn't make more of him. Maybe they are worried it might become a destination for Australian tourists rather than a mecca for gardeners and foodies. Either way this beautifully reconstructed space is worth a visit. I ought to admit that I was against the reconstruction because the original garden had a pristine beauty that I still remember very fondly. But as reconstructions go this is definitely a hit.

The Garden Museum as it was

40: THE INVISIBLE BAYNARD CASTLE

It may not look much, but this brutalist BT building (see photo on next page), Baynard House, which City workers pass by oblivious of its history, is a scheduled ancient monument. It is interesting not for what you see but for what is buried underneath – the remains of the fascinating Baynard's Castle, which was destroyed in 1666 in the Great Fire of London.

The first structure was built for Ralph Baynard, a henchman of William the Conqueror, but in around 1275 the land was handed over to the Dominicans so that they could extend their adjacent monastery at Blackfriars, and so a second castle was built nearby.

In the 1970s and 1980s, frantic excavations under Baynard House and the City of London School involving umpteen volunteers revealed extensive remains of the second castle, covering an area 65 metres long and up to 55 metres wide. They included foundations and sections of walls which were sealed and will now lie forever buried and out of public view unless the current building is demolished.

Baynard Castle, the only castle in London, has its own place in history as the venue for a meeting between a group of noblemen and Richard, Duke of Gloucester, most notably in 1483. The Duke of Buckingham presented a petition and, in Shakespeare's words, proclaimed Richard King Richard III: "I salute you with this royal title: Long live kind Richard, England's worthy king!"

It was in the hall of Baynard's Castle that Edward IV (1442-1483) assumed the title of king and summoned the bishops, peers and judges to meet him in council.

Baynard Castle Then

The castle later passed to Henry VI, who granted it to Richard, Duke of York. In about 1500, Henry VII transformed it into a royal residence and stayed at the castle on several occasions.

It was considerably extended in the 16th century and Henry VIII, ever generous with other people's property, passed it on to several of his wives, including Catherine of Aragon.

Seldom has something as invisible as Baynard's Castle played such a significant role in English history.

Footnote: The official description by the archeologists is as follows: "It was built with four wings around a central courtyard. The foundations of the north wing include the remains of the walls, gatehouse and gate tower. On its southernmost side, which originally fronted the river, is part of the 16th century foundations of a series of five small projecting towers between two large multi-angular end towers. There is a cobbled landward entrance in the north wall. A riverside entrance in one of the small south towers is attested in documentary sources".

Baynard Castle Now

41: FINDING LONDON WALL

London used to be surrounded by a wall that was built by the Romans around 200 AD and had later medieval additions. That very old London still is. But the wall has got lost and you have to look carefully for remnants – of which there are still plenty.

Its course runs in a roughly horseshoe shape from around Blackfriars station northwards via the Old Bailey and the Museum of London before turning east along the road called London Wall and then meandering its way to the Tower of London. Following it is like chasing a serpent which disappears underground only to reappear before diving out of sight again. The locations of three of the most visible bits are as follows:

**Bank of America Merrill Lynch,
Newgate Street.**

It would be difficult to find a more dramatic contrast between old and new London than this. Above ground, the throbbing trading floors of the US investment bank. Below it, an ancient section of Roman-built London Wall, now lying 20 feet beneath the streets of the city having been buried under layers of City development. The wall helped protect the City of London from its enemies.

You need to have permission to see the full glory of this extensive chunk of wall, but you can get a good idea of what it is like through a window in the square. Go down an alley

London Wall under the Merrill Lynch building

London Wall by Tower Hill Underground Station

next to the Viaduct pub at the junction of Giltspur Street with Newgate Street (where it joins High Holborn). Walk down the alley and turn left into the courtyard opposite Caffe Nero. A little way along on the left you can peer through the window and see the wall. This is what remains of a four metre high wall and bastion built from stones carried by sea from Kent.

There is another bit of the wall in the basement of the Old Bailey nearby along the passageway where prisoners once walked to the gallows, but you will need to be on one of the official Old Bailey tours in order to see it.

Museum of London Archaeology (MOLA) area.

This is where one of the bastions or forts was located, which defended the wall. Start at Noble Street where remnants are visible (with a lot more underneath if you catch one of the MOLA tours). Then, on the other side of London Wall, there are more remains of the bastion and wall. If you double back and go down Wood Street to the churchyard of St Giles Cripplegate there is a generous expanse of the medievalised wall. There is yet another section in the underground car park, which runs the length of this part of London Wall road. Further along London Wall, part of the medieval wall (with Roman foundations) has been incorporated at All Hallows church.

Tower Hill Underground station.

The most dramatic section of surviving wall can be seen when you are exiting the station. It is the eastern end of it, Roman and Medieval, 33 yards long and standing at pretty much its full height of almost 12 yards. If you navigate around Coopers Row and the Grange Hotel, you can see more of the wall subtly blending in with modern buildings. A little further on, at One America Square, there is another large section, preserved on the lower floor of a commercial building.

42: THE STATUES OF VAUXHALL BRIDGE

Vauxhall Bridge definitely qualifies as a hidden gem, though you would never think so from walking across its mundane, deteriorating surface. It is almost designed not to be appreciated, because you can't easily see its treasures – eight marvellous, twice life-size sculptures hanging on the sides of the bridge, seemingly risking life and limb.

Made by two distinguished artists, F.W. Pomeroy and Alfred Drury, they hymn the praises of British creativity in the fields of pottery, engineering, architecture, agriculture, education, fine arts, science and – wait for it – local government. It is the only bridge in the whole country with statues on it, according to Historic England.

You get a fleeting glimpse of them if you pass under the bridge in a boat, but not enough time to savour them. Most people don't even notice. They are probably best seen from a drone. Apparently, they were only added as an afterthought when the bridge was, unusually, completed under budget.

In 1963 there were plans to replace Vauxhall Bridge with a modern version of the old London Bridge, complete with seven floors of shops, offices, hotel rooms and leisure facilities. But this barmy scheme, which would have ended the life of the statues, was abandoned because of costs. We must be thankful for small mercies.

43: THE REMAINS OF THE FIRST SOMERSET HOUSE

Somerset House – nowadays a vibrant creative centre – was constructed in the 1770s on the site of an earlier Tudor palace built by the rapacious – it's not too strong a word – Edward Seymour, the eldest brother of Jane Seymour and the first Duke of Somerset. Remnants of his palace, one of a number of aristocrats' mansions that lined the banks of the Thames, can still be found on the site, as indeed can earlier Saxon remains.

Somerset bludgeoned his way to becoming Lord Protector of the nine-year-old Edward VI after the death of his father Henry VIII and set about constructing a palace big enough for his image of himself.

It was built on robbery. He pillaged local inns, churches and other places without compensation to build his grandiose home. He stole stone from the charnel house of Saint Paul's and parts of the Priory of Saint John of Jerusalem at Clerkenwell. According to the writer Thomas Pennant, he was only stopped from stealing stone from the monastery of Westminster Abbey by being bribed with 14 manors. When he tried to demolish the nearby St Margaret's Church it provoked a riot by locals and he backed off.

Later, providence came to the rescue: Protector Somerset was executed on Tower Hill before his palace was completed, an event that was lamented, according to Pennant, but only because his overthrow was brought about by "a man more wicked, more ambitious and detested than himself". Those were the days.

Somerset House then became an occasional residence for royalty, including Elizabeth I, before being pulled down in 1775. It was replaced by the current Palladian design, which until recently housed government services, giving it some claim to be the first dedicated office block ever built.

Fascinatingly, there are still traces of the original building to be found if you know where to look – or if you get onto a conducted tour. The most dramatic lie under a glass floor, appropriately in the archaeology department of King's College (see photo). They include a Tudor wall on the left and chalky medieval remains next to a bed of stones beneath which was uncovered a rubbish tip dating to the time the Saxons established the trading port of Lundenwic along the Strand.

At the eastern end of the building yard, where King's students park their bikes, is a late 17th century wall – the only free standing remnant of the old palace. (see photo) On the other side is the entrance to what for years has been known as the Roman Bath, partly because it was mentioned by Dickens and other authors. However, King's professor Michael Trapp has established that, although it has been used as a cold bath for periods, it was in fact a much taller structure which fed water into spectacular fountain in the Somerset House gardens.

44: THE HAUNTINGLY BEAUTIFUL TEMPLE CHURCH

On March 15, 1927, the choir of Temple Church recorded O For The Wings Of A Dove by Felix Mendelssohn with a 15-year-old boy called Ernest Lough as the soloist. Young Ernest is believed to have had to stand on a couple of books in order to reach the microphone. The recording became a global hit, one of the first to reach a million sales – incredible for a classical record in those days. It eventually sold nearly seven million copies. For many years afterwards, visitors from around the world flocked to the site of the original recording. Lough was one of the church's loyal parishioners, and is buried in its yard.

More recently, Temple Church has achieved notoriety by being featured in Dan Brown's bestselling thriller The Da Vinci Code and its movie adaptation, thereby attracting yet more hordes of visitors, albeit for fictional reasons. This is all for the good, otherwise tourists would be unlikely to stumble across this marvellous building hidden in the time warp of the Inns of Court, whose outside walls date back to its consecration in 1185.

The church served the Knights Templar, who were military monks pledged to protect pilgrims making their way to the Holy Land. The order was founded on the site of King Solomon's Temple in Jerusalem, the model for other circular churches the Templars built in the big cities of Europe. At first, the knights were backed by popes and kings, but eventually the huge wealth they accumulated – which effectively meant they were the world's first international bankers – attracted enemies. Edward II confiscated the London Temple and later Henry VIII did the same. James I granted the Temple Church in perpetuity to the emerging Inns, as long as they maintained the edifice – which they do to this day.

Among the dignitaries buried in this hauntingly beautiful church – as a horizontally laid statue – is William Marshal (c 1147-1219), a legendary warrior who helped the hapless King John govern England for a time after he took the throne in 1199. Marshal was a comparatively poor knight who ended up as the first Earl of Pembroke and Regent of England, serving under no less than five Angevin kings altogether. He was largely responsible for saving the dynasty of the Plantagenets, which would survive for 250 years.

45: THE THAMES WATERMEN'S SEAT OF POWER

This tiny bit of masonry on the wall of the Real Greek restaurant on Bankside near the Globe Theatre is all that remains to remind us of what was once London's biggest workforce and one of the most successful trade unions ever seen on the planet. All that is left is part of one of the seats where the watermen used to rest in Shakespeare's time – though it would have been nearer the river then.

The watermen earned their bread by ferrying people across the Thames in their wherries – small, passenger boats – to visit the theatres or engage in some nefarious pursuit. It was the only way of crossing the river apart from the narrow, congested and expensive London Bridge or the ferry at Lambeth, which was for horses.

There are reckoned to have been about 2,500 ferrymen operating along the Thames for hundreds of years. Their longevity was helped by the City of London, which had a monopoly on the revenues from London Bridge and was therefore happy with the status quo. This combined with the consequent massive industrial power of the waterman to prevent the construction of any new bridge across the Thames until 1750, when Westminster Bridge was built.

Watermen were tough, rough-hewn men, often veterans of overseas campaigns, who could be press-ganged into the navy at any moment and vied with each other when jostling for business at the foot of one of the numerous landing points on the river.

The most celebrated of watermen was the people's poet John Taylor, who fought for the democratisation of the watermen's guild and is one of the first people to have written of Shakespeare's death, in a 1620 poem called *The Praise of Hemp-seed* where he noted: "Spenser, and Shakespeare did in art excel".

Among Taylor's other achievements was travelling in a paper boat from Central London to Queenborough in the Thames estuary and penning one of the earliest palindromes: "Lewd did I live & evil I did dwel".

In another book, Taylor backed the watermen's disputes with the theatre companies when from 1612 they moved their premises from the south bank to the north, thereby depriving the ferries of traffic. He harangued the coachmen who were taking business from the wherries too.

The prevention of bridge building on the Thames was undoubtedly a restraint of trade, which ought to have been removed. It stands as a unique example of capital – the City of London – joining forces with labour – the wherrymen – to preserve a lucrative monopoly.

46: THE GRAY'S INN TIME WARP

On December 28 1594 a play was performed in the hall of Gray's Inn, one of the four Inns of Court, by what the hall's diary described as "a company of base and common players". After a riotous evening of drunken revelling the official report dismissed it as The Night of Errors. But those "base and common players" were in fact William Shakespeare's troupe, including Shakespeare himself, and the play was The Comedy of Errors. On special occasions it is still possible to see the play staged in the very hall – albeit reconstructed – where it was once put on with Shakespeare in the cast.

Gray's Inn could almost drown in its own literary history. Its Elizabethan alumni include George Chapman, the playwright whose translation of Homer were drooled over by John Keats, and Thomas Middleton, who co-wrote Macbeth and is now enjoying a renaissance in his own right. But its most celebrated resident was Francis Bacon, whose statue adorns Gray's Inn's South Square (see photo). It is a tad ironic that the large garden at the back of the Inn which almost certainly inspired Bacon's famous essay Of Gardens, which began "God Almighty first planted a garden, and, indeed, it is the purest of human pleasures" was only constructed after he had acquired the neighbouring parkland and cleared the "lower orders" away. Paradise comes at a price for some.

Gray's Inn is curious. The footprint of the building is almost exactly as it was in medieval times, but it has been so heavily rebuilt that hardly any of the stonework is original. If you look at the hall and chapel from the north, they are built roughly where the town house or "inn" of its first owner Lord Grey of Wilton (in Herefordshire) would have been. But little remains from medieval times except a holy water font embedded in the wall, recycled bricks inside, some majestic stained glass (not least of Francis Bacon) and possibly some window frames. However it is likely that the screen in the hall – dating to the 1590s – could have been there at the time of Shakespeare's performance.

If you come into Gray's Inn by way of Gray's Inn Road you will be entering one of the time warps of London. Suddenly, the roar of City's traffic dims to near nothingness and you can walk through territory little changed for hundreds of years and with barely a moving car in sight. Every evening a curfew bell is still heard in South Square, one of only two in London (the other being in the Tower of London), that preserve the tradition of a "curfew" or "curfeu", a word derived from the French "couvre feu" or cover the fire, which, had it been observed in 1666, might have prevented the Great Fire of London.

These days, the curfew in South Square is generated electronically rather than with an actual bell, but at least an old tradition is being maintained.

47: BEDLAM'S PROGRESS

Many years ago I worked in the City office of the Guardian newspaper in Salisbury House, between London Wall and the lovely garden of Finsbury Circus. I had no idea until decades later, when I looked at an old map, (see image) that it was on the exact site of the second Bedlam lunatic asylum.

A monumental building, which included parts of the original London Wall, it was designed by the amazing polymath Robert Hooke, whose only sin was to have been a contemporary of Christopher Wren and Isaac Newton, who outsmarted him in fame though not in talent.

The original Bedlam (or Bethlehem) Hospital, built in 1247, was around the corner in Bishopsgate where Liverpool Street Station is now located. It had gained a terrible reputation because of appalling living conditions and a dreadful practice whereby members of the public paid to see the inmates suffering.

It was, however, the first institution of its kind in Britain – and possibly anywhere else – so it was at the start of a long learning curve. The management sought "people of quality" to visit as well as "the lower orders" in a kind of primitive business plan to generate compassion and increase donations.

In the eighteenth century, according to some estimates, anything up to 90,000 Londoners a year paid a penny to visit the asylum and watch the antics of the inmates, who were often chained to a wall in their cells, as depicted by William Hogarth in A Rake's Progress, in which the louche son of a rich merchant ends up in Bedlam. The satirist Jonathan Swift suggested that "as all the politicians were mad, they should recruit for Parliament from inside".

Bedlam was moved to St Georges Fields in Southwark where it lasted until 1930 in a building that was taken over a few years later in 1936 by the Imperial War Museum, which is still there. Today, Bedlam exists in its fourth home as the Bethlem Royal Hospital and Maudsley NHS Foundation Trust in Bromley, where it is a world leader in the treatment of mental illness.

"BEDLAM" IN THE EIGHTEENTH CENTURY.—Bethlehem Hospital was originally at Bishopsgate, being removed to Moorfields in 1675 and in 1815 to the site in South London which it is about to vacate. Our print shows the old Hospital at Moorfields, where in the eighteenth century it was customary to allow the public to see the lunatics chained to the walls. Over a long period the institution was popularly known as "Bedlam."

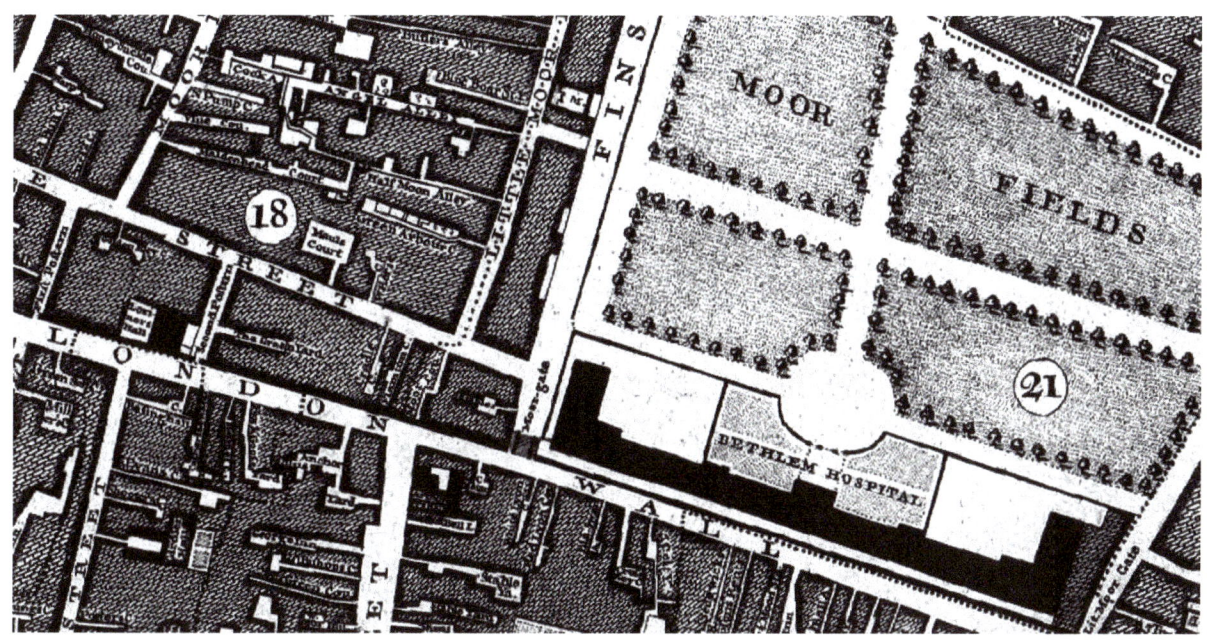

48: THE FISHMONGERS' HALL

For centuries the Fishmongers' Hall on the north side of London Bridge was the tallest secular building in London. Look at it now! It is more like one of the smallest as it gets lost in the dash for the sky.

The Worshipful Company of Fishmongers has been active for well over 700 years, mainly because for a long time it had a monopoly of fish sales in London. Even today, unlike many other livery companies that have morphed into social and charitable institutions, the Fishmongers Company maintains one of its founding missions, monitoring the quality of fish at Billingsgate.

The livery companies, with their opulent halls and the churches mainly built by Christopher Wren, are the two great survivors of ancient times in the City of London. Since it is much easier to enter a church than a livery company, I jumped at an opportunity to visit the Fishmongers' Hall. And I was not disappointed.

There are lots of interesting artefacts inside, not least the famous portrait of the queen by Pietro Annigoni which, surprisingly looking back on it, was controversial when it was painted in the 1950s. The Fishmongers commissioned the painting but inadvisedly sold the image rights to the Annigoni estate. This means that when films are shot in the Hall the makers have to pay a sizeable chunk of royalties to the estate if they want the painting in the background. In the background of the portrait on the left is a tiny figure in a boat, meant to be Annigoni who, like Alfred Hitchcock, enjoyed appearing in his own productions. He also did a similar portrait of a slightly scowling Duke of Edinburgh which is kept in a smaller room. Wonder why.

On the stairway of the Hall there is a wonderfully detailed statue carved from an elm tree of Sir William Walworth, a grandee of the Company, raising his dagger to kill Wat Tyler at Smithfield during the Peasants' Revolt of 1381. Until recently it was thought to be the actual dagger used by Sir William but it turns out it is of more recent origin.

There is plenty of silverware around and also a marvellous relic of the medieval London Bridge in the form of a large armchair hewn out of wood from the bridge. The slats across are carved in the shape of the old bridges. Thus is preserved a long link with London Bridge which separates the Fishmongers' Hall from the old Billingsgate market where it ploughed its trade.

The original building was one of the first to be burned down in the Great Fire of 1666. The present Greek revival version was designed by Henry Roberts. He is not a well-known architect, but his helpers included the illustrious George Gilbert Scott and he worked under the supervision of Sir Robert Smirke, whose works include the main block and facade of the British Museum.

49: THE THAMES FORESHORE

Few things are taken more for granted by Londoners than the foreshore of the River Thames. It is lost not only in memory but also in real time twice daily as the tidal river rises and falls by seven metres to cover up the foreshore completely. It is reckoned to be the longest archeological site in any capital city.

Mudlarks – who have to be registered – regularly find fragments of history there, from pipes to pottery still washed up on the banks each day. More importantly, the Museum of London, aided by volunteers, has been uncovering thousands of artefacts and mapping amazing archaeological treasures from Teddington to Greenwich and beyond.

If you are watchful about rising tides and wear appropriate footwear, you can go down some of the regular steps to the foreshore and rummage among the historic fragments, some of which may have been washed up that very day. But there are rules about what you can take away and it might be better to go on one of the fascinating walks organised by the Thames Discovery Programme. I wrote this poem after one such walk.

Observe, twice daily; the angry sea drives
The Thames back upstream then quickly subsides
Straining the banks that can barely cope
Shaking the foreshore like a kaleidoscope
Leaving freshly churned history on the beach
Medieval pipes, bricks, tiles, shards each
Could tell a story if only it could speak
Who last smoked this pipe? What mansion unknown
Was stealthily stripped of this half-hewn stone
Who built by Vauxhall bridge those submerged posts
Which emerge like 7,000 year old ghosts
And then only at the lowest of low tides
But of the gems the Thames so deftly hides
Watch your step you might be treading we're told
On micraster fossils a million years old
Curated by the river over the centuries
By this, our Thames, free museum of memories.

A Museum of London foreshore tour

50: THE RING OF FORTS

It is difficult to believe, but London was once protected by a vast ring of fortifications, which have completely vanished. It is without question the largest bit of Lost London ever found – or rather not found, because no-one has ever discovered any remains. They don't come any more lost than that.

The forts were built in the 1640s during the civil war to protect London against invasion by King Charles I's royalist army, which had retreated to the country but was preparing an attack on the capital. It must not be confused with the London Wall built by the Romans, much of which still exists. Cromwell's fort cordon was over three times bigger than that wall, with the section north of the Thames stretching in a sort of semi-circle from Wapping in the east to near Vauxhall Bridge in the west before rounding off at Southwark.

We know from contemporary accounts that it was constructed by thousands of citizens who dug ditches, trenches and a series of forts along the perimeter including at Shoreditch (top end of Brick Lane), Mount Pleasant, Hyde Park Corner and Constitution Hill before dropping down to what was known as Tothill Fields, south of today's Victoria where I now live.

To find the nearest fort to my home I consulted George Vertue's map of the fortifications (below) which was drawn some time later, in 1738, and is almost the only map of the wall extant. My local fort is simply marked as being in Tothill Fields. But where? The redoubtable Ian Mansfield, author of Ian Visits, who has walked around the presumed lines of the fortifications, says that Vauxhall Bridge Road was the likely line of the wall where it meets Rochester Row, an ancient trackway where later maps

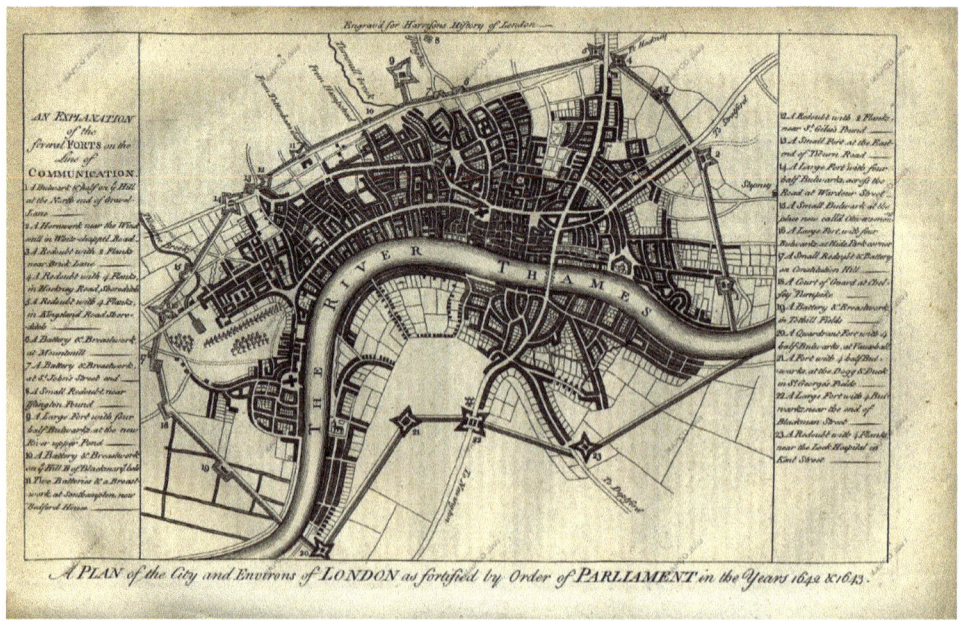

A PLAN of the City and Environs of LONDON as fortified by Order of PARLIAMENT in the Years 1642 &1643.

Lillington Gardens - Once a site for one of the forts

"show a distinctive earth disturbance at the end of Rochester Row".

Guy Mannes Abbot, writing in the Westminster History Review, puts the site of the fort further down Vauxhall Bridge Road where the prize-winning council estate Lillington Gardens Estate now is (see main picture).

Either of these sites could be the right one, not least because both of them follow the course of the River Tyburn, whose presence would have made the fort more formidable. The Tyburn still runs underground – albeit merged with Joseph Bazalgette's sewage system – from the junction of Francis Street with Kings's Scholar's Passage along the western side of Lillington Gardens (Tachbrook Street) to the Thames west of Vauxhall Bridge.

The main reason there is no trace of these monumental structures is that parliament ordered their destruction. Since then, there has been no reason to rebuild them. But if the Mayor of London wants to protect London from an onslaught by Brexiteers, he knows where to get the plans.

51: THE WORLD'S FIRST CIRCUS

If you stroll over Westminster Bridge to the eastern end of St Thomas' Hospital – near where the Florence Nightingale Museum now is – you will be standing on the site of the world's first circus. Of course, circuses in some form had existed for many centuries. The word itself is of Greek origin and exhibitions of strange animals were held in ancient Egypt. But it is generally agreed that the modern circus was born on this London spot on 9 January 1768 when Philip Astley (1742-1814), born in Newcastle-under-Lyme, pioneered it in the form of a modern arena surrounded by tiers of seats from which to watch trick horse-riding and other acrobatic exercises. Astley reckoned that a diameter of 42 feet for the circus ring was needed so horses could move comfortably, a standard that is still used today. Tumblers, tightrope walkers and clowns were added later.

Astley's success soon spawned imitators. A rival, Charles Hughes, who had once worked with Astley, set up a Royal Circus a short distance from Astley's Amphitheatre of Equestrian Arts. Hughes, who was the first to use the word "circus" in this context, took his troupe to entertain Catherine the Great in 1790 and is credited with planting the idea of circuses in Russia. Meanwhile, John Bill Ricketts, a former student of Hughes, went to America and established a circus in Philadelphia. A performance in 1793 was attended by George Washington and a commemorative plaque now stands on the site – which is more than can be said for Astley's original.

Later on, the barnstorming US showman PT Barnum became more successful than Astley, but there is no doubt who was the true architect of circuses. Astley established wooden amphitheatres around Britain and 18 in other European cities. He opened his first Paris circus in 1782 and is buried in the Pere Lachaise cemetery in Paris. In 1844, long after Astley's death, the circus was still up to its tricks. The Annual Register reported that "an immense number of people" lined the Thames to watch a clown from Astleys sail from Vauxhall to Westminster Bridge in a washing tub pulled by two geese and then walk casually into the circus. That must have been one of the greatest PR stunts of its time.

Amazingly, the world's first modern circus was situated only a few hundred yards from what is claimed to be the world's first serious music hall, which I wrote about elsewhere. Astley's circus has long since disappeared but it lives on in literature having been mentioned by Jane Austen, James Joyce, Charles Dickens and Tracy Chevalier.

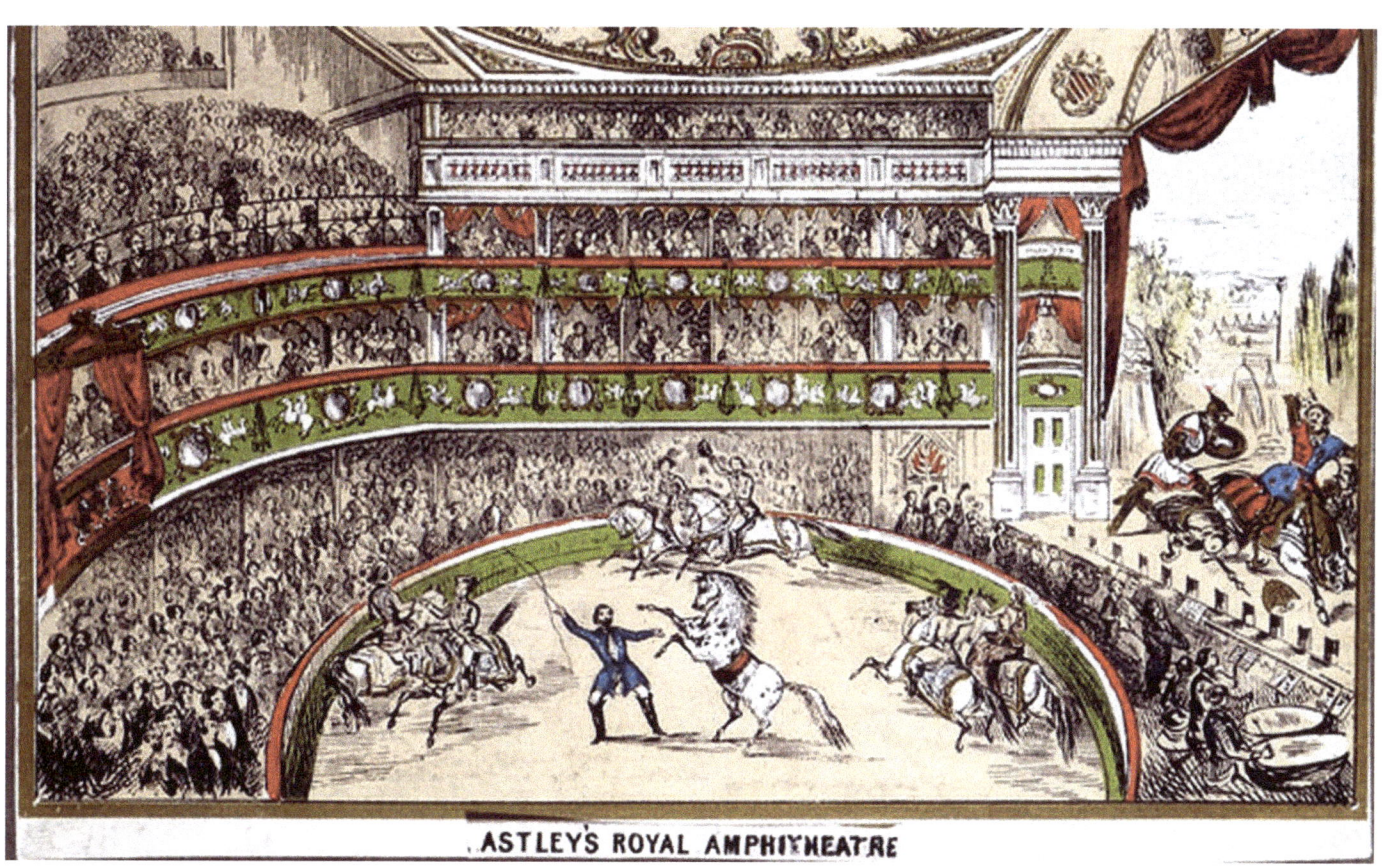

ASTLEY'S ROYAL AMPHITHEATRE

52: THE DEVIL'S ACRE

When Charles Dickens called the streets around Old Pye Street (south of today's Victoria Street) "The Devil's Acre" he knew what he was talking about. Several other parts of London could claim to be the most destitute – Shoreditch, Saint Giles and Turnmill Street for a start – but none were quite as abominable as this territory a few hundred yards away from the sublimity of Westminster Abbey and the Houses of Parliament.

Indeed, it was its proximity to the Abbey that caused many of its problems. For centuries a large area of land outside the Abbey, thanks to a decree of Edward the Confessor, was a sanctuary where criminals were safe from the long arm of the law. It thus became a magnet for disreputables and the tradition lingered long after the abolition of sanctuary.

In the first edition of his Household Words, Dickens described the neighbourhood as "begirt by scenes of indescribable infamy and pollution; the blackest tide of moral turpitude that flows in the capital rolls its filthy wavelets up to the very walls of Westminster Abbey."

Horrific overcrowding – sometimes as many as 12 people to a room and with up to half the population engaged in thieving according to some reports, it is not surprising that it became a no-go area for the police.

In St Anne's Lane, off Old Pye Street, a contemporary described a side court which had "every feature of a sewer, and found a long puddle of sewage soaking in the hollow centre. The passages of the low black huts on either side were like old sooty chimneys, and the inhabitants were buried out of sight in the gloom."

Further down Old Pye Street in Perkins Rents was a pub called One Tun which has rightly been described as a school for pickpockets. It may well have been an inspiration for Dickens when he wrote Oliver Twist, though there are other candidates. It was rescued by philanthropist Adeline M. Cooper, who raised money to convert the pub into a ragged school.

The Devil's Acre was rescued partly by the construction of Victoria Street around 1850 with its associated slum clearance and partly by the emergence of other philanthropists such as William Gibbs and George Peabody, who built modernised blocks of flats around Devil's Acre for the poor and which are still very much functional today.

Well, actually, they were for the poor but not for the very poor, as you had to have a job to afford the affordable rents. And since they were far nicer and bigger – only a few to an apartment rather than over a dozen in the slums they replaced – it made conditions even worse for those ejected from the slums who had nowhere else to go. They were a marvellous advance but, as with so many reforms, there were unforeseen consequences. Meanwhile Devil's Acre is long gone, a bit of Lost London we are happy to say "Good Riddance" to.

Gustav Doré's drawing of the slums in Devil's Acre (the building at the back is still there)

53: CARDINAL WOLSEY'S WINE CELLAR

The Tudor wine cellar of Cardinal Wolsey – later snatched by Henry VIII along with the rest of Wolsey's York Palace when the cardinal failed to get the monarch a divorce – is one of London's spectacular buried treasures. Sadly, very few people get to see it because it is below ground in the bowels of the Ministry of Defence on Horse Guards Avenue, to the right of the main entrance. Special permission is required to view it and tough security procedures must be gone through.

The amazing thing is that it is there at all, having survived several serious fires over the centuries and, more critically, the 1940s plans for the new Ministry of Defence building which included its destruction. Only after protests by Queen Mary (widow of George V) was it saved. I hope they gave her a decent drink. The rescue involved encasing the cellar in steel and concrete and lowering it by six metres so it didn't interfere with the contours of the new building. It is the last intact piece of Henry VIII's Palace of Westminster, once bigger – though much uglier – than Louis XIV's Versailles. It was the main palace of the admittedly peripatetic English monarchs for 200 years.

When visiting, what struck me after negotiating a series of stairways was not just the unexpectedly large size of the cellar itself but the way it is presented. It is done in museum style, with large reproductions of paintings and maps, and numerous boards explaining the historical background to it as you walk around the outside of the mausoleum-style structure that now encases it. This was an impressive bit of engineering for the time. It took 90 men 18 months, but provided the ministry with an extra 1,335 square feet of office space. The justification for doing this was that otherwise the cellar would have protruded 10 yards into Horse Guards Avenue. What would have been so wrong about that?

Stepping into the cellar is like entering a time capsule. In the depths of a building where battles are planned and nuclear tactics discussed are the intact remains of a piece of Tudor times. It is just as it was 600 years ago bar a few replacement stones, a lick of white paint on the walls and some more recent wine barrels installed at each end to recreate part of the atmosphere of a bygone age. There is a stark beauty to the columns and the vaulted ceiling made of sculptured bricks, which come together in "V" shapes.

There has been speculation about what sort of wines were stored here to slate the Cardinal's thirst. England – and London – were not short of vineyards in those days, but it is presumed that Tudor snobbery – sorry, taste – would have ensured that most of the wines came from France including, possibly, from the then (still) white wine region of champagne. That would have been a memorable experience.

There is also a bit of unfinished business. The wine cellar was very close to one of the halls of Wolsey's Palace where, in later years, some of Shakespeare's plays were produced. I read somewhere that part of the wall of that hall can still be seen. Does anyone know where it is?

Wolsey's wine cellar

54: THE ORIGIN OF PARLIAMENT

If you fancy a cup of coffee in the wine cellar, now called the Cellarium, of Westminster Abbey – and why not? – it is worth going upstairs to the upper café where, if you glance out of the window, you will see a very old wall. This is not any old wall. It is all that remains of the refectory where monks ate their meals in medieval times. But it wasn't just a dining room, it was also the place where the embryonic House of Commons – doing a kind of AirBnb with the Abbey – met for over 60 years. Members would have had to move out when the monks wanted to eat.

It wasn't the first Commons meeting place, but it was the first that its members could call home. The first meeting of the lower house was in the elaborate Painted Chamber over the road in the Royal Palace and after that there was a long spell in the Abbey's Chapter House – a beautiful building which still exists today – but the acoustics were poor and the monks did not like their prayers and rituals being interrupted. So the Commons moved into the much more commodious refectory where, according to historian Alasdair Hawkyard, they met almost without interruption from 1483 until after the dissolution of the monasteries in 1548, when the Commons was moved to St Stephen's Chapel. It met there until Parliament was burned down in the fire of 1834.

The site of the original Commons can merely be glimpsed from the Cellarium, because it is actually the back garden of Ashburnam House, which is part of Westminster School and can only be seen out of term time on an official visit. The former floor of the refectory is now covered by a lawn, but the north wall is there in all its faded glory.

Somewhat bizarrely, on the right side of the photo are several Eton fives courts – yes right in the middle of Westminster. They are of comparatively recent construction and should not distract our attention from what is in the background – the wall that launched the House of Commons.

The wall that gave birth to Parliament

55: TRACES OF THE GREAT EXHIBITON

It was – and still is – a Wonder of the World. When the Crystal Palace was constructed in Hyde Park in 1851 by the formidable Joseph Paxton to house the Great Exhibition of industrial artefacts from around the globe, it was the biggest building on Earth. You have to run nearly a mile to get around the site. Go there and see.

Over six million visitors, equivalent to a quarter of the nation's population, made the journey there. It marked the first time that people of all classes mixed together on a big scale (well, after the first few weeks, during which the price was so high only the rich could afford to go). It marked the high point of Britain's industrial power, when we were self-confident enough to invite the rest of the world to come and match our products.

The Palace was, amazingly, built in only nine months from prefabricated standardised bits of glass and iron – eat your heart out, IKEA – and, wait for it, not only made a handsome profit (£186,400), which helped to finance the museums of South Kensington, but it is still making a profit of over £2.4 million a year today. The money is distributed to worthy

THE CRYSTAL PALACE IN HYDE PARK FOR GRAND INTERNATIONAL EXHIBITION OF 1851.
Dedicated to the Royal Commissioners

innovative causes. The finance was raised largely by public subscription. No other industrial exhibition was able to equal that achievement.

It was, of course, a temporary structure which was moved to South London after only six months, where it lent its name – which the magazine Punch had coined – to the area and the football club around it before it was burned down in 1936. Virtually nothing of it remains in Hyde Park now, apart from the Coalbrookdale Gates, which were moved to their present position at the south end of West Carriage Drive after they failed to attract a buyer at a post-Exhibition auction.

The only other remnant there, apart from some underground pipes, is a latrine which, according to the man who uncovered it, Edward Strickland, may have been used by the workers building the Exhibition building. Some people think it may be the origin of the phrase "spend a penny", as 675,000 pennies were spent there, though there are other candidates for that prestigious coinage.

Until recently there was nothing at all to show exactly where the Crystal Palace stood, but now there are five plaques dotted around the huge expanse of what is now called the old football pitches. These give its almost exact dimensions, though it is a bit like hunt the thimble to find them.

Nobody in the cafe near the Exhibition Road end of Hyde Park had even heard of them when I asked, and were quite surprised when I located one of the plaques on the floor of the terrace where they regularly serve coffee and snacks (see photo). It's always the same. The nearer you to something the less likely you are to see it. Crystal clear.

Latrine

56: LONDON'S FIRST SHOPPING MALL

The sixteenth century Royal Exchange building is situated in the City of London between the Bank of England and the Mansion House. If you wonder why this historic building has been turned into a succession of posh shops the answer is that that is how it started.

When the formidable merchant Sir Thomas Gresham built the nation's first stock exchange or Bourse there in 1567 so that traders could meet in one central place instead of in the surrounding streets, he also turned the first floor into an array of 150 shops or stalls, mainly catering to well-to-do women. It thus has a strong claim to be Britain's first shopping mall. It was said you could find more coaches parked there than outside church doors. The building was officially opened in January 1571 by Queen Elizabeth I who gave permission for use of the title Royal and a license to sell alcohol.

If can be argued that Sir Thomas's vision laid the foundations for Britain's financial supremacy. But the interesting thing is the extent to which then – as now – that success depended on foreigners. Sir Thomas saw the commercial opportunity provided by the arrival of immigrants piling into London to escape the clutches of the Inquisition. He got permission from the City's ruling aldermen to "employ such strangers about the making of the said Burse, as he might think proper."

The works were "under the guidance of a Flemish architect, and conducted by a Flemish carpenter", according to John William Burgon, biographer of Sir Thomas, who also claimed that, apart from wood from Suffolk "nearly all of the materials of which the edifice was composed were brought from Flanders."

Labourers protested at the immigrant influx and, according to Burgon, the bricklayers of the city had been guilty of "many misdemeanours, both in words and deeds" towards Sir Thomas – jealous, probably, of the foreigners he had begun to employ. Not only that but half of the merchants trading in the Exchange were foreign too, including from Holland France and Germany, as Sir Thomas sought to wrest financial and trading success away from Antwerp and Venice.

Burgon concluded: "His (Gresham's) wish to see the arts and artisans of the Low Countries transported into England was actually fulfilled and so completely that our commercial greatness may be said to have arisen on the ruins of that of Antwerp. The Flemings came over in immense numbers, established their manufactures, and enriched the country to a prodigious extent. A census taken in 1567 found that of 4,851 strangers in the city no less than 3,838 were Dutch at a time when London's population was around 255,000."

57: FLEET PRISON

One of the capital's many debtors' jails was later the site where a famous political party was born.

The nondescript modern building Five Fleet Place on Farringdon Street is sitting on a lot of history. It is worth viewing it from across the road to take in the fact that the block on which it now stands was for over 900 years the site of the notorious Fleet Prison, where debtors and others were incarcerated. Later, it was on this site that the Labour Party was founded. It is strange for us to imagine a prison on the main road whose inmates could beg from the windows or even walk around outside if they had bribed their (privatised) warders enough. The River Fleet – or Ditch as it was known because of all the sewage dumped in it – ran outside the prison under the road: indeed it still does, flowing down the route of Farringdon Road and Farringdon Street to the Thames at Blackfriars.

You could start a university with some of the inmates of Fleet prison. Alumni include: William Penn, the future founder of Pennsylvania (banged up for his unorthodox religious beliefs); John Cleland, author of Fanny Hill; John Donne, the poet (imprisoned for illegally marrying his wife); and Charles Hall, an early economist and socialist who would have been well pleased to know that the Labour Party would eventually begin in the same place. In fiction, Samuel Pickwick was imprisoned in the Fleet in Charles Dickens's The Pickwick Papers, and in Shakespeare's Henry IV Part II, the Chief Justice orders his men: "Go, carry Sir John Falstaff to the Fleet; Take all his company along with him."

The Fleet was a debtors prison as long ago as 1290 and existed even earlier than that. It was destroyed during the Peasants Revolt, led by Wat Tyler, in 1381, burned down during the Great Fire of London in 1666 and destroyed yet again during the Gordon Riots of 1780 (though the rioters gave advance warning to the prisoners in order to minimise casualties). It was finally demolished in 1846. In 1872 the Congregational Memorial Hall was constructed on the site and it was there, on February 27, 1900, that the Labour Party was created during a conference held by all the leading socialist groups and trade unions. All that remains of all this today is a rather dour plaque.

From a drawing by Shepherd

FLEET PRISON AND FARRINGDON STREET

58: QUEEN ANNE'S MANSIONS 'MONSTER BLOCKS'

A rogue banker caused outrage by building a 141-foot residential block in Victorian times, but nobody could do a thing to stop him

With so much controversy about the exploding height of buildings it is good to remind ourselves of the one that started it all – Queen Anne's Mansions opposite St James' Park station, the first high-rise flats in London. In those days we didn't build big. For centuries the tallest secular building in London was the Fishmongers Hall by London Bridge which is now a dwarf among the buildings around it.

In the mid 1870s, Henry Hankey, a dodgy City banker, erected Queen Anne's Mansions, to an unprecedented – wait for it – 10 storeys high, rising in part to 12 storeys. In 1877, at some 141 feet tall, it was more than twice as high as normal flats of that time. And he did it without bothering with the tiresome task of asking permission.

Twelve floors may not seem large to us today, as developers line the whole of one side of Victoria Street with 20-storey plus giants, but it was hugely controversial then. The Metropolitan Fire Service warned that its hoses could not reach the top of the building in the event of fire. Queen Victoria objected because she could no longer view the Houses of Parliament over which she presided from Buckingham Palace. The Builder magazine described it as "monster blocks of dwellings" while the Times dismissed it as "the most elevated thing in bricks and mortar since the Tower of Babel". (Richard Dennis's excellent 2008 paper on "Babylonian Flats" is the source for the facts and quotes above).

When Hankey started to expand the building along Petty France, the architect of the Grosvenor Hotel (the one by Victoria Station) James Knowles – who admittedly lived next door to the mansions – wrote to the Metropolitan Board of Works saying that the mansions would "constitute an eyesore so offensive as would disgrace the whole neighbourhood of Westminster… and turn this quarter of London into a laughing stock". Goodness knows what Mr Knowles would make of the current redevelopment of Victoria Street. He would be lost for words.

Eventually, the London County Council gave up its attempts to prove that Hankey's building was illegal by trying to make sure nothing like it would happen again. In an Act of 1890 the maximum height of new buildings was to be 90 feet – later reduced to 80 feet in an ensuing Act in 1894.

Queen Anne's Mansions continued to be a paradigm of ugliness in the early 20th century. A drawing of "one of the most inexcusable buildings in modern London" was included in 1905 in Henry James's English Hours. Of course, one solution was to live in the mansions so you could get its wonderful views without having to look at the building itself. it was adopted by many people, including MPs who railed against it in Parliament.

The mansion block lasted until the 1970s when it was pulled down and replaced by an even bigger and if not uglier, then certainly more brutalist building – the new Ministry of Justice headquarters, designed by Sir Basil Spence.

Whether, in the long term, the original mansion block was a hero or villain depends on your point of view. It was almost universally reviled, but the reaction to it kept London's skyline much lower than would otherwise have been the case for quite a few years. Win some, lose some.

Queen Anne's Mansions

59: THE BROADWOOD PIANO FACTORY

It was Beethoven's pride and joy. He thought of it as "an altar on which I will place the choicest offerings of my mind to the divine Apollo." It was a favourite of Mozart and Chopin. Listz played one on his last visit to London.

This was the John Broadwood piano, made by the oldest, largest and most celebrated piano manufacturing company in the world, which by 1842 was producing 2,500 pianos a year. And where was it based? Not in France nor Germany but at 69 Horseferry Road in Victoria, between a brewery and a marble works opposite the corner of today's Monck Street where the huge Westminster Gas and Coke Company pioneered the world's first public supply of gas.

London in the 19th century was the global centre of piano manufacturing with over 130 factories, mainly located in Islington. But Broadwood chose Horseferry Road, an ancient route leading from Westminster to the horse ferry at Lambeth (by today's bridge) where tolls would be paid to the Archbishop of Canterbury at Lambeth Palace – a nice little earner, especially during the centuries when the only fixed crossing across the Thames was London Bridge.

The Broadwood factory, which made all the components of its pianos on the premises – a true craft industry – is long gone. The company still exists, though nowadays it manufactures abroad. The site is now a modern office block complete with coffee shop and betting shop. Progress.

60: HOW ELECTRICITY FLOWED FROM MAYFAIR ART

If you had the idea of creating the country's first electricity grid you probably wouldn't think of starting it at an art gallery. But that is what happened at the Grosvenor Gallery in Mayfair, which was set up in 1877 to take paintings rejected by the staid Royal Academy. It was there that John Ruskin famously said that Whistler's painting Nocturne in Black and Gold was "flinging a pot of paint in the public's face." Whistler sued and won, but after being given a miserable farthing in damages was propelled into bankruptcy.

In Oscar Wilde's The Picture of Dorian Gray, Lord Henry says that the painting of Dorian is so good it should be sent to the Grosvenor Gallery because the Royal Academy is too large and vulgar: "Whenever I have gone there, there have been either so many people that I have not been able to see the pictures, which was dreadful, or so many pictures that I have not been able to see the people which was worse. The Grosvenor is really the only place."

The Grosvenor, which was at 135 New Bond Street – occupied today by a Belstaff fashion store – did turn out to be somewhere special for a second reason when Sir Coutts Lindsay, who built it, decided in 1883 to use recently invented electricity generators to light the gallery. This proved so successful that neighbours wanted to be supplied too and, with the help of Sebastian Ferranti, he eventually delivered power from Regent's Park to the Thames and from Kensington to the City of London. Who could have guessed that such sparks would fly from of an institution of the avant-garde?

The Former Grosvenor Gallery

61: PENAL FOUNDATIONS OF WESTMINSTER CATHEDRAL

It's not every day you stumble across a buried prison near your front door. It happened to me a few years ago when workmen were digging up the road to renew the electricity cables. They had opened a long stretch along Thirleby Road, SW1, which clearly exposed the foundations of the famous Tothill Fields Prison as could be seen from old maps.

The prison once stretched between Francis Street and today's Victoria Street, covering the ground on which Westminster Cathedral was subsequently built. The cathedral's archivist tells me that the nine foot bed of solid concrete on which the house of correction was built forms a large part of the massive foundations of the cathedral, though it is no longer visible as further thick layers of brick and marble rubble were laid on top. Clearly, it is solidly based, as you would expect from so meticulous an architect as John Francis Bentley.

BOYS EXERCISING AT TOTHILL FIELDS PRISON.

Remnants of the old prison dug up by workmen

Tothill Fields was no ordinary jail. It was built in 1834 near the site of an earlier (1618) penitentiary on an eight acre site employing "open" principles as a panopticon (roughly translated as "see all"), very vaguely in keeping with theories espoused by Jeremy Bentham. The idea was that all of the prisoners could be viewed from a central point by a warder while not being able to see each other. They were not allowed to talk to each other either. It was pulled down in 1877 and the inmates moved to the much bigger Millbank Penitentiary, which occupied the site on which the Tate Gallery now stands.

It was not regarded as a success partly because it was – for its age – quite liberal-minded and nurtured a high proportion of re-offenders, who preferred life inside the prison gates to the violent destitution outside. In 1850 the regime was changed and male convicts were no longer held there. It became a prison just for women and boys under the age of seventeen. Henry Mayhew, the social reformer who had visited the prison in 1861, praised the staff for maintaining discipline without much need for physical punishment. Small wonder it proved so popular with recidivists.

62: THE AGELESS BEAUTY OF THE BLEWCOAT SCHOOL

The tiny Blewcoat School behind the Albert pub off Victoria Street is an enchanting building, with its beautiful time-worn brickwork and a statue of a pupil, complete with blue coat, standing in a recess beneath the original clock. If not exactly lost, it is certainly hidden. The amazing thing is that it is still there after nearly 350 years, even though it must feel totally lost among the huge office blocks that have sprung up around it.

The building is owned by the National Trust but it is now empty following the demise of a recent tenant – an up market wedding dress outfitter. But at the time of writing the Trust has allowed an imaginative designer to present an astonishing array of plants and twig – baskets outside that would grace a gallery such as Tate Modern. It is the only ancient building left in this part of Victoria, apart from another school – Grey Coat Hospital, which – unlike Blewcoat, which has long since closed – is still functioning today, as a successful Church of England academy for girls.

Both schools sprang from the education "turf wars" of the 17th century, when catholics and protestants vied to enlist poverty-stricken children growing up in slums at a time when there was no state education.

The garden of the twig magician

An excerpt from a parchment roll from around 1700 says it all:

> In the late reign, the Roman Catholick Priests and Jesuites were busie in making Proselytes and to that end set up Free Schools in the Savoy and other places in and about the City of London inviting all poor children to be educated by them gratis.

Anglicans responded in kind – if street kids were to be given an education for nothing, then it had better be Anglican and not RC. Local tradespeople in Westminster coughed up the money to provide religious and secular education for children living in horrific slums like those in Old Pye Street and Duck Lane (now St Matthew's Street) where the original Blewcoat was founded in 1698. It moved to its present location in Caxton Street in 1709, financed by local brewer William Greene.

The Blewcoat and Grey Coat weren't the only schools to hoist their colours. There was also a Green Coat School (where the Greencoat Boy pub now stands in Greencoat Place), a Brown Coat and a Black Coat, all three of which amalgamated to form today's Westminster City School for boys, also now an academy, which has close historic ties with Grey Coat.

The Blewcoat building is easily missed by the thousands of people who flock past en route to St James's Park station, but it is absolutely worth a detour as it is one of the very few buildings of such great age to have survived in an area where office blocks are built only to be demolished a few decades later. You don't have to believe that the school bears the imprint of Sir Christopher Wren – though it might well do – to let its fascinating history sink in.

63: THE ROYAL AQUARIUM

There is no larger lost building in central London than the Royal Aquarium. Opened in 1876, it was inspired by the 1851 Crystal Palace in Hyde Park and was almost as big, stretching from the edge of Parliament Square right down one side of Tothill Street to Dartmouth Street, near St James's Park station.

It hosted all sorts of attractions, including a very large angled glass and iron roof, clearly influenced by Joseph Paxton's for Crystal Palace, and a grand hall which was 340 feet long and 160 feet wide. Arthur Sullivan – of Gilbert and Sullivan fame – looked after the music and John Everett Millais, the paintings. It housed a 400-piece orchestra, a large reading room, a chess area, a roller skating rink, a palm court, sculptures, exotic trees, fountains and the biggest collection of circus and freak acts you would find anywhere.

These included the tightrope walker The Great Farini, Zazel the Human Cannonball, and a music hall where George Robey made his debut. Next door was the Aquarium Theatre, later re-named the Imperial Theatre. In 1907 this was demolished brick by brick and rebuilt as the Imperial, Canning Town, eventually becoming the Imperial Cinema before it was burned down in 1932.

The noble vision of the Royal Aquarium was to encourage "public instruction and entertainment" but standards soon deteriorated in an attempt to arrest a fall in customer numbers. The founding rule that "no lady unaccompanied by a gentleman would be admitted after dusk" lapsed into the admittance of lots of women, whose prime interest was fishing rather than aquariums.

One such lady, Emily Turner, was lucky. She was picked up there by a notorious serial killer Thomas Neil Cream masquerading as "Major Hamilton". He offered to set her up with rooms in Lambeth. He gave her pills which made her ill, but happily she survived. However, she refused to identify Cream in court for fear her lifestyle would become public.

A curious fact about the Aquarium is that it took only eleven months to build. Sadly, it proved uneconomic in the long run. It was closed in 1903 and sold to Wesleyans, who built the Methodist Central Hall on part of the site.

Its menu of high-minded art, music and literature was not what most people wanted in those days, and even its efforts to go down market with music hall acts and low level entertainment could not save it. But what a piece of Lost London it is. Imagine how popular a citadel to the arts would have been if it had survived. Like so many other things, maybe it was simply ahead of its time.

93

64: THE NOTORIOUS NEWGATE PRISON

The Old Bailey is known the world over as Britain's top criminal court. What is less well-known it is that it is built on the exact site of the notorious Newgate prison, which dates back to medieval times – and that parts of the old prison are still visible.

In its time Newgate held within its mawkish walls a wide variety of inmates, from notorious murderers to literary giants. Its alumni include Daniel Defoe, John Milton, Oscar Wilde and Jack Sheppard, the inspiration for the highwayman Captain Macheath in John Gay's The Beggar's Opera.

One of its most distinguished inmates was the Quaker William Penn, the future founder of the US state of Pennsylvania who was a drafter of an early version of the US constitution. In 1670 Penn, charge with unlawful assembly, was acquitted by a jury, only for the judge to order it to return a guilty verdict instead. When the jury refused, its members were promptly imprisoned by the judge, who also happened to be Lord Mayor of the City. However, the Chief Justice

Part of the old London Wall in the basement of the Old Bailey

later overturned this decision, thereby enshrining in law a jury's right to judge by its own convictions and not be over-ruled. It is ironic that this basic principle of English law – which has been strictly implemented at the Bailey ever since – was triggered by the actions of a man who was incarcerated in the jail that used to stand in the same location.

Many of the stones of Newgate were recycled in the new building. One of the walls in the courtyard is just as it was when it was a prison. An underground tunnel linking the Bailey with St Sepulchre's church opposite is claimed to have been built so priests could administer to the prisoners without having to weave their way through thousands of ghoulish spectators awaiting an execution. The atmospheric Viaduct Tavern opposite (formerly a gin palace) claims to contain cells from the old prison, though historians are not agreed on this.

What is not in dispute is that the bowels of the Old Bailey also contain a large chunk of London Wall, built by the Romans to enclose the city they built. Convicted murderers would pass it en route to Dead Man's Walk. And the gallows.

65: THE GREAT EASTERN STEAMSHIP

The Great Eastern steamship, built by the amazing Isambard Kingdom Brunel, was one of the wonders of its age. Constructed on the banks of the Thames at Millwall in 1858 to carry 4,000 passengers non stop to Australia, it was, at 692 feet, the longest ship the world had ever seen and remained so for over 40 years until the RMS Oceanic pipped it in 1899. It was also the first ship to be built almost completely of wrought iron and had three different modes of propulsion – propellers, sails and paddle wheels – to ensure she kept moving.

Although the ship was scrapped in 1890, the remains of the slipway on which it was launched can still be seen at low tide in Millwall, a shortish walk from Island Gardens DLR station. I took this photo of it at low tide, though the water was higher than expected because of rain, so only part of it was showing.

It almost boggles belief that Brunel built this monster on the banks of the Thames and had to launch it sideways from its moorings because there was not enough space on the river to do it in the conventional manner. Small wonder it took multiple efforts over several months to finally get it into the water.

The Great Eastern under construction on the Thames

The remains of the launching pad for the Great Eastern still visible today

The Great Eastern – the third of the large ships designed by Brunel – had a chequered career. While it was being built, Brunel's budget was cut from £500,000 to £250,000, entailing many economies including abandonment of plans to build a new dock. Bad luck followed it when it entered service, ranging from the bankruptcies of the various companies that owned it to boiler explosions and hitting an uncharted rock while negotiating entrance to New York harbour.

After being sold at auction, she found a new life laying transatlantic cables from Europe to America. In 1887 the ship was sold again and went to Liverpool where she was broken up. A sad end to a massive pioneering project by one of the greatest engineers Britain has produced (though he was the son of a Norman immigrant and did much of his schooling in France). The Great Eastern's worst mistake was to have been born decades ahead of its time.

66: THE STATUE THAT WAS TOO BIG FOR ITS BOOTS

At nine metres high, the Duke of Wellington statue built to commemorate his victory at the Battle of Waterloo was the largest equestrian statue in Britain. Designed by Decimus Burton and built out of metal from cannon captured during the Napoleonic Wars, it was placed on top of what was originally called the Green Park Arch, another Burton design, at Hyde Park Corner in 1846. It isn't there any more.

The statue's great size attracted widespread hostility. The Duke himself, who was also twice Prime Minister and three times leader of the Lords, felt rather differently, and the statue was deferentially left in place until 30 years after his death in 1852. When the arch, now known as the Wellington Arch or Constitution Arch, was moved about 100 yards to its present location in 1882-83, the giant statue was not replaced, and in 1885, it was moved to a new site near the garrison church in Aldershot, where it still stands today.

The larger than life Duke of Wellington

The Duke's Replacement

In London a smaller – though still large – statue of the Duke on horseback was positioned nearby, opposite his residence, Number One, London while the arch is now topped by a four-horse chariot or quadriga. There was a second Burton arch in vicinity of the first. That too was relocated. Today, we know it as Marble Arch. As for Wellington, he left his mark on the English language as well as the battlefield and politics. It was he who coined the phrase "Publish and be Damned" in response to a mistress threatening to spill the beans.

67: THE SPARKLING DUCK ISLAND

Duck Island is very small island and is located at one end of the lake in Saint James's Park, behind the cottage that looks like a Swiss chalet. It is hidden from view by a ring of trees and undergrowth and is not open to the public. Its name derives from the fact that in the days when St James's was an enclosed park, decoys were built to attract ducks for the royal table.

Small though it is, the island once had its own governor. In the early 1660s Charles II appointed Charles de Saint-Evremond, a French aristocrat who had fled the wrath of Cardinal Mazarin in France during the 1660s, to be in command of Duck Island on £300 a year. It must be the smallest amount of land ever given to a governor.

Saint-Evremond, curiously, is buried in Poets's Corner in Westminster Abbey. One of the things Charles II liked about him was that he introduced him to French champagne, which quickly became a court favourite.

This is where it becomes interesting. In those days, champagne was a still white wine. That is because French glass was made in wood-burning furnaces and too fragile to cope with secondary fermentation in a bottle, which caused the bottles to explode.

In England, however, because government edict had decreed that wood was needed to build ships, our glass furnaces were changed to being coal-fired, which meant bottles were much stronger.

In December 1662, while the governor of Duck Island was doubtless rhapsodising about the wonders of still champagne, an interesting lecture was delivered at the Royal Society whose offices these days are located on the other side of the Mall, just a few hundred yards away. Sir Christopher Merrett explained to fellow RS members how sparkling wine and other drinks were being made in England by allowing secondary fermentation in the bottles. In other words, what we today we call the "méthode champagnoise" was pioneered in England. It was another 20 years before Dom Perignon, whom most French people still believe invented champagne, actually got around to using it.

Saint-Evremond has slipped back into the news recently. Tattinger, the renowned French champagne house became the first champagne company to plant a vineyard – 100 acres – in England to take advantage of the growing success of English sparkling wine. And what will they call their first English sparkling? Why Domaine Evremond, of course. Plans are afoot to restore Duck Island to something approaching its former glory.

Let's drink a glass of sparkling to that.

68: THE WESTMINSTER ABBEY ANCHORAGE

The photo shows the entrance to one of the least known hideaways in Westminster Abbey. And hideaway it certainly was, in the best possible sense of the word. It was through the doorway on the right of the photo that the Abbey's anchorite would pass, seldom to see the light of day again. He – or very occasionally she – would retire for a life of prayer and contemplation except for food deliveries and unusual occasions.

One such moment was when Henry V, mourning the death in 1413 of his father (which took place in Westminster Abbey as it happens), went to the anchorite with the purpose of, as Shakespeare put it, "laying bare to him the secret sins of his whole life".

Previously, during the Peasants' Revolt against the poll tax in 1381, Richard II left the Tower of London to escape the violence and visit the shrine of Edward the Confessor at the Abbey, where he had his confession heard by the anchorite, a word that comes from the Greek word "to withdraw". (One of the most unusual anchorites was St. Simeon Stylites – 390-459 – who apparently spent three years in a hut before establishing his dwelling on top of a 60 foot column).

The anchorage at Westminster is close to Poet's Corner on the right hand side of the chapel of St Benedict, founder of the Benedictine order, which ran the monastery at Westminster until Henry VIII's dissolution in the 1530s. It had four stone walls with a window on to St Benedict's Chapel so the occupant could partake in services. He would be served with food by an attendant, who would also deal with matters of personal hygiene.

Anchorites have largely disappeared from religious life. It could be argued, though, that they have reappeared, involuntarily, in secular form as a consequence of the Covid-19 epidemic, which has led to lots of people, particularly older ones, being isolated in small rooms, often left to themselves throughout the day and night alleviated only by carers or relatives bringing food.

Anchorites, of course, did this as a conscious choice to achieve spiritual fulfilment, whereas with modern day anchorites it often leads to depression.

The doorway to the anchorage, which has a bust of a monk above it – presumably St Benedict – was only rediscovered in 1878 during cleaning work, when a stone tablet was removed. The location of the cell had remained a mystery since being demolished at the dissolution of the monasteries. Even today you get an eerie feeling looking at this door to eternity.

69: THE DUKE OF YORK'S COLUMN

The top of the Duke of York's column off The Mall, can, unlike Nelson's Column, be accessed by a spiral staircase. But it has been closed to the public for over 120 years. I stumbled across this curious fact reading the redoubtable Augustus J C Hare's account of Trafalgar Square, which he was not a fan of. In 1896, he described it as a "dreary expanse of granite" with the "miserable buildings" of the National Gallery flanked by a "hideous hotel and a frightful club". He considered Nelson's Column "a very poor work, which, however, does not signify much as it can only be properly seen from the top of the Duke of York's column, which no one ascends".

This whetted my appetite to see a view of London that hardly anyone has seen for well over a century and – to cut a long story short – managed to blag permission to ascend the column's 168 Aberdeen granite stairs, accompanied by two attendants.

At the top, we were hit by a wonderful panoramic view of London from an angle I'd never seen before. I looked immediately for Nelson's Column, only to find that what would have been Hare's untrammelled view of Trafalgar Square was obscured by the British Council building, a Johnny-come-lately structure. This apart, the platform revealed an unfolding panorama rarely seen from the west of the capital.

It is easy to see why it is still closed to the public, as there is a clear risk of suicides. But it is less easy to understand why the Duke of York (1763 – 1827) got a column in the first place, let alone one with a coveted spiral staircase.

The Duke of York's column

Nelson's Column as seen from the top of the Duke of York's column

He was appointed Commander in Chief of the army by his doting father, George III, but failures on the field of battle in France and Holland made him widely regarded as unfit to command an army in the field. He was a notorious philanderer and gambler, with the dubious honour of being satirised in the famous nursery rhyme:

Oh, the grand old Duke of York, he had 10,000 men.
He marched them up to the top of the hill.
And he marched them down again.

When he died he left debts of £401,169 – tens of millions at today's prices – leading some to suppose that he was put on top of a column to dodge his creditors. However, he did bequeath a lasting legacy for which the nation was grateful, by reducing corruption in the granting of army commissions (though this didn't stop his mistress earning a bob or two that way) and established a military college that became Sandhurst.

The column, built, appropriately, from York stone at the foundations as well as Aberdeen granite, was paid for by soldiers in the army donating a day's pay – by conscription rather than subscription, one presumes – amounting to £21,000 for its construction, which began in 1831. The statue of the duke was raised to the top three years later.

The public used to be allowed to climb to the top from from between noon and 4:00pm from May until to Sept for the price of six (old) pence, until a spate of suicides led to its closure in the late 18th century. On a clear day you can see for miles.

70: ALBION MILLS

It is difficult to believe, but a site at the southern end of Blackfriars Bridge was for a brief period a wonder of the industrial world. Albion Mills was built at the start of the Industrial Revolution by the great engineer Matthew Boulton between 1783 – 1786, helped by James Watt.

A five-storey building, it was the world's first commercial flour mill to be powered by steam engines. Erasmus Darwin called them "the most powerful machines in the world".

The trendy upper classes liked to drive to Blackfriars in their coaches and gawp at this spectacle of a new age being born – and on this occasion in the south of England, not the north.

Harder eyes saw the enterprise in a different light. Albion Mills was widely resented, especially by local millers and millworkers, whose wind-driven mills were put under sentence of death by the new age of steam. When Albion Mills caught fire at 6.30am on 2 March 1791 in a spectacular conflagration which the primitive fire service couldn't adequately deal with, it was widely presumed to be the work of revenging local arsonists.

But a closer inspection by Samuel Wyatt, the architect of the building, and John Rennie (who was later to build Waterloo Bridge and the replacement for the old London Bridge) found that the fire was started accidentally by a problem with grease on a corn machine near a kiln.

Albion Mills was almost certainly the inspiration for William Blake's "dark satanic mills", as he and his wife moved to nearby Lambeth in 1790 and would have seen the building, and maybe even the fire, on his walks.

In 1802 William Wordsworth produced his famous sonnet Composed Upon Westminster Bridge, September 3, 1802, with its famous opening lines, "Earth has not anything to show more fair." This was an industry-free poem. The derelict remains of Albion Mills, which was not demolished until 1809, would have still been nearby, as were other mills conveniently lost to the eyeline of Britain's most prominent romantic poet.

71: CHELSEA PHYSIC GARDEN

This is the nearest you will ever get to a Paradise garden – well, at least in your lifetime. It is as if Noah had called in his favourite plants and trees from around the world and hidden them in a secluded few acres in Chelsea. The Chelsea Physic Garden is not exactly lost, but it is assuredly hidden and still unknown to millions of Londoners.

The garden's high prison-like walls help to create a genuine microclimate, which seduces you as soon as you walk through a tiny entrance in Swan Walk among dangling pomegranates. Turn right and you will pass a banana tree and an olive tree (the oldest flowering one, it is claimed), the most northerly grapefruit tree and even – strictly come legal – proud looking cannabis plants. From there you are on your own to stumble across the secrets of this intoxicating place, including a Grade II listed rockery,

complete with clamshells from Captain Cook's Endeavour and Icelandic larva brought to the Garden in 1772 by the great plant adventurer Sir Joseph Banks (pictured in his rockery opposite).

In its day its day the Garden was the central seed market for the British Empire. For instance, in 1733 it sent a packet of long strand cotton seeds to the new colony of Georgia, the first to be grown in America. By the Garden's account, this small packet, "Became the parent of the subsequent great American cotton crops; a mainstay of the economy ever since". Cotton was also, as the Garden freely admits, intimately linked to the slave trade, with all that that entails.

These are but some of the plants and trees ranging from mulberries to ginkgos and even a row of manicured grape

vines that assault the eye as you wander around – and all of them serve a purpose, whether medicinal, environmental, historic or economic.

The Garden owes its existence to the philanthropy of Sir Hans Sloane – he of Sloane Square – who bequeathed it in perpetuity for a peppercorn rent of £5 a year on condition it was maintained as a physic garden. He also bequeathed artefacts which helped to found the British Museum. They don't make philanthropists like that any more.

But, sadly, as with so many philanthropists, there is also a side story here as Sir Hans was well aware of the slave trade from his visits to the West Indies. In 1695, in London, Sloane married Elizabeth Rose, widow of Dr Fulke Rose, a leading slave owner and became a beneficiary of her 33 per cent share of the profits from her husband's estates.

On the brighter side there is a fine café at the Garden, serving snacks and very good lunches with tables spilling onto the lawns in summertime. It is difficult to think of a nicer place in London to have lunch and a glass of wine on a sunny day.

72: LONDON ROOTS OF HARVARD, SMITHSONIAN & YALE

What have some of America's noblest institutions – Harvard University, Yale University and the Smithsonian Institute – got in common? Answer – they were all founded by Londoners, though these stories have all become a bit lost in time. We often hear of American philanthropy in England, supporting the Peabody estates and the Wellcome Foundation to give two good examples. We hear far less of the philanthropy that has travelled in the other direction. Yet the bequests across the water of three London men were, and are, quite remarkable.

First off the mark was John Harvard (1607-1638), who was reared in Borough High Street, then part of Surrey. His father owned a butcher's shop there and an adjoining pub, where there is a plaque commemorating him. Harvard's parents were rich enough to send him to Emmanuel College, Cambridge. He later emigrated to New England, and settled in Charleston, Massachusetts, where he became a church teacher and preacher.

Two years before his death – at the age of just 30 – a college was founded at what was originally called Newtowne and then had its name changed to "Cambridge". Harvard made a deathbed bequest to it, which resulted in its name being changed again, to his.

The second great benefactor was Elihu Yale, who was actually born in America of an ancient Welsh family but left for England at the age of three. He was educated in London before spending a long period with the (British) East India Company in India, making a lot of money, often in controversial circumstances. Yale returned to London in

1699. The Yale family lived in Queen's Square, London, when they were not at the family seat in Wrexham, where Elihu is buried.

In 1718, Yale was persuaded to support the fledgling Collegiate School of Connecticut, which needed funds for a new building. He gave books, goods and artefacts, which the school sold to raise the cash it needed. Yale had hoped he might benefit from regular disbursements. Those never happened, but the new building was named after him and so, eventually, was the entire school, which became Yale College. Some believe another other donor, Jeremiah Dummer, had been more generous than Yale, but the trustees of the school feared Dummer College would not be a great name for a place of learning.

The third benefactor was the most amazing of all. James Smithson (1765-1829), the Paris-born illegitimate son of the Duke of Northumberland, gave $500,000 – reckoned by some to have been the equivalent of 1/66th of the whole US budget – to found what became the Smithsonian, the biggest museum and research institution on the planet.

And he did this without ever having set foot in America. Why? No-one knows exactly, but it was almost certainly to further education and research in this new democratic country along the lines of what the Royal Institute and the Royal Society (of which, as a scientist, Smithson was a member) were doing in London. It remains one of the most astonishing acts of philanthropy ever recorded. Smithson is remembered by a blue plaque at his home in Bentinck Street, W1.

HISTORIC SOUTHWARK

THE "QUEEN'S HEAD INN" OWNED BY THE
FAMILY OF JOHN HARVARD, FOUNDER OF
HARVARD UNIVERSITY, FORMERLY STOOD HERE

73: PRINCE ALBERT'S MANSIONS FOR THE POOR

You could easily fail to notice this unassuming building in Kennington Park Road near the Oval, but it has a fascinating history and is of great relevance today.

It was completed in 1851 by order of Prince Albert, consort of Queen Victoria, and was intended to form part of the Great Exhibition in Hyde Park as an example to the world of what a dwelling for the "labouring classes" could look like at a time of social deprivation. This was a time when many of the workers who made the industrial revolution were living in distressed conditions, often with multiple families in one room.

Albert had a genuine concern for the well being of the poor and this housing – a forerunner of experiments like the Peabody estates – had innovative features designed by its distinguished architect Henry Roberts. The building was divided into four flats and included such things as sound-resistant hollow bricks, which did not absorb water, and internal toilets.

But there was a problem. Although Albert was the brains behind the entire exhibition, his committee did not want the model building to be inside the gigantic Crystal Palace. They argued that a brick building would look out of place in a revolutionary iron and glass edifice which seemed to float on air. And there was a further reason: the exhibition committee felt that showcasing social distress was not, er, something they wanted to draw attention to in an exhibition heralding Britain's industrial strengths.

Eventually, Albert negotiated a compromise. The model dwelling was erected a just few hundred yards away from the glass extravaganza. It was to be of the Exhibition, but not in it. Despite this status as a sort of changeling child, it attracted over 250,000 visitors, including the queen, Charles Dickens and many from overseas. Roberts's designs gave philanthropic housing a big boost, and influenced social housing in Britain, on the continent and even in America.

When the Great Exhibition had finished, the main structure was famously transported to Sydenham, where it remained until it was destroyed by a fire in 1854. Meanwhile, Albert's model dwelling was dismantled brick by brick and rebuilt a few miles away in Kennington Park Road. It is the only edifice from the Great Exhibition that has survived to this day.

Albert's house stands on the edge of Kennington Common, where thousands of Chartists gathered in 1848 before presenting a petition to parliament demanding basic rights. The authorities feared violence and brought in tens of thousands of police and army personnel to quell a riot that never happened.

What did happen was that most of the Chartists's demands – secret ballots, payment for MPs, equal constituencies and manhood (not yet womanhood) suffrage – have been achieved. But the problem of providing affordable homes for the London poor is still a big, unsolved one. Prince Albert would not be amused. Meanwhile, this model dwelling, currently occupied by Trees for Cities, stands as a true Albert Memorial of which the Chartists would surely have approved.

74: THE DISAPPEARING RIVER TYBURN

Nothing in the metropolis is more lost than the historic rivers that once fed the Thames. And none is more historic or more lost in geography or imagination than the River Tyburn, which once flowed openly from Hampstead's hills across Regent's Park and Green Park to form an eyot called Thorney Island. On these few acres stood Westminster Abbey and its monastery, the royal palace (until Henry VIII moved out), the emerging Houses of Parliament and Westminster School. No parcel of land in Britain, and maybe anywhere, contains more history in such a small space.

I say "once flowed" but, of course, the Tyburn still does until it goes underground and gets swallowed by Sir Joseph Bazalgette's amazing sewer system and its interceptor channels, which pipe what is left of the Tyburn to sewage works in East London at a point shortly before it used to empty itself into the Thames. The only bit of it that occasionally reaches the Thames now is the western extension from around Buckingham Palace to a few hundred yards west of Vauxhall Bridge, where you can still see the outlet through which surplus water enters the Thames during storm conditions. You can also still see the sluice gate keeper's house, now converted into a des res called Tyburn House close by the exit.

Archaeologists are still arguing about the eastern route of the Tyburn after it leaves Buckingham Palace to flow roughly under Tothill Street to old Westminster, as new archaeological digs throw up new evidence of the mix of Thames and Tyburn waters which spawned lots of small eyots. But if you walk from the Embankment opposite Victoria Tower Gardens along Great College Street, the original medieval wall along which the Tyburn route ran is still there on your right.

And when you get to the entrance to Dean's Yard, you are passing over the remains of an ancient bridge near which the remains of a 14th Century pillar can still be found in the bowels of Church House. Thereafter, the Tyburn skirted the walls of the old monastery, along what used to be called Longditch (today's Storey's Gate) and partially up Whitehall before turning right into the Thames before reaching Downing Street.

Whether the Tyburn can still be called a river when it contains so much sewage and doesn't properly reach the Thames is a matter for linguists as well as archaeologists, but there is no doubt that waters still emerge from the Hampstead hills and, in storm conditions, produce a lot of water that in olden days would have been part of the Tyburn. You don't need much imagination to sense that it is still there.

Model of medieval Thorney Island

75: SHAKESPEARE'S BOAR'S HEAD

Every Shakespeare buff knows that the Boar's Head pub in Eastcheap was where Sir John Falstaff and Prince Hal caroused in Shakespeare's Henry IV under the watchful eye of Mistress Quickly.

This was, of course, an invention. There is no evidence that an inn of that name existed in the early 15th century, the time the play was set in. But there was definitely a Boar's Head at or near the building shown above in Shakespeare's time. In fact, it was almost certainly his local.

The original pub was destroyed in the Great Fire of London in 1666 and subsequently rebuilt. The present building at numbers 33-35 Eastcheap was built in 1868 as a vinegar warehouse and references Shakespeare's play with the effigy of a boar peeping out of bushes half way up the wall. Ian Nairn, the idiosyncratic architecture critic, described the building (now offices) as "the scream you wake on at the end of a nightmare".

That boar is a fake, but the building previously on the site (which was not a pub, at least not in its later years) sported a bust of the actual boar's head from the pub that was there in Shakespeare's time. The original is now in the keeping of the Globe Theatre.

We know from parish tax records that Shakespeare lived very close by, in the parish of St Helens after he moved from Shoreditch in about 1592. It is not known exactly where he dwelled but he departed in 1596, leaving unpaid tax debts behind him. Parishes were often quite small, as their boundaries were set with reference to the number of people that could be comfortably accommodated in its church building. It may not sound very romantic but Shakespeare would have lived somewhere between the NatWest Tower, the Walkie Talkie, the Gherkin and Richard Rogers's Lloyds building.

These buildings almost suffocate St Helen's, a gem of a church, much of which is as it was in Shakespeare's time. There is a recent stained glass window commemorating the playwright inside, one of the very few images of him in London on semi-public display. In the courtyard of St Helen's was Crosby Place, where Richard III once lived and Thomas More wrote Utopia.

Using artistic licence, Shakespeare set the death of Henry VI in 1481 and his marriage to Anne at this place though neither event actually took place there. Richard, Duke of Gloucester said: "At Crosby House, there shall you find us both." You would never have found the actual Duke of Gloucester there, but you might have encountered William Shakespeare.

Site of the Boar's Head with effigy halfway up

76: KENNINGTON PALACE

If you are interested in buried history, look no further than the triangle formed in Kennington by Sancroft Street, Courtenay Street and Kennington Lane. Not that there is anything to see. The ruins uncovered during excavations in the 1960s have long gone. There aren't even any paintings or prints in existence to show us what this pageant of history used to look like. But it was definitely there.

Kennington Palace was built between 1346 and 1362 by Edward, the Black Prince, whose military victories at Crecy and Poitiers made him a household hero. He would have become king of England had he not died a year before his father Edward III. His son Richard became king instead.

Richard II spent much of his childhood at Kennington Palace and visited it regularly as king. It was barely half a mile from the Thames along what is today called Black Prince Road at the start of which he left a boat. Henry IV and Henry V lived for periods in the Palace too, as did Catherine of Aragon when she came to London to marry Henry VIII's elder brother Arthur.

The excavations revealed a string of separate buildings rather than a unified palace, dominated by an 80 foot long Grand Chamber with a hall, pantry, stable and sundry other rooms, including the Queen's Chamber, which jutted out under today's Sancroft Street. If you stroll to the backyard of St Anselm's Church you will be standing where about a third of the excavations took place, while at the other end the gated entrance to the estate at the junction of Sancroft Street and Cardigan Street would have given you a view of the entire palace now, sadly, left to our own imaginations.

The history of the palace came to an abrupt end when Henry VIII demolished it to provide materials to build his new palace at Whitehall, the biggest, and almost certainly the ugliest one in Europe.

Although there are no memories of Kennington Palace left, apart from Black Prince Road and the Black Prince pub which stands on it, there is one uninterrupted continuity: this triangle of land has had the same owner since it was built. The Black Prince was the first Prince of Wales and the land – and plenty else in the area – is still owned by the current Prince of Wales.

Site of the main excavations

77: THE MOVING STATUES OF TRAFALGAR SQUARE

Few things in London look less lost than Trafalgar Square, with its imposing column commemorating one of Britain's genuine heroes, Lord Nelson. But even here nothing is what it seems. Nelson's column was never intended to be there. It was an afterthought, imposed by a parliamentary committee to the chagrin of the architect Charles Barry. He had intended to build the Royal Academy in the square to complement William Wilkin's National Gallery on its north side. It then took 30 years for the column to actually be built – a solid construction unlike the Duke of York's column nearby, which is hollow with an internal staircase.

The name Trafalgar Square was an afterthought too. It was originally going to be called King William IV's Square. Poor William. He not only lost his square but his plinth as well. What is now called the Fourth Plinth on the north-west side of the square – these days a permanent home for temporary statues – was originally intended for a bronze statue of him, but no one could raise the money for it. The plinth therefore remained empty until 1998, when the Royal Society of Arts (RSA) suggested the idea of rotating a series of modern sculptures. They generate praise and scorn in equal measure, but have the exhilarating effect of starting open air conversations about art in the middle of a capital city.

It goes on. The National Gallery itself was never intended to look quite like it does. Wilkins was very miffed when forced to incorporate columns and capitals from the nearby Carlton House (roughly where the Duke of York's column now is in The Mall), which had been lying in storage since its demolition. This gave rise to widespread criticism at the time that the square lacked grandeur. Well, you can't win every battle.

The little noticed bronze statue of George IV on the north-east of the square was never intended to be there either. It was originally planned for the top of the Marble Arch – at a time when the arch itself was going to be outside Buckingham Palace – but George was plonked on this plinth as a temporary resting place and has been there ever since.

Another statue that has gone walk-about is that of General Gordon. There used to be an 18 foot high (pedestal) statue of him in the square between the two fountains before it was removed in 1943 and re-sited on the Victoria Embankment a decade later. And the fountains themselves are not the original ones, which were erected there to prevent large numbers of potential rioters assembling. They were given to Canada as a gift and replaced by new ones, designed by Sir Edwin Lutyens in 1937-39. A shorter journey was made by the earth excavated from the square – it was taken to nearby St James Park to level the land.

If Trafalgar Square is beginning to look like a game of musical statues, we may be tempted to look for continuity at the statue of the executed Charles I situated at the southern end of the square looking down Whitehall to his place of execution outside Inigo Jones' Banqueting Hall. It is the oldest equestrian statue in London, created by a French sculptor Hubert La Sueur in 1633.

Except that it hasn't been there for the whole of that time. After the Civil War, Cromwell's parliament ordered it to be melted down. For its present presence we have to thank a brazier – a man appropriately called Rivet – who, instead of melting it down, hid it and sold it back to Charles II

after the restoration of the monarchy. The statue too was restored to its original location has remained there ever since, on the site of the original Charing Cross, created by Edward I in the early 1290s as a memorial to his wife Eleanor. It can be regarded as the geographical centre of London, as distances from the capital are measured from a point beneath the statue.

A royal presence there is fitting, because Trafalgar Square is actually owned by the Queen, though the roads around it are controlled by Westminster Council. The square is now a revered place, especially since the northern end has been pedestrianised, transforming it overnight into a bubbling public space for gossiping and entertainments of all kinds from opera to food markets and celebrations of the Chinese New Year.

There may be a moral to this story. Maybe we should rotate all our statues on a regular basis, so that new ones can replace the giants of old who have long-since faded from the popular imagination.

78: MAPPING THE SLAVE TRADERS' HOMES

The blobs on the map look like something that has escaped from a Damien Hirst painting, but they represent something much more serious. Each marks the location of a house once owned by someone who made a fortune from the slave trade. They cover a very small area of London – just the streets around Portman Square and Welbeck Street – but they are part of a much bigger London map.

Britain's involvement with the slave trade was, at least until recently, rarely taught about in schools, having been in effect airbrushed from our history and almost totally lost from memory. But we are now becoming more aware of our shameful role in it, not least because of research done at University College London (UCL), which has been listing all the houses – and there are lots of them – in Central London and elsewhere that were owned by slave traders.

This was made possible because when slavery ended in 1833 (26 years after it was officially abolished in 1807), slaveowners – ludicrously, instead of bring imprisoned for their foul deeds – were able to claim compensation. The transatlantic trade led to the deaths of at least 10-12 million Africans and quite likely many millions more over a period of more than 300 years.

UCL researchers have identified 45,000 claims worth an amazing £20 million – over £2 billion at today's prices – paid out by UK taxpayers, half of which can be linked to London properties. The map shows those occupied at that time by slave owners in Fitzrovia alone. Details of the project, including an interactive version of the map complete with names, can be found online.

James Blair of Portman Square was one of the biggest beneficiaries. He received £83,530 (worth tens of millions today). UCL say that about 40 per cent of the recipients were women and a very small minority were "of colour", presumably the sons or daughters of slaveowners.

Most of them would have been churchgoers, rarely questioning what God up there might have thought of what they were doing to his fellow creatures down here. The fact is that many of the stately homes in London and elsewhere in the country were financed by the slave trade and subsequent compensation for its ending.

The trade wasn't, of course, confined to London. Liverpool became the global centre of the slave ship trade and made many people rich, including Sir James Penny – after whom Penny Lane of the Beatles song may have been inadvertently named – who was one of the most prominent shipowners and defended the slave trade in parliament right until the end.

It is eerie to walk about these parts of London knowing that some of the finest homes in them were built with wealth created by the slave trade. So many people were involved: some directly as plantation owners and many others simply as consumers of sugar and spices which were produced by slave labour. Once you discover this part of their history, walking those streets of London never feels the same again.

Map of slave owners living around Portman Square who claimed compensation

79: THE CHURCH OF ST MAGNUS THE MARTYR

If you want to follow in Shakespeare's footsteps, stroll through the yard at the side of the ancient church of Saint Magnus the Martyr on the northern side of today's London Bridge.

The path it stood on led to the ancient, original London Bridge – the one which stood for 600 years until the 1830s. The church served as a gateway to it. Shakespeare would have had to used this route on his way from Bishopsgate and Shoreditch – where he lived and worked for a while – to the theatres on the South Bank.

The original church was destroyed by the Great Fire of 1666 but rebuilt under the direction of Christopher Wren between 1671 and 1687, and the bottom of its tower was reconstructed in the 1760s. The new London Bridge was built barely 30 yards to the west of the church.

In the foreground of the painting we see the The Monument, commemorating the Great Fire, designed by Wren and Robert Hooke. Today, if you walk from it along Fish Street Hill you can see across Lower Thames Street to the path that leads to the churchyard, where you will find two large chunks of stone from the original London Bridge.

The Monument in front of St Magnus

The new London Bridge takes shape next to the old one.

Inside the church there is a large wooden model of the bridge, which provides an authentic idea of what it looked like, including all the houses that were built on it. Outside in the yard there is an even older link with ancient times in the form of a blackened chunk of wood from the piles of an old Roman quay which was excavated here around 1830.

It is a reminder of the enduring history of this fascinating church, which is named after Magnus Erlendsson, Earl Of Orkney (c 1080-1115), who was executed following a power struggle with his cousin. But that's another story.

80: THE LAMBETH ROOTS OF ROYAL DOULTON

Few places better illustrate dramatic changes in the landscape of London than the road between Lambeth Bridge and Vauxhall Bridge on the south bank of the Thames. Walk along it today and you pass end to end hotels and luxury flats, apart from the headquarters of the International Maritime Organisation. If you had done the same journey in the 19th century, it would have been end to end factories, wharves and potteries. Especially potteries.

Potteries in Lambeth can be traced back to Tudor and even Roman times. But their presence achieved revolutionary status with the arrival of the Doulton family, who, in around 1826, teamed up with John Watts to form Doulton and Watts and eventually the Royal Doulton company. After a slow start it expanded, gobbling up rivals, to transform the whole stretch from Lambeth to Vauxhall into the home of an internationally successful pottery industry. In its early days, the company supplied drains, pipes and sanitary ceramics for the industrial revolution. One of its factories was dedicated to making drainpipes, which were loaded onto Thames barges and exported all over the world.

The most fascinating stage of the development of Doulton was when it linked up with Lambeth School of Art, run by a pioneering headmaster John Charles Lewis Sparkes, who, realising the difficulty of getting money out of the government, started to cultivate local firms, Doulton included. This led to an extended period of co-operation between the two, which gave a huge impetus to the company's foray into artistic ceramics.

According to Hannah Renier in her book Lambeth Past, by 1885 there were no less than 250 artists in Doulton's pottery department and all but 10 had come from the art school. This was an extraordinary collaboration between art and industry and would have delighted Prince Albert, Queen Victoria's husband, who was the mastermind of the Great Exhibition of 1851 and the subsequent development of museums like the Victorian and Albert, dedicated to industrial design. How fitting that the road where Doulton had its main factory – long since demolished – is now the Albert Embankment.

In 1956, Doulton had to move its activities elsewhere as a consequence of clean air regulations, ending 400 years of pottery manufacture in Lambeth. It is now owned by a Finnish company, Fiskars Corporation. However the former head office (attached to what used to be the art studio) is still there in Black Prince Road in all its art deco glory. Further down the road are some lovely examples of Doulton artwork on the walls.

Had I been told in the 19th century that all of the industries that peppered the south bank of the Thames would disappear, I would have feared for the future of London. But somehow we survived. Let's hope we do in future.

81: BLACKFRIARS MONASTERY

The recently completed £1 billion European headquarters of Goldman Sachs in Farringdon Street is situated on the exact footprint of the first medieval Blackfriars monastery. It was built for mendicant Dominican friars in 1224. They moved 50 years later to their main home near today's Blackfriars station, a few hundred yards down the same street on the opposite side of the River Fleet.

But the apparent contrast between God and Mammon is not as clear cut as it may seem. Goldman Sachs turned out to be mendicants of a kind on an industrial scale when they received $10 billion in emergency support from the US Treasury during the 2008 financial crisis. Nor were the monks model mendicants. Piers Plowman, the 14th century poet, accused them of debauchery and luxurious living on a grand scale.

Nothing remains of the original monastery and there are only scattered remnants of the second one, which occupied a vast eight-acre walled estate stretching to the Thames from Ludgate Hill. Fragments found in dozens of archaeological digs were destroyed or left buried under new buildings.

Remains of the original monastery

The only bits of the original building still visible form part of a wall along Ireland Lane (see main picture) and the remains of a window preserved behind glass in one of the office blocks, which you need permission to see. Otherwise, apart from a window arch in the garden of the Selsdon Park hotel and a column at St Dominic's church up in Haverstock Hill, nothing is left of this historic 13th century monastery, which once had close links with the Crown.

Its great hall was once used to host meetings of parliament, which was convenient for Henry VIII whose main London palace, Bridewell, was a few yards away on the other side of the Fleet. Shakespeare's play Henry VIII was once staged in the very hall where that monarch's divorce petition against Catherine of Aragon had been debated decades earlier. It included some of the actual words used during the original trial.

From 1536, after the dissolution of the monasteries, Blackfriars became a highly desirable residential neighbourhood where aristocrats and cronies of the monarch, as well as the likes of Ben Jonson, lived in relative tranquility until that man Shakespeare arrived.

82: SHAKESPEARE'S BLACKFRIARS THEATRE

There is not even a plaque to draw attention to it, but it was arguably the most iconic place in William Shakespeare's life. When you consider that he is the most written about writer in the world, it is bizarre that there is nothing to record the site of the Blackfriars Theatre, the playwright's main money earner, which was situated in the former Blackfriars monastery. If you want to know what the playhouse looked like you will have to go to Staunton in Virginia where Shakespeare-loving Americans have built a replica. The only clue to its former presence in London is that the spot it stood in lies in what is now called Playhouse Yard.

The monastery building actually contained two separate theatres. The first staged performances by boy actors, children of the chapel royal, from 1576 until 1584 and the second was built after the actor and impresario James Burbage purchased the Upper Frater or refectory rooms in 1596. Burbage was a leading member of the Lord Chamberlain's Men, the company to which Shakespeare belonged. They had been forced to leave the Curtain Theatre in Shoreditch after a dispute with their landlord, and Burbage's intention was that his new Blackfriars playhouse would be the company's new home.

But they were thwarted by a lobby to end all lobbies – a very powerful group of Puritanical Blackfriars residents led by the formidable Lady Elizabeth Russell, a confidante of Queen Elizabeth, whose single-mindedness makes Mrs Thatcher look like a girl guide. She not only harnessed her gold-plated address book – which listed her brother-in-law the all-powerful Lord Burghley as well as Elizabeth herself – to her campaign, but also managed to persuade other locals to join in. These included Shakespeare's childhood friend Richard Field and Lord Hunsdon who as patron of The Lord Chamberlain's Men would have benefitted financially from a Blackfriars venue. But not in her backyard.

Lady Russell's petition to the Queen succeeded, so instead of moving to Blackfriars after their eviction from Shoreditch, Shakespeare's troupe had to revert to Plan B and move across the Thames to build the Globe Theatre, a replica of which – built by an American! – is the best known symbol of Shakespearean drama in the world. The new Blackfriars did not go unused, however. It too put on shows by boy actors, which were thought generally harmless. But times changed, Lady Russell met her demise, and from 1609 or 1610 "Shakespeare's company", now known as the King's Men following the crowning of King James in 1603, at last began performing there. They continued to until 1642.

Unlike the Globe, the Blackfriars was an expensive, candle-lit, all-weather indoor venue seating 700 people, who paid five times as much as the Globe across the river. It proved highly profitable for Shakespeare as actor and part owner. It is a sobering fact – recounted in detail by Chris Laoutaris in his fascinating book Shakespeare and the Countess – that if the troupe had not been driven out of Blackfriars there would have been no Globe. Amazing thought. London is often accused of hiding its history but seldom has anything been as deeply buried as memories of the Blackfriars Theatre.

Playhouse Yard - site of the Blackfriars Theatre

83: THE PERFIDIOUS ROGUE OF DOWNING STREET

Everyone knows that there is only one Downing Street, the traditional home of British Prime Ministers just off London's Whitehall. However, New York has two Downing Streets – one in Brooklyn and the other in Greenwich Village. They can be checked out on Google Streetview. And there is a direct connection: it is a man called George Downing (1624-1684), an extraordinary character whom Samuel Pepys once described as a "perfidious rogue".

Downing was probably born in London in 1624, but joined his mother's family in America in 1638. He became one of the first nine students to attend Harvard, sponsored by the soldier John Okey and, soon after finishing, became the first tutor there (Harvard's founding benefactor was another Englishman, John Harvard from Southwark, by the way). A few years later he sailed as a preacher to the West Indies on a slave ship and eventually ended up back in England, where he became chaplain to Okey's regiment, fighting on Oliver Cromwell's side in the Civil War.

Downing was one of the people who urged Cromwell to take the crown. But when Cromwell died and Britain's enthusiasm for republicanism waned, Downing did the only honourable thing a perfidious person could do. When the monarchy was restored, he jumped ship to support Charles II, having already cleared his path at a secret meeting with Charles in Holland while he was still on Cromwell's payroll.

Charles dispatched him to the Netherlands, where one of his jobs was to organise a spy ring and hunt down the remaining regicides at large who had killed his father, Charles I. One of those he captured was none other than Okey, the man who had sponsored his education in America. Okey was executed and buried in the Tower of London, rather than the graveyard of St Margaret's Westminster where most of the regicides were interred, to minimise popular reaction.

To be fair, Downing did help institute some major financial reforms and was one of the key people supporting the reform of the Treasury and establishment of what became the Bank of England. He was also instrumental in doing a deal with the Dutch, as a result of which Britain acquired ownership of New York in exchange for Surinam. He amassed a huge fortune by fair means and foul.

A grateful Charles rewarded him with a knighthood and a parcel of land adjoining St James's Park, including what was renamed Downing Street after he commissioned a row of smart terraced houses there. Judging by the recent double dealing among cabinet members it looks as though the ghost of George Downing still haunts Number 10.

Downing Street from the back

84: THE MEDIEVAL TOWER OF LAMBETH

St Mary's church in Lambeth was rebuilt by the Victorians, but its tower is a medieval gem that offers a breathtaking view of an unusual aspect of London. In its present form the tower dates from 1377, though it was founded as a wooden structure in 1062 by Countess Goda (or Godgifu), a sister of Edward the Confessor and daughter of King Ethelred. While Edward was building Westminster Abbey on the other side of the Thames, Goda was constructing St Mary's. Apart from the crypt of Lambeth Palace, it is the oldest structure in Lambeth and one of the oldest buildings in all of London.

The church used to be intimately linked with neighbouring Lambeth Palace, with which it still shares a wall (see picture opposite). This may help explain why among the 26,000 people buried in and around the church there are six and a bit archbishops of Canterbury (don't ask). It has been been known for ages that they were there, but it was only recently, when builders unexpectedly came across an underground cavern, that five of the actual coffins were found, one of them with a gold mitre on top.

For a small fee you can climb a stone spiral staircase to reach the top of the tower from where a spectacular panorama takes in parliament and Westminster Abbey on one side and the the garden and buildings of Lambeth Palace on the other. It was almost certainly from here that be great engraver Wenceslas Hollar drew his Prospect of London and Westminster in 1647, though he used some artistic license in placing the tower of St Mary's a good 50 yards in front of the position from where he was drawing.

Also buried or commemorated here are Countess Goda herself; Hardicanute, the last Viking King of England, who died in Lambeth in 1042 while standing up and drinking at a wedding; Thomas Howard, the 2nd Duke of Norfolk (born 1443), grandfather to Queens Katherine Howard and Anne Boleyn; and Sir Arthur Sullivan (1842-1900), who composed light operas with William Gilbert, who was baptised there.

It is also the resting place of Elias Ashmole (died 1692), who moved into the "Ark" created by the Tradescant gardening family, whose members are buried there too. The Ark contained all the plants and artefacts they had collected on their voyages. Ashmole transported them in controversial circumstances to Oxford in order to found the Ashmolean Museum. Also resting at St Mary's is the astrologer Simon Forman, a contemporary of Shakespeare who was consulted by many prominent people of the time and William Bligh of Mutiny on the Bounty fame.

The tower (right) almost glued to Lambeth Palace (left)

85: QUEEN MARY'S STEPS

Whitehall Palace has effected one of the great disappearing acts of English history. It was built by Henry VIII, starting from 1530, by means of expanding York Place, which he confiscated from Cardinal Wolsey. It became the biggest – and ugliest – palace in Europe, with over 1500 rooms rampaging down Whitehall from today's Trafalgar Square almost to Parliament Square. Henry married Anne Boleyn and Jane Seymour there and, in 1547, died there too.

Today, nothing is left of it in public view except the steps shown in my photo opposite, with the accompanying river wall at the junction of Horse Guards Avenue and the Victoria Embankment. The steps were reconstructed by Christopher Wren to enable Queen Mary (she of William and Mary) to descend from her private quarters to her carriage on the river. The Thames in those days, before Joseph Bazalgette built the Embankment, was much wider.

Surprisingly, the earlier and much more ancient original Palace of Westminster, an 11th century royal dwelling which occupied the area around Westminster Abbey and where its successor of the same name hosts parliament today, still boasts two brilliantly preserved historic buildings: Westminster Hall, with the biggest hammer beam roof in the world, and the boutique Jewel Tower of Edward III. Henry abandoned that residence in 1512 after most of it was destroyed by a fire.

There are remnants of Whitehall Palace off limits to the public, such as Cardinal Wolsey's wine cellar and bits of its former "real tennis" courts and occasionally, if workmen dig deep when laying cables, you can see the remains of Tudor brickwork underneath. Otherwise, Britain's largest ever palace has been erased from history.

86: THE HUGE NORTHUMBERLAND HOUSE

Many buildings have been lost from around Trafalgar Square, but none as enormous as Northumberland House, the last and biggest of the majestic aristocratic houses that once dominated the whole of the southern side of the Strand.

It started life as Northampton House before becoming Suffolk House and then Northumberland, when it was sold to the Earl of Northumberland in 1640. It remained in the family until 1866, when, by that time owned by the then Duke of Northumberland, it met a force even greater than itself – the Metropolitan Water Board in 1874 under the leadership of Sir Joseph Bazalgette, who wanted to build a road from Trafalgar Square to his newly planned Embankment. What Bazalgette wanted, Bazalgette got. The Duke accepted an offer of £500,000. As a small gesture to history the new road was named Northumberland Avenue.

Northumberland House from Trafalgar Square

Northumberland House from the river

The only way to appreciate what the Strand looked like in those days is to view it from across the river (see picture above) and imagine that the entire Thames frontage was taken up with huge mansions owned first by bishops and later by aristocrats who wanted to be a short journey by water from the power and patronage of Whitehall. None survive to this day apart from Somerset House, which was a much later reconstruction.

Northumberland House may have gone but parts of it live on in other areas of London, not least the lion – almost 22 feet long and 5.5 feet high – which used to sit proudly at the top of Northumberland House and which is now keeping watch at the top of Syon House (another family property) near Brentford. Part of the bottom of Northumberland House can also be seen today in the East End. An archway designed by William Kent is now the main entrance to the Bromley-by-Bow Centre where it was moved in 1998. If you want to know how the aristocracy lived inside the building, there is a sumptuous interior wall from Northumberland House in the Victoria and Albert Museum.

87: THE ROYAL UNITED SERVICES MUSEUM

This is a tale of a lost museum. In its day it was regarded as the biggest and most important in the country, apart from the British Museum. It was started by the Duke of Wellington in 1831 and housed 9,000 artefacts, including Napoleon's horse (well, its skeleton) and a telescope designed for the one-armed Lord Raglan during the Crimean War.

I first learned of the Royal United Services Museum in H V Morton's wonderful book In Search of London, published in 1951. Morton described it as "the most surprisingly housed museum in the world". I couldn't wait to visit and wondered how I could have missed it during my frequent walks along Whitehall.

There are two reasons for that. One is that the entrance is marked merely by a slightly confusing set of initials — RUSI, a modest label for the Royal United Service Institute, the oldest think tank for defence in the world. The second reason is that the contents of the museum, which was housed from 1895 in Inigo Jones's magnificent Banqueting House, complete with the Rubens painting on the ceiling next door (see picture), were dispersed in 1962 to other museums and galleries. The RUSI building is, however, still attached to the Banqueting House as a kind of Siamese twin with connecting doors.

RUSI remains home to some of the busts snd paintings from the museum and also boasts a Grade I listed window on a shared wall with the Banqueting House, on which can still be seen blackened scars caused by the fire of 1698, which destroyed Henry VIII's Whitehall Palace.

The rest of the contents were dispersed to the British Museum, the Victoria and Albert Museum and the Army Museum, among others. When it was at the Banqueting House, the museum was a history of war told in objects ranging from a bottle of port and bits of masts rescued from Nelson's flagship Victory to the skeleton of Napoleon's horse – called Marengo after his victory at the Battle of that name. Marengo's frame is now restored and can be viewed in the Battle Gallery of the Army Museum in Royal Hospital Road.

The original Royal United Services Museum catalogue is available online. The thousands of artefacts also include a scale model of the Whitehall Palace, a German crossbow, the Duke of Wellington's umbrella and remnants of battles from Crecy to Alamein. There was, apparently, even a piece of ration bread issued to British troops on the day of the Battle of Waterloo.

The origin of the museum can be traced back to 1829, when an article in Colbourn's United Service Journal written by "an old Egyptian campaigner" suggested a society which would "apply the new lessons of science to the military art". The RUSI would doubtless argue that that is part of what it is still doing today.

The interior of the RUSI museum in the Banqueting House

88: THE THREE TUNS PUB

The piece of Lost London that most frequently haunts me is the Three Tuns pub on Snow Hill, buried close to today's Holborn Viaduct. Archaeologists from the Museum of London were let loose on the site a decade ago, prior to a new office block being built at 60 High Holborn. What they discovered was a revelation – substantial remains of a medieval inn that had been expanded during the Tudor and later periods. It was a very modern inn, with its own wine bar and micro brewery.

Some of its walls were 2.5 metres high, and in an ideal world its extensive remains would have been preserved intact within the new development for public access, or even rebuilt as a pub within the new building (now occupied by Amazon). It is almost certainly the oldest inn in Central London. Snow Hill was the main road from St Paul's to the west of London, taking in the gallows at Tyburn. It followed a steep incline past the pub to a bridge over the River Fleet, then up again. It was the construction of Holborn Viaduct that raised the level of the road and left the pub below ground for future generations to discover.

And so they did. The archaeologists, led by Dave Saxby, uncovered a cornucopia of artefacts, including clay pipes, blue panels, charred bricks from the 1666 Fire of London, writing, water tanks and furnaces and carved bones from nearby Smithfield market. Also unearthed was was the inn's logo with three barrels and the words "at the 3 Tuns, Holborne Bridge".

PS: At the end of the 17th century, Richard Ames wrote an epic poem about the difficulty of getting a decent glass of claret in London. He visited dozens of pubs in search of one, including another on Snow Hill called The Castle, where criminals on their way from Newgate to execution at Tyburn were allowed to stop for their final bevy. Ames was about to enter when he realised Tyburn-bound prisoners were already there, and he decided to beat a retreat. He wrote in 1691:

"On Snow Hill at the Castle, two fellows in Halters,
Just going to Tyburn and reading their Psalters,
Made the cart stop, and drink of a pint of Canary,
To attend their sad face with a countenance merry,
To find no claret there, though we had a suspicion,
Yet declined we to enter, by odd superstition,
That if we drank there, it would follow of course,
That in a few sessions their turn would be ours."

89: ELEANOR'S CROSSES

King Edward I, also known as Longshanks, is mainly known today for two things, one romantic, the other utterly discreditable. The romantic bit was authorising the construction of 12 large, ornate crosses between 1291 and 1294, marking the nightly stopping points on the journey of the body of his beloved wife Eleanor of Castile on its journey from Lincoln, where she died, to Westminster Abbey in London. The last of these was erected at the London village of Charing in the middle of today's Trafalgar Square. Yes, Edward was the man responsible for putting the "cross" in Charing Cross.

If you look at an old map of London there is generally a small drawing showing its location in what was then the Royal Mews, where the equestrian statue of Charles I now stands. Made of marble, it was the most lavish of all his crosses – a work of love, but also a public demonstration of his kingship paid for directly or indirectly by the people.

It lasted for over 300 years before being destroyed in 1647 by Cromwell's cronies during the Civil War and becoming for a short while a fishmonger's stall. When the restoration saw Charles II become king in 1660, the site of the cross was utilised in a gruesome way when eight of the regicides who had killed Charles's father were executed there. A Victorian replica of Eleanor's Cross can be seen today in the forecourt of the nearby Charing Cross Hotel, which gives a good impression of the original's size and grandeur (see photo below).

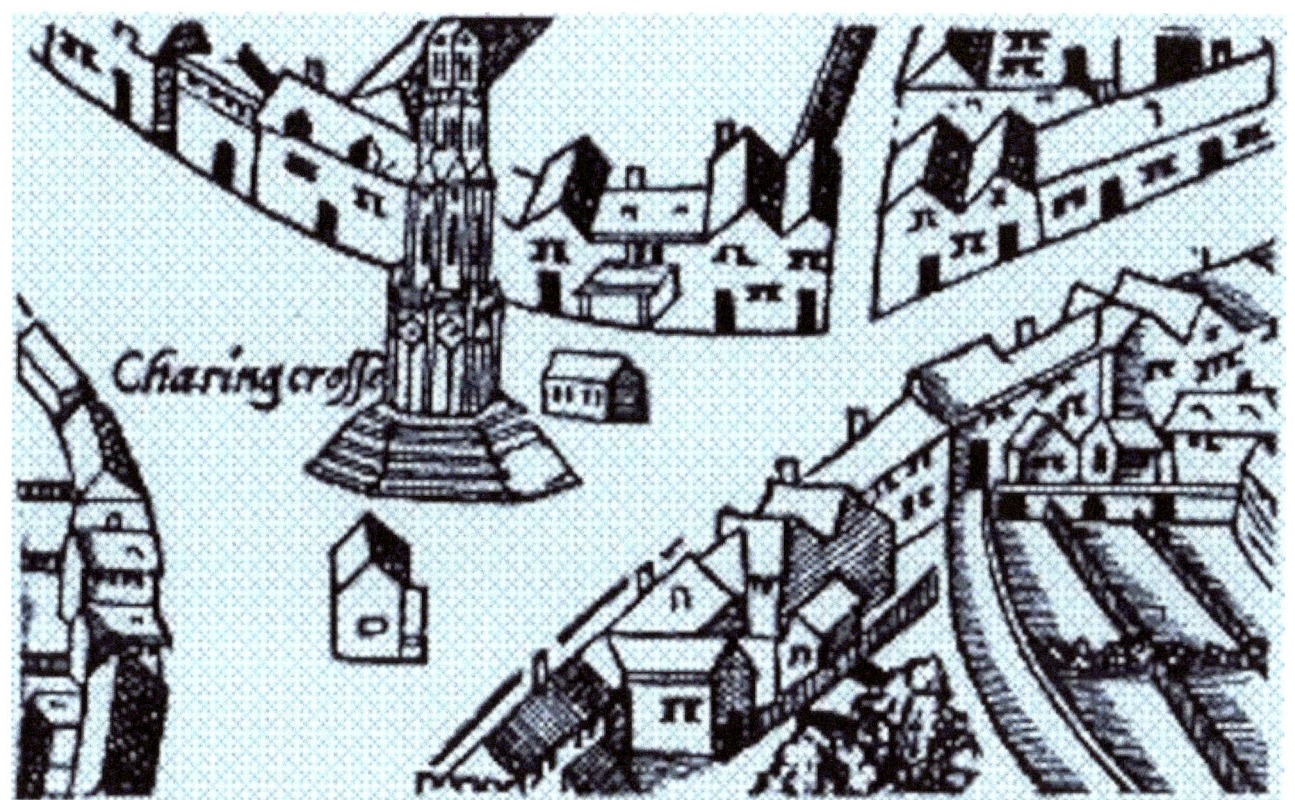

In 1675, an equestrian statue of Charles I, which had been made in 1633 and then hidden after Cromwell had ordered its destruction, re-emerged and was reinstalled on the site of Eleanor's Cross looking down Whitehall at the Banqueting House where he was beheaded. History has a strange way of taking revenge.

But what of the other side of Edward I, the one that is remembered with revulsion? In 1290, the same year that he mourned Eleanor's death, he authorised the expulsion of the Jewish population from England. The country's main influx of Jews had come with William the Conqueror in 1066 and their ability to lend money at a time when lending for profit was strictly forbidden by the church played a leading role in the financing of economic growth. But it also generated hostility. Jews were directly answerable to the king and did not enjoy any of the privileges of Magna Carta.

The expulsion order for the Jews lasted for over 350 years until it was rescinded in 1656 by none other than Cromwell. The few square yards that were home to Eleanor's Cross and then Charles I on horseback have seen more history than most other places of similar size.

90: THE COCKPIT STEPS

One of the least lamented lost bits of London is the cockpit. Fighting with cockerels – with rampant betting – was the sport of the day in Tudor times and lasted until it was made illegal in 1833. Every town had a cockpit and London, quite a few.

One of the most notorious was located between Old Queen Street and St James's Park in Westminster, now commemorated with its own street sign, Cockpit Steps. Although the pit is long gone, these steps are more or less as they were when it was in regular use. It was known as a royal cockpit because it was frequented by aristocracy as well as "lower" classes.

The site is opposite a pub of more recent vintage called The Two Chairmen. That is appropriate, because many of the spectators at cockfights would have been borne there in a sedan.

The pit's location is a bit surprising as it was only a few hundred yards away from another, genuinely royal, cockpit built by Henry VIII after he had moved his royal palace from nearby Westminster Abbey to Whitehall. It was located in an octagonal building between Downing Street and Horseguards Parade, the remains of which still exist.

A contemporary account of a cockfight on 18 June, 1710 near Gray's Inn by Zacharias von Uffenbach describes a typical scene thus: "The people, gentlefolk as well as commoners, act like madmen and go on raising the odds to 20 guineas and more. As soon as one of the bidders calls 'done'... the other is held to his bargain. Then the cocks are taken out of the sacks and fitted with silver spurs. As soon as the cocks appear the shouts grow even louder and the betting is continued. When they are put onto the table, some attack at once while others run away from the rest and try in their fright to jump down from the table among the crowd."

Cockfighting was a brutal sport, but it operated within very strict and often complex rules which are credited with being an important staging post in the development of rules for all sports. Birds paired against each other had to be of equal weight and properly reared, starting with the lighter weights.

The arena at Cockpit Steps appears to have been moved at a later time to Tufton Street just south of Westminster Abbey, but the road sign at the top of the steps still gives passersby a rare hint of what life was like in bygone days.

91: THE DEEP ROOTS OF THE LONDON PLANE TREE

Nothing is more London than the London plane tree. Its gnarled branches finger the sky and its spreading leaves act as lungs for an increasingly polluted city.

Plane trees have been around for millions of years. Romans watered their roots with wine, endowing them with divine powers. Returning Greek armies gave alms in recognition of their power and under whose dappled, protective branches Hippocrates taught medical advances.

But that wasn't our London plane whose origins are shrouded in mystery. We know the London plane is a hybrid of the Oriental plane and the Western (or American) Occidental plane, and that it only came into existence in the middle of the 17th century – but probably not in London.

Some say it came from Spain – hence it's common name Platanus Hispanica – others that it came into being by hybridisation in the garden of John Tradescant in Lambeth or at the Oxford Botanic Garden, Britain's oldest botanic garden where both Platanus orientalis and Platanus occidentalis were recorded by Jacob Bobart the Younger in 1676. However, a similar variety was also recorded in the Botanic Garden at Montpellier in France some years earlier – so take your pick.

Sadly, the popularity of the plane tree is threatened. Thanks partly to the squeeze on council expenditure, the default tree for planting is no longer the plane but the ginkgo, which doesn't need to be regularly pollarded and, having survived the Ice Age, and the age of the dinosaurs, has proved one thing beyond doubt – it has longevity on its side.

Typical London Plane

92: ST GILES AND GIN LANE

If you peer at William Hogarth's 1751 masterpiece of degradation Gin Lane, the only part of the scene depicted that exists today is the spire of St George's church in Bloomsbury, which peeps up in the background as some kind of beacon of hope. The people in his picture needed that, but all they got was cheap, untaxed gin, virtually on tap. It provided momentary distraction from the poverty, criminality and prostitution around, and from the profits of farmers selling the grain from which the gin was made.

Degradation had been part of the DNA of this part of London ever since the Great Plague started there at the end of 1664. It was reckoned that every fifth shop sold gin to the helpless inhabitants, most of whom were addicted. A survey of the rookeries in 1849 found as many as 50 or even 90 people lodging in a single four room house, many of them Irish people fleeing the potato famine in their homeland.

When Frederich Engels visited the Saint Giles neighbourhood around 1884 he found "hardly an unbroken windowpane", walls that were crumbling, doorposts and window frames loose and rotten. He observed: "Indeed, in this nest of thieves doors are superfluous, because there is nothing worth stealing." He found piles of refuse and ashes lying all over the place and the slops thrown out into the street collected in pools emitting a foul stench. "Here," he said, "live the poorest of the poor." In London, The Biography, Peter Ackroyd observed that, "Only sex and drink could make the conditions bearable."

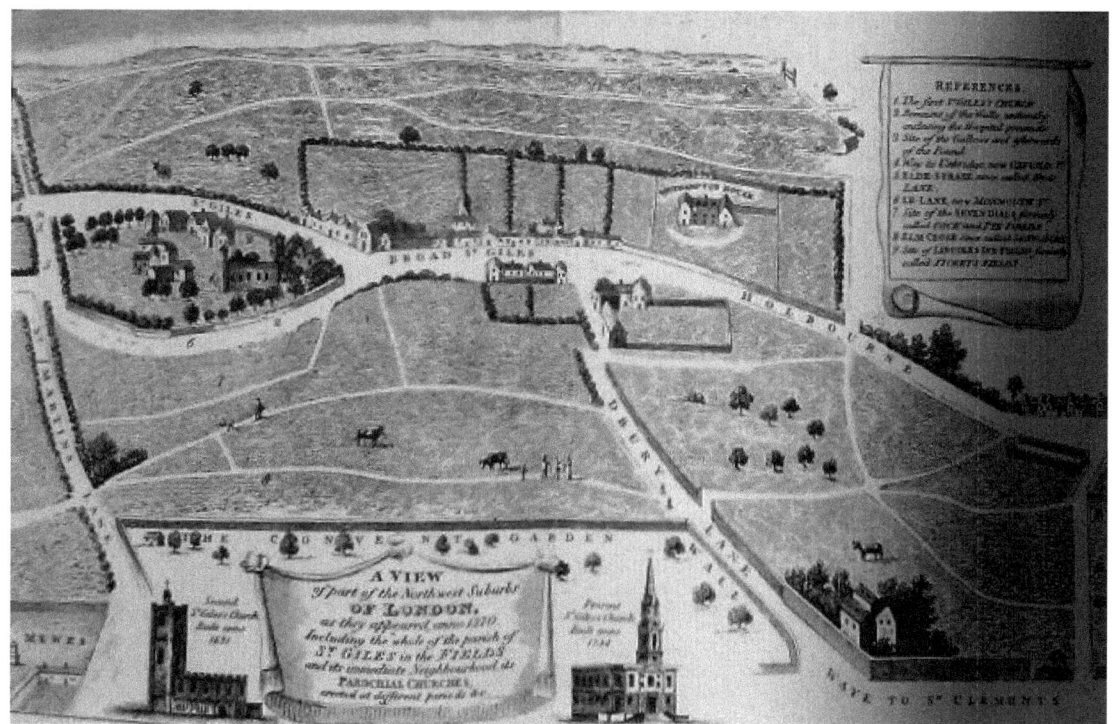

St Giles in happier distant times

As in so many other places in London, poverty rubbed shoulders with riches. The church of St Giles-in-the-Fields had to minister to the down and outs as well as its more illustrious residents such as Lord Byron, Shelley and Andrew Marvell, author of "To His Coy Mistress".

One of the hapless tasks of the church wardens was to buy a final drink at the Angel pub next door (then called Resurrection Gate) for criminals as they were conveyed from Newgate Prison to the gallows at Tyburn. This is said to be the origin of the phrase "one for the road", though other pubs on the same route also claim this dubious honour.

It would need a book to record all the people of note who lived here within spitting distance of the urban poor. They range from the second Lord Baltimore, founder of Maryland in America (though he didn't actually go there), who is buried in the churchyard, to Luke Hansard who started the practice of taking down verbatim the words uttered by MPs in parliament.

The tide started to turn between 1842 and 1847 when a new major road, Oxford Street, was run through St Giles, leading to the demolition of the worst lanes. However, as when Victoria Street was built further south through the slums of "The Devils' Acre", the initial result was to worsen the situation for the poorest, because although the lucky few were moved from high to low density, the poorest were left, displaced from overcrowded accommodation with nowhere to go.

Looking at Renzo Piano's multi-coloured luxury development in St Giles today, it is difficult to imagine the squalor it has replaced. Saint Giles-in-the-Fields is the only link with the past, still quietly doing all the things it was doing hundreds of years ago – except giving a last drink to prisoners on the way to Tyburn.

93: EAST INDIA COMPANY'S LEADENHALL STREET HOME

This building was the headquarters of the biggest company the world had ever known. At its peak it even had its own huge army, estimated at anything up to 260,000 men – twice the size of the entire British army at the time, and three times what it is today. Such was the power of the East India Company, an astonishing relic of Britain's imperial history, which once accounted for nearly half of all world trade.

It started as a joint stock company in the reign of James I and, until it was in effect "nationalised" in 1858, was privately owned – think Facebook with its own military capability. But its vast home in Leadenhall Street has long since been demolished, leaving no trace. The building was 200 feet long and built of stone. Its portico had six large Ionic columns on a raised basement. It gave an air of much magnificence, according to London writer Walter Thornbury, yet "the closeness of the street made it somewhat gloomy".

The site now houses the hi-tech building of Lloyd's of London, whose forebears doubtless insured some of the activities of the East India Company. Roger Williams, in his fascinating book England's Lost Global Giant, points out that if the East India HQ had lasted another hundred years it would almost certainly have been listed.

Although it started in 1600 as an attempt to break into the lucrative spice trade in Asia, the East India Company gradually became more and more political, and by the 18th century it was, in effect, running a privatised British Empire, extending its influence from India into China. One of its employees was the author Charles Lamb, who ruefully observed: "My printed works were my recreation; my real works may be found on the shelves in Leadenhall Street filling some hundred folios".

The company's demise followed the Indian Mutiny of 1857, when the Bengal Army mutinied, triggering a national uprising. A two-year internecine war persuaded parliament it was time for a change of governance. The company was stripped of its powers and replaced by the British Raj, managed from Whitehall.

The balance sheet of the company remains controversial. It was very successful – thanks to having been granted a monopoly in bringing spices, cottons and silks to Britain – and it revolutionised our drinking habits by introducing tea from China. But it also became riddled with corruption from the top downwards. It ruthlessly subdued and pauperised much of the population, and turned huge numbers of Chinese into opium addicts.

The HQ of the East India Company in Leadenhall Street

94: RAGGED SCHOOLS

London's "ragged" schools, where philanthropists financed basic education for the poorest of the poor, are thankfully a thing of the past. But in their time they filled a vital need that governments were not yet prepared to provide.

The schools are long lost, yet some of the buildings remain, often converted for other uses like the one in Newport Street, Lambeth, built in 1851 by Henry Beaufoy in honour of his wife, to help educate the children of the destitute. It is now an atmospheric café and gallery called Beaconsfield and well worth a visit.

If, however, you want to experience something of what it was like in those dreadful days, the Ragged School Museum in Mile End, not far from the station, is a must. It is housed in one of the early schools founded by that amazing Irishman Thomas John Barnardo, who provided education for destitute children irrespective of religious belief or nationality. Barnardo's homes still do enormous good work for poor children.

On entry, you are propelled into the past with classrooms much as they used to be, and which are used to conduct lessons with visiting schoolchildren who are apparently enthralled by the experience of being taught (by actors) in a strict Victorian manner.

Known as the Copperfield Road Ragged School, it opened in 1877 in converted warehouses along Regent's Canal. By the time it closed in 1908, thousands of local children had been educated here, with many of them being found jobs. Ragged schools, which started at the end of the 18th century, spread nationally, helped by social reformers like Lord Shaftesbury and Charles Dickens.

Story boards around the museum recall the terribly overcrowded conditions in which families had to live in those days. During the cholera epidemic of 1866, three times as many people died in the East End than in the whole of the rest of London.

The museum buildings are clearly in need of refurbishment and ambitious plans have been submitted to the Lottery Fund to make better use of the spacious building, including a canal-side café. It is to be hoped that they will be successful. We should never be allowed to forget the history of ragged schools.

95: THE GATEHOUSE PRISON

If you linger by the Martyrs' Memorial column outside Westminster Abbey you will be standing on the site of the notorious Gatehouse Prison. Built in 1370 as the gatehouse of the Abbey, it served for many years as a double-fronted jail for secular and religious offenders.

At times, it might have been called the Poets Prison. It was here that Richard Lovelace, while imprisoned for trying to get rid of the Clergy Act of 1640, wrote these famous lines:

> "Stone walls do not a prison make,
> Nor iron bars a cage;
> Minds innocent and quiet take,
> That for an hermitage.
> If I have freedom in my love,
> And in my soul am free,
> —Angels alone, that soar above,
> Enjoy such liberty."

It was here too that Sir Walter Raleigh penned his last poem on the final night of his life before his execution around the corner in Old Palace Yard on October 29, 1618. It ended:

> "While we live, the waking sense
> Feeds upon our difference,
> In our passion and our pride
> Not united, but allied.
> We are severed by the sun,
> And by darkness are made one."

Among other alumni of the Gatehouse were Samuel Pepys, who spent three weeks there "on suspicion of being affected to King James", and the celebrity dwarf Sir Jeffrey Hudson, who was imprisoned for his Popish tendencies.

The Gatehouse was demolished in 1776 following complaints by Dr Johnson and others, having lasted for 406 years.

The Gatehouse Prison

96: THE OTHER CRYSTAL PALACE

Everyone knows about the Crystal Palace. It was erected for the Great Exhibition of 1851 in Hyde Park before being relocated to Sydenham. But hardly anyone knows about a second Crystal Palace, which started life in Dublin to help house the 1865 International Exhibition of Arts and Manufactures, only to be taken down a few years later, shipped to London, and re-erected next to Battersea Park.

Renamed the Albert Palace, its grand opening took place in 1885. It stood along what was then Prince of Wales Road and is now called Prince of Wales Drive. Augmented with stone from the old law courts at Westminster (which had been demolished two years earlier), a tea room and the Connaught Hall Concert Room, it reached an amazing 675 feet in length.

The project had plenty of attractions including a permanent orchestra, cat shows, bird shows, flower shows and an Indian village full of spinners, weavers and carpet makers. There was a diving bell, gymnastic displays and ballooning, though sadly these were not enough to make it viable for one simple reason: punters were reluctant to pay the admission charge when so much around them was free, namely Battersea Park itself.

The glass white elephant was permanently closed by 1888 and slowly decayed before being demolished by the end of the century. If you want to see a remnant of it, go to Fort Augustus Abbey in Scotland, where its huge organ was transported to. Otherwise, its memory lives on in the name of Albert Palace Mansions, which were built on the site in 1897.

THE ALBERT PALACE, AT BATTERSEA PARK.

97: A MEETING AT THE COLONIAL OFFICE

Downing Street has seen some quirky encounters but none quite as quirky as one on September 18, 1805 at the Colonial Office, which was located at the end of it at that time (see image). Sir Arthur Wellesley – not yet the Duke of Wellington – fresh from his victory at the Battle of Assaye, had come to report to the secretary of state. For some unexplained reason he was running late and the person who was due to see him before Wellington was still in the waiting room.

Wellington immediately recognised that person as Lord Nelson (clue: he had only one arm and one eye) but Nelson did not recognise Wellington as they had never met before and there were, of course, no photographs around in those days.

What happened next is best described in Wellington's own words as recorded by the diarist John Wilson Croker some years later:

"He could not know who I was, but he entered at once into conversation with me, if I can call it conversation, for it was almost all on his side, and all about himself, and in really a style so vain and so silly as to surprise and almost disgust me. I suppose something that I happened to say may have made him guess that I was somebody, and he went out of the room for a moment, I have no doubt to ask the office-keeper who I was, for when he came back he was altogether a different man, both in manner and matter. All that I had thought a charlatan style had vanished, and he talked of the state of this country and of the aspect and probabilities of affairs on the Continent with a good sense, and a knowledge of subjects both at home and abroad that surprised me equally and more agreeably than the first part of our interview had done; in fact, he talked like an officer and a statesman."

The conversation continued for nearly three quarters of an hour. Wellington said he had never had a chat that had interested him more and never before seen "a more sudden and complete metamorphosis" of a person. If the secretary of state had not kept them waiting he would have had a completely different view of Nelson. What on earth he was doing that made him keep two of Britain's most successful military commanders waiting can only be guessed at.

The pair would never be offered another opportunity to meet. The then Wellesley went on to greater things, culminating in the Battle of Waterloo. Nelson died a month later at the Battle of Trafalgar, the most successful naval encounter in Britain's history.

The Colonial Office has long since been demolished but one memento of the historic meeting that took place in it remains. In the map room of the Ministry of Defence the actual mantelpiece at which the two great men conversed has been conserved, though it is not open to public view.

The old Colonial Office at the end of Downing Street

98: PAVLOVA ON THE PALACE

One of the more incongruous statues in London is that of the famous Russian ballerina, Anna Pavlova. It sits – or rather stands – opposite Victoria Station on top of the Victoria Palace theatre, better known for musicals like Billy Elliot and Hamilton than for ballet.

It was erected in 1911 after racehorse owner and theatre impresario Alfred Butt, later a Conservative MP, had the theatre built on the site of the Royal Standard Music Hall, which Butt had purchased in 1910. He engaged Frank Matcham, the celebrated theatre architect, to build the Victoria Palace, after which he commissioned a statue in memory of Pavlova's early performances at the new theatre.

The statue has been there ever since – except for a gap of 63 years from 1939, when it disappeared without trace. The most likely explanation is that it was melted down for re-use during the Second World War, but there is no proof of

this and it may well have been hidden away somewhere (as the statue of Charles II in Trafalgar Square was when Oliver Cromwell ordered its demolition during the Civil War).

Whatever the explanation, a new statue, fashioned using photos of the original, was erected in 2006. The effigy appears to be floating in air, even though hardly anyone seems to notice because it looks so small from the ground. Actually, it is twice the size of the real life Pavlova, who lived in London during her later years and by all accounts couldn't bear to look at it. She would hide her face when she passed by it in a carriage as she thought it was superstitious to have a gander.

Now that the restoration of the Victoria Palace is virtually complete you can see Pavlova in all her glory once again. But to fully appreciate here, you will need a telescope or a camera with considerable magnification.

99: THE PIMLICO ROOTS OF WIMBLEDON

At the western end of Churton Street in Pimlico at number 46 there is an Italian restaurant called Cacio & Pepe. Previously, it was a Vietnamese restaurant. Nothing unusual about that in a street with shops and restaurants churning fairly regularly.

However, although there is nothing to show for it in the way of plaques or anything like that, well over 100 years earlier there was a shop at this address that had a strong claim to be where a new game called "lawn tennis" originated.

It was launched and patented in February 1874 by Major Walter Clopton Wingfield, a well connected Welsh army officer. Originally, believe it or not, it was called "sphairistike or lawn tennis" after the Greek word for ball playing skill. It sold as a £6 kit from French & Co at 46 Churton Street, complete with racquets, balls and a set of rules.

As with so many inventions, there are others with competing claims, not least Harry Gem, a solicitor who helped found the world's first tennis club, the Leamington Tennis Club, in December 1873 with a Spanish friend. However, it was Wingfield who first formalised the rules and standardised the sets of equipment.

It was only a few years later in 1877 that the All England Croquet Club, located near the railway tracks in Wimbledon, changed its title to include "lawn tennis" in its name, and many other croquet lawns were turned into tennis courts.

The game was soon spread to America by Mary Ewing Outerbridge of New York, who was introduced to it in 1874 by a friend of Wingfield's in Bermuda. She returned to the US with a kit and established America's first tennis club at the Staten Island Cricket and Baseball Club.

The shop in Churton Street Pimlico

Lawn tennis could not have happened without two other discoveries, as Simon Inglis points out in his marvellous book Played in London. The invention by Edwin Beard Budding (1796–1846), an engineer from Stroud in Gloucestershire, of the lawn mower enabled grass to be cut smoothly, unlike the rough finish of the hand-held scythe which preceded it, while the application of "vulcanisation" by the American Charles Goodyear – he of motor tyres fame – led the way for air-filled rubber balls.

Wingfield wisely dropped the name sphairistike, but his pioneering efforts led him to be known as the "Father of lawn tennis". He would be rather surprised to see what his invention has led to at Wimbledon.

100: WHERE TO LOOK FOR LONDON BRIDGE

The original London Bridge with houses on top – without which London would never have existed – lasted an amazing 600 years until 1831. In that year, it was pulled down to make way for Scottish civil engineer John Rennie's London Bridge, which survived a mere 130 years before being sold to a chainsaw millionaire and transported to America in 1967. But although the first two London Bridges were demolished, they have not disappeared from the city. A surprising amount of their remains can still be found, if you are prepared to look for them.

This is particularly true of Rennie's bridge, which was not completed until after his death. Although the London Bridge at Lake Havasu is now the second most popular tourist attraction in Arizona (something called the Grand Canyon is the first) its creator purchased only the outer stone of the one that spanned the Thames, for use as cladding. The rest was built from reinforced steel, so lots of the stone from Rennie's bridge was left in London.

THE WEST SIDE OF OLD LONDON BRIDGE AFTER THE REMOVAL OF THE HOUSES
From a drawing by Joseph Farington, R.A.

The biggest chunk, which didn't need to be moved, still forms part of the present bridge. You can walk under it on Montague Street, close to Southwark Cathedral (see photo). If you continue from there a few yards further under the bridge, towards Tooley Street, you will come across two parallel lines in the road. These mark the actual – very narrow – width of the original London bridge. And if you track back under the bridge you will soon pass a number of large stones on your right, which were further parts of the Rennie bridge. There are more of these in front of Evans Cycles at 6 Tooley Street.

Other parts of Rennie's bridge have travelled out of London, including huge chunks in the Waltham Abbey area, some of which have been made into sculptures. I made a (mainly interactive) map of many of them some years ago which can be found online and in previous articles I have written.

Of particular interest are the remains of the original bridge, which was regularly reconstructed over the six centuries for which it stood. The best preserved are four of the shelters which graced the bridge, dating from the late 1750s. Three of them are easily accessible. One is at the entrance to Guy's Hospital (with a statue of John Keats sitting in it, see photo) and two are at the eastern end of Victoria Park.

A lot of the original bridge's stonework was taken downriver in 1833 to build an impressive mansion at Greenhithe in Kent for James Harmer, a fascinating radical lawyer and proprietor of the Weekly Dispatch. Original stones can also be seen on the northern side of London Bridge in the churchyard of Saint Magnus the Martyr. Some of the parapets are preserved in Myddelton House Gardens in Enfield and, further afield, there is a dourly handsome chunk of stone in a public space at Amersfoort in Holland.

Among other interesting relics of the old bridge is a fine carving of the royal arms of George II (later altered to those of George III), which was once above the southern gatehouse of the bridge, but is now fixed on the front of the King's Arms pub in Newcomen Street.

In the Fishmongers' Hall right by London Bridge is a ceremonial chair commissioned in 1832, whose back depicts the first two London Bridges and whose seat is made from the foundation stone of the original. Visitors to Kew Gardens sitting on a bench by the lake may be surprised to find that it rests on several granite blocks from Rennie's bridge, while residents of Heathfield Road in Wandsworth appear ignorant of the fact that the wall protecting their gardens comes from the original London Bridge. When I visited it a few years ago, one of the residents was disposing of part of the wall unaware of its provenance. That could be the story of most Londoners. We love the city but are unaware of much of its history.

101: ST ETHELDREDA'S CHURCH

In order to get to this bit of Lost London you would, until quite recently, have had to pass through a part of Cambridgeshire. That is because it was not only owned by the bishops of Ely, whose London establishment it had been for centuries, but also an enclave within their diocese which therefore fell within the county they came from. Though physically inside London, it was not within the city's jurisdiction.

Even today you have to pass by a gatehouse, watched over by a beadle before entering a time warp of Ely Place – still a private street, where stands St Etheldreda's church, which was built next to the bishops' residence, Ely House. It is one of the very oldest buildings in London and the oldest Roman Catholic church in England. Also there is Ye Olde Mitre tavern, perhaps the most hidden pub in the capital. It was licensed by Cambridgeshire until the 1960s.

ELY HOUSE, 1784.

The church is one of the very few medieval structures in London surviving from the reign of Edward I (1274-1307). Nearly all of the walls and the crypt beneath – where you can still see the original beams on the ceiling – are very old.

It was Ely House where Shakespeare gave John Of Gaunt (who lived at Ely Place when his palace in the Strand was burned down during the Peasants' Revolt) one of the finest speeches in the English language. It is the oration in Richard II, the first lines of which are known by heart by many English speaking people.

"This royal throne of kings, this scepter'd isle,
This Earth of majesty, this seat of Mars,
This other Eden, demi-Paradise,
This fortress built by Nature for herself,
Against infection and the hand of war,
This blessed plot, this Earth, this realm, this England"

Medieval chronicles mention the cloister and the gardens of St Etheldreda's, saying how wonderful they were with their fields of saffron and strawberries. These are mentioned in Shakespeare's Richard III, when the Duke of Gloucester says to the Bishop of Ely:

"When I was last in Holborn,
I saw good strawberries in your garden there,
I do beseech you send for some of them."

167

Ye Olde Mitre is hidden behind the church and only accessible through narrow alleyways (one from Hatton Garden and the other from Ely Place) Built by Bishop Thomas Goodrich in 1546 as a place to feed his workers, it has been heavily reconstructed, but some pub buffs regard it as a candidate for the oldest pub in London.

In the right hand corner of the small bar there is part of what is claimed to be a cherry tree around which Queen Elizabeth I is said to have danced, and which also marked the boundary between the garden of Sir Christopher Hatton, one of Elizabeth's favourites, and that of the Ely bishops. Why not!

102: THE SOCIETY FOR THE DIFFUSION OF USEFUL KNOWLEDGE

Number 59 Lincoln's Inn Fields has managed to avoid celebrity status apart from being next door to the home of Spencer Perceval, the only British Prime Minister to have been assassinated. But in the 19th century it was the head office of a remarkable Victorian experiment set up by a remarkable Victorian man.

It was a kind of pre-internet Wikipedia called The Society for the Diffusion of Useful Knowledge, which, between 1826 and 1848, spread knowledge about useful subjects not just to Britain but to a network of educators, scientific institutions and publishers all over the world.

Among its publications was the The Penny Magazine, which sold 200,000 copies in its first year, and was followed by the Penny Cyclopaedia and the Library of Useful Knowledge, which sold over 33,000 copies at sixpence a pop. When the Society closed in 1848, its founders said it was because the job was done. Others thought the admirable material was sometimes a bit esoteric for the working classes and lower middle classes at which it was aimed. But it was a

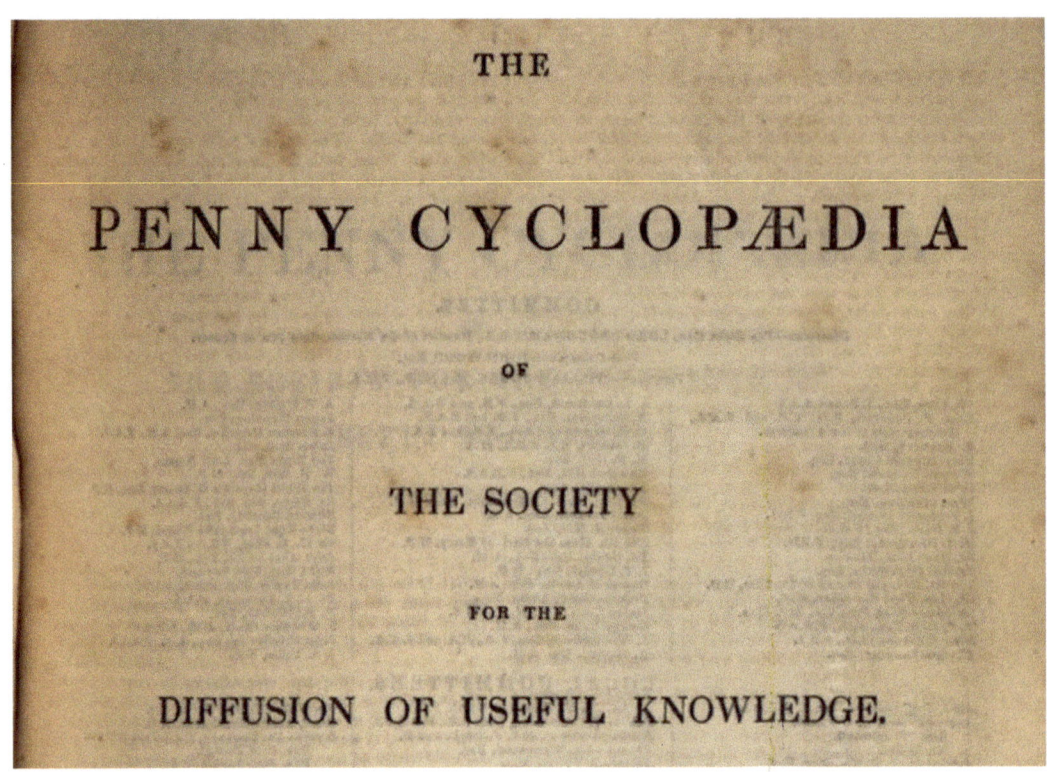

THE

PENNY CYCLOPÆDIA

OF

THE SOCIETY

FOR THE

DIFFUSION OF USEFUL KNOWLEDGE.

remarkable experiment at a time when mass schooling did not exist, and it was influential around the world.

The Society was a secular organisation set up by many of the same people behind University College London, founded in opposition to Oxford and Cambridge, which admitted only religious believers. Its driving force was the remarkable Lord Brougham, also notable as an MP, a political reformer, a slavery abolitionist, an inventor and a Lord Chancellor.

You might think this list of achievements would merit a statue of Brougham. But he hasn't got one, at least not in London. To see one, you will have to go to the south of France, where there is a very large one of him in the celebrity resort of Cannes, which Brougham more or less invented as a tourist resort for him and like-minded folk to enjoy. There is a plaque in his honour on his London house, 5 Grafton Street, but as he lived most of his later life in Cannes, that doesn't amount to much.

Brougham also invented the Brougham Carriage, which only needed one horse to pull it, instead of two plus coachman and groom. A later motorised version influenced General Motors and Ford, who used his name.

The Society for the Diffusion of Useful Knowledge was not without its critics. Religious groups complained about its secular nature and the book trade claimed that the society "have done, and are still doing, more to ruin the book trade than all the change of times, the want of money, the weight of taxes, and even the law of libel have accomplished". You can't please all of the people all of the time – even if useful knowledge is being diffused.

103: THORNEY ISLAND

There is a lost island in Central London that hardly anyone knows about, including many of those who live or work on it. Meet Thorney Island, formed in ancient times by the convergence of the Thames with the River Tyburn, on which Parliament, Westminster Abbey, the old Royal Palace and Westminster School stood, making up surely the densest concentration of "history" anywhere in the country.

All but the palace – which Henry VIII moved a short distance north to Whitehall – are still there. So is the Tyburn, which rises on the Hampstead hills and meanders under Mayfair and Green Park down to Buckingham Palace, where it bifurcates, one leg leading towards Vauxhall Bridge and the other to Westminster and the lost island we're discovering here.

The Tyburn has long since been absorbed by Sir Joseph Bazalgette's amazing sewer system, but some of its waters still reach Thorney Island via the sewers, especially after heavy rainfall, before being channelled through interceptors, which take it downstream to the East End for treatment. No traces of the Tyburn reach the Thames at Westminster, but a few hundred yards west of Vauxhall there is an outlet to it, which takes surplus storm water the sewers can't cope with.

Thorney Island was where the first parliaments met, in the chapter house of the Abbey and in the monks's refectory. Remnants of the refectory wall can still be seen (see photo) if you peer out of the window in the upstairs section of the Abbey's cellarium café (which was once the monks' wine cellar).

Another gem of Thorney Island is the Jerusalem Chamber – part of the dean's private quarters. It can be seen peeping up behind the Abbey gift shop. It was there that much of the hugely influential King James Bible was written, and where Henry IV died, both in reality and in Shakespearean fantasy.

Every monarch since the William the Conqueror has been crowned in the Abbey, where many of them now rest in sepulchral splendour. There was once some kind of Roman structure on Thorney Island, but the authenticated origins of the Abbey are from the late 10th century, when St Dunstan and King Edgar founded a community of Benedictine monks on the site.

Thorney Island was also home to the Cotton Library, a collection of manuscripts owned by the antiquarian Sir Robert Bruce Cotton, which was kept in Ashburnham House, nowadays a part of Westminster School. Cotton's collection later formed the basis of what is now the British Library, and is still kept there today.

Westminster School itself has produced more than its fair share of literary and scientific figures. They include Edward Gibbon, John Dryden, Christopher Wren, Robert Hooke, Ben Jonson etc, etc. The first head office of the Fabian Society was also located there.

Thorney, however, is not the only island in the capital – London itself, north of the Thames, is a man-made one, because of the canals running from Limehouse to Brentford which surround it. But it doesn't have the history of Thorney Island, which gained its name in medieval times because of the brambles growing there.

These were almost certainly hawthorn bushes or trees, and there are a couple of hawthorns today in the Abbey Garden (open to the public for free most weekdays) in the middle of the original island, offering a metaphorical link to a unique piece of history. For more information, visit the website of the Thorney Island Society.

104: SHIPBUILDING ON THE THAMES

Nothing has been lost in London that is larger than its once mighty shipbuilding industry. During the early 19th century the capital had the biggest shipbuilding industry in Britain and that probably meant in the world as well. But of all the hundreds of ships associated with the Thames, three stand out: one because it was built there, one because it sailed from there, one because it was broken up there.

Brunel's Great Eastern was the one was built on the Thames. Started in 1858, it was so big it had to be slid sideways into the river from its Millwall mooring. It was not only the world's biggest ship at the time, but it maintained that status for nearly 40 years.

The one that was broken up on the Thames was the Chatham-built Temeraire, now known universally as the Fighting Temeraire because of J M W Turner's iconic painting showing the ship being pulled by a tug boat for demolition at Beatson's breaking yard at Rotherhithe. Local mudlark Alan Murphy assures me that the painting must have been executed at the end of Beatson's yard, facing a bend in the river.

Turner, of course, used artistic licence to make his point. The ship was towed by two tugs, not one, and did not have such stately masts as in the painting. And it was day time when it arrived, not night time. But strict accuracy would have deprived Turner's work of its iconic hint about the sunset of Empire.

THE TÉMÉRAIRE 106 guns

This vessel, now lying at the wharf of Mr John Beatson of Rotherhithe (who has purchased her of H.M. Commissioners for the purpose of breaking up) is the largest ship ever conducted so high up the River Thames, being in fact the largest ever sold by government. The name of the Téméraire is immortalized by the distinguished part she bore in the memorable Battle of Trafalgar when she was commanded by Captain Eliab Harvey.

The Temeraire itself performed many roles, from a prison ship to a victualling depot, but it has a special place in history because it fought side-by-side with Nelson's HMS Victory at the Battle of Trafalgar. Without the Temeraire being so positioned, it is possible the battle would not have been won. Like the Victory, it needed up to 5,000 oak trees for its construction, many of them well over 100 years old. It was built to last. You can still see remnants of it in the form of a communion rail and two bishop's chairs at St Mary's Church, Rotherhithe.

But Rotherhite's most iconic ship was neither built nor broken up there. The Mayflower, which carried the Puritan Pilgrim Fathers to Massachusetts in America, set sail from Rotherhithe in 1620 for Plymouth (in England) before heading for the already established Plymouth in America, where the settlers founded a colony that became America and a key part of the British empire.

The Mayflower arrived back in England on May 6, 1621. Christopher Jones, its captain and part-owner, died the following year and is buried in St Mary's at the heart of old Rotherhithe. His widow, Josian, inherited the ship, which was eventually broken up and probably sold off as scrap. A full-sized replica, built in England, was restored in America in time for the 400th anniversary of the historic event.

The sailing is commemorated by the Mayflower pub in Rotherhithe which, although of recent origin, looks the part and is visited regularly by American tourists to pay their homage.

105: THE LION BREWERY OF WATERLOO

One of the saddest of London's lost buildings is the former Lion Brewery, which once dominated the view south of the Thames by Waterloo Bridge. The building itself was handsome rather than beautiful. What gave it grandeur was the huge statue of a lion – one of two at the brewery – surveying the river from the roof of the building – a true British icon.

It is difficult to complain too much about this loss, because the brewery, founded by James Goding in 1836, had fallen on hard times and the building itself was derelict. It was demolished in 1949 to make way for the Royal Festival Hall, the only lasting memory we have of the 1951 Festival of Britain. The shot tower on the left of the photo was demolished with all the other exhibits.

The lions themselves weren't destroyed. They merely went for a walk: one to Waterloo Station and afterwards to the southern end of Westminster Bridge, where it still proudly stands stripped of its red paint and, in deference to Victorian values, its private parts. The other one, now painted gold, stands sentinel outside Twickenham rugby football stadium, doubtless an inspiration when the (human) British Lions play there.

Both of the lions were made of the highly fashionable artificial Coade stone manufactured in a factory almost next door to the brewery. At the time, the ingredients of Coade stone were kept secret like the core of Coca Cola is today. But the stone, manufactured by the redoubtable Mrs Coade, one of the great entrepreneurs of the time, has proved its claim that it weathers better than natural stone, as is evident from hundreds of examples up and down the country.

There is one other curious memory of the Lion Brewery that still exists. Hoare and Co, the banking dynasty, which was one of the oldest businesses in London purchased it in 1923. They already owned the (unconnected) Red Lion Brewery down river at Lower East Smithfield which was once the biggest brewery in London with a history going back to Tudor times.

Charrington, the huge brewery chain, purchased the breweries from Hoare in 1933. They later ceased brewing at the Lion but kept one of Hoare's trade marks, a Toby Jug, and even extended it to their Toby Inn pub food chain. Hoare's Bank is still going strong today at its offices in Fleet Street. The big brewers have long since left Central London which is a great shame. But at least there are numerous micro breweries springing up to take their place.

106: THE TOMB OF THE BARE-KNUCKLE FIGHTER

If you want to be entombed in Westminster Abbey you need to be a king, a queen, a prince, a duke, a lord, a baronet, a famous musician, a distinguished soldier, a celebrated scientist or a world renowned poet. Or perhaps a bare-knuckle fighter – Jack Broughton, pugilist extraordinaire.

Broughton died in January, 1789, aged 86, and his body is buried in the west cloister next to that of his wife Elizabeth. When it was first laid down, Broughton's stone had a gap after his name. It was intended to say "Champion of England" there, but the Abbey's dean, Arthur Penrhyn Stanley, apparently vetoed this, and it was not until almost 200 years later, in 1988, that the words were belatedly etched on the stone.

A champion Broughton certainly was. For almost 18 years he fought top boxers and was undefeated until lured back from retirement in 1750 to fight the unfancied Jack Slack, a Norwich butcher to whom he lost. This outcome had repercussions, not least because Broughton's patron, the infamous Duke of Cumberland, son of George II, who had butchered the Scots during his victory at Culloden, had bet a small fortune on Broughton winning. He wrongly accused him afterwards of deliberately throwing the fight and had bare fisted fighting outlawed for a while as a result.

Broughton was the thinking man's pugilist. He was the first to draw up comprehensive rules to make bare knuckle fighting less vicious. This initiative would eventually lead to the introduction of the Marquis of Queensberry rules in the 1860s. He built and ran a successful prize ring in Oxford Street near Hanway Street. He was also, in an earlier part of his life, a wherryman ferrying punters across the river. Broughton was the first person to win the Doggett's Coat and Badge by

winning the Doggett's race, claimed to be the oldest boat race in the world, still held each year on the Thames in Central London.

Even so it is a big jump from those accomplishments to a burial place in Westminster Abbey. It happened partly because Broughton became one of the king's Yeomen of the Guard after his retirement from boxing. He was also a verger in the Abbey, though that doesn't normally confer burial rights. What is not in dispute is that he was surely the first and last bare knuckle fighter to be buried there.

107: EDWARD III'S THAMES-SIDE MANOR HOUSE

Any surprise at stumbling across the remains of this medieval manor house of Edward III, on the Thames Path where Bermondsey meets Rotherhithe and in sight of the Gherkin, is drowned by the immediate thought – what on earth is it doing there at all?

One thing about Edward – the man who plunged Britain into the 100 Years War with France with initial victories at Crécy and Poitiers – is that he was not short of palaces. He spent vast sums on them, mainly financed from the astonishingly large sum of £250,000 he obtained as a ransom for the captured French King John. With this, he turned Windsor Castle, his birthplace, into one of the biggest palaces on earth.

When he was not at Windsor he could be seen at Eltham Palace or at Sheen, which was his favourite and where he died. Oh, and his main gaff was supposed to be at Westminster, which he expanded considerably, including by constructing the Jewel Tower, one of Westminster's the few remaining medieval buildings.

Not content with all these, Edward also built this Thames-side manor house. But why? Some have thought it must have been a hunting lodge, but there is nothing to show that there was ever a park attached where deer could roam. In any case, Edward had already built a number of hunting lodges elsewhere. The most likely theory is that it was built so Edward could indulge another of his favourite hobbies, falconry, for which the marshlands would have been ideal.

It was only in the 1970s and 1980s, when warehouses where demolished on this stretch of the river that archaeologists at the Museum of London excavated the remains in order to preserve them and make them available to the public.

The picture above, taken from the information board at the site shows that there was a moat on three sides, with the north side leading out to the Thames and affording a landing spot for Edward after a comparatively short journey from Whitehall. What was going on inside Edward's head when he decided to build this can only be imagined. Perhaps when you have so many magnificent palaces it is sometimes good to have a bolthole get away from them.

108: JACOB'S ISLAND

In the 19th century there were numerous candidates for the unwelcome title of the worst slum in London. Shoreditch, Turnmill Street in Clerkenwell and Hogarth's Gin Lane were strong candidates as was the Devil's Acre – a phrase popularised by Charles Dickens – west of Westminster Abbey, where 40 policemen were once rebuffed when they tried to arrest a resident.

But if you add health to degradation as a social barometer, Jacob's Island in Bermondsey – also popularised by Dickens – was right at the bottom of the pit. It was an area bounded roughly by today's Bermondsey Wall West, George Row, Wolseley Street and Mill Street where, despite extensive gentrification, the plaque commemorating Jacob's Island has itself been defaced. Old habits die hard.

Contemporary descriptions chart the depths of hopelessness better than makeshift ones from today. In 1849 the Morning Chronicle called it "the very capital of cholera" and "the Venice of drains" while the reformer Henry Mayhew described the ditches as red from houses discharging their waste directly into them, and "the water harbouring masses of rotting weed, animal carcasses and dead fish." All people had to drink was the toxic waters of the Thames.

Small wonder that Dickens in Oliver Twist had Bill Sikes living and dying there (from a dramatic fall from the roof into Folly Ditch). His description was so accurate that years later Dickens's fans would visit what they were convinced was the actual house from which Sikes fell.

During the previous century it had been a fashionable area for the well-heeled, but the advent of industrialisation, shipbuilding and its dependent industries with attendant casualisation of labour and low wages quickly turned it into a rookery and slum.

The tide turned again in the early 1980s when this part of Bermondsey was one of the first places to be turned into expensive loft apartments, luxury flats and bijou residences, many of them passively overlooking the river that once made the area prosperous and full of activity including shipbuilding, ship breaking and the docks. One can only hope that the cycle of deprivation doesn't come around here again.

109: THE GREAT DUST HEAP

For some of the biggest bits of lost London there is only one proper reaction. Good riddance. And of none is this more true than the Great Dust Heap – perhaps one should say mountain – which dominated the landscape in front of what today is King's Cross station. It was the eyesore of eyesores and almost certainly the inspiration for the huge fortune that John Harmon made from dust in Charles Dickens's Our Mutual Friend.

An article in Household Words by R H Horne describes it thus: "About a quarter of a mile distant, having a long ditch and a broken-down fence as a foreground, there rose against the muddled-grey sky, a huge Dust-heap of a dirty black colour – being, in fact, one of those immense mounds of cinders, ashes, and other emptyings from dust-holes and bins, which have conferred celebrity on certain suburban neighbourhoods of a great city…"

And where there's muck, there's brass. An army of foragers regularly descended to pillage broken pottery, earthenware, oyster shells, discarded pans anything which could be sold on to make a few pennies. But the main value of the dust heap was ignored.

It was the cinders from household fires, which could be recycled into bricks and other valuable building materials. Contemporary accounts – including W J Pinks's venerable survey of Clerkenwell – report that the dust heap was sold – wait for it – to the government of Russia to help the re-building of Moscow after the war with Napoleon for an estimated price of £20,000.

The land on which it stood was sold to the Panharmonium Company whose owner, an Italian music teacher Gesualdo Lanza, planned to build a large theatre within specially laid out pleasure gardens with a music gallery, ballroom, drama school, picture galleries, reading rooms and other features including a refreshment area. There were even plans, years before King's Cross was opened in 1852, to include an overhead railway from which carriages were to be suspended (image above).

The site was roughly where Crestfield and Belgrove streets are today. If you look from the end of Argyle Square you will have most of the site stretching out before you. It appears that only a small theatre in Birkenhead Street – possibly the drama school – was completed. Bang went north London's answer to Vauxhall Gardens.

110: IN SEARCH OF POCAHONTAS

Pocahontas was an unlucky princess. She wowed London when she arrived from Virginia with a retinue in 1616 on the arm of Norfolk adventurer John Rolfe. She had reputedly saved the life of Captain John Smith, one of the earliest settlers in Virginia, in 1607. She was brought to London as a kind of ambassador for the Virginia Company, hoping to attract new investment. She was feted by London society and met Queen Anne, wife of James I several times.

A lovely nude statue of her by David McFall, which once graced the front of 38 Red Lion Square in Holborn, hasn't been heard of since it was sold at auction at Christies 1996. The actual body of Pocahontas was buried at St George's Church, Gravesend, in 1617 where she died of a disease – possibly pneumonia or smallpox – which struck her at the very start of what was meant to be her voyage home.

A century later, the church was destroyed in a fire and rebuilt on a different site. No-one knows for certain where the old church was located. It is thought her body might be lying beneath nearby Domino's Pizza. There is a more recent statue of Pocahontas in the church yard, donated by the people of Virginia.

Why was the statue in Red Lion Square? It was commissioned in 1954 to grace the new head office of Cassell Publishers. The spot was chosen because their previous head office had been in Ludgate Hill on the site of an ancient inn called the Belsavage or Belle Savage where Pocahontas had stayed during her visit to London. In 1575, the poet George Gascoigne referred to the "veine delights" of Belsavage fayre".

In the 18th century the essayist Joseph Addison renamed it "La Belle Sauvage" ("The Beautiful Savage") in praise of a heroine nurtured in a natural environment, but the actual name can probably be traced back to a proprietor of the inn called Savage.

McFall's statue was moved from Red Lion Square to Greycoat Place, Victoria and then to Villiers House in the Strand before being auctioned. No-one seems to know where it is now. It could be in a private house or a gallery or maybe even in America. It would be fitting if this lovely sculpture could be displayed once again as a public sculpture in London to commemorate a historic happening.

111: ELIZABETH WOODVILLE'S WESTMINSTER ABBEY SANCTUARY

When you enter Westminster Abbey's gift shop you are unlikely to notice the stone building peeping above it. Yet the right hand side of this turreted wall – where the tops of four windows are visible – has a tale to tell. It occupies one of the least know parts of the Abbey precincts and is not open to the public. It looks like the smaller version of an Oxbridge college hall and is used by the pupils of Westminster School for meals during term time and for the rest of the year reverts to its historic owner the Dean of Westminster.

It forms part of his private suite of rooms known as Cheyneygates, which is claimed to be the oldest residence in London in continuous occupation. It was to this room that Queen Elizabeth I would come to hear pupils of Westminster School perform plays in Latin, as stipulated by her as the school's founder. But its bigger claim to fame is from a much earlier time. What happened there then changed the course of history. William Shakespeare is our witness.

It was here where the formidable Elizabeth Woodville took refuge to avoid the wrath of Richard III. The Abbey was one of London's sanctuaries, providing a space anyone from a criminal to a poet could enter but where the Crown could not trespass.

Elizabeth was a queen in her own right as the wife of Edward IV. She was also the mother of another king, Edward V, who was born in the sanctuary and had a daughter who was married to yet another king, Henry VII, which resulted in Elizabeth being declared Dowager Queen. But it is for her stay at the Abbey – to which she twice repaired to avoid prison during the Wars of the Roses – that she is chiefly remembered.

After Edward IV was forced to flee the country, Elizabeth escaped from the Tower of London at night and claimed sanctuary in the Abbey on 1 October, 1470. Edward V later became notorious as one of the Princes in the Tower who were – almost certainly – murdered on the orders of Richard III, who was desperate to eliminate rival claimants to his throne. This is the story told so dramatically by Shakespeare in his play Richard III.

Elizabeth was duped into letting her son leave the sanctuary during her second stay there, in order to join his brother in the Tower, on the spurious grounds that he would be looked after and that sanctuaries were for criminals, not innocent children.

The hall that was familiar to Elizabeth I - and Elizabeth Woodville

As the Duke of Buckingham put it to Cardinal Bourchier in Shakespeare's play:

> "This prince hath neither claim'd it (sanctuary) nor deserv'd it,
> And therefore, in mine opinion, cannot have it.
> Then taking him from thence that is not there,
> You break no privilege nor charter there.
> Oft have I heard of sanctuary men,
> But sanctuary children ne'er till now."

This gives only a fleeting glimpse of an extraordinary life. Elizabeth retired to the royal apartments in Bermondsey Abbey in 1490, where she died two years later, apparently destitute. She is buried beside her husband in St George's Chapel at Windsor.

112: JAMES I'S MULBERRY TREE MISTAKE

The Chalrton Mulberry (photo credit: MorusLondinium.org)

It is not often that London loses an industry before it has even begun, but that is what happened when James I decided in the early 1600s that England needed its own silk industry to rival the success of those of France and Italy.

At first, all went swimmingly. James ordered thousands of mulberry trees on his own account, which were planted on several acres covering part of the garden of today's Buckingham Palace, extending over Constitution Hill to the edge of Green Park. He also persuaded prominent noblemen to plant thousands more. All was set fair except for one thing: James had ordered the wrong kind of tree. Silk worms thrive on the leaves of white mulberries, but the ill-advised James had chosen black ones, which were ill-suited to England's cool climate. What happened to them? Are any of them or their descendants still around?

Today, there are 40 mulberry trees in the garden of Buckingham Palace, which houses the National Collection of mulberries, curated by the Palace's head gardener, Mark Lane. None of them, however, are direct survivors of James I's endeavour, except for one grown from a cutting from the famous heritage mulberry at Charlton House. This is believed to have been planted at the behest of James, presumably as part of his plan to get the nobility involved. The website MorusLondinium.org describes the Charlton mulberry as "an extraordinary tree" which, at over 400 years old, is one of the oldest trees in London and the strongest candidate to have been planted as part of James's original project. Pity about the colour of its fruit, though.

Mulberry trees had existed in London long before James became interested them. Archaeological digs have uncovered seeds planted by the Romans to create a food source, and they were grown in monasteries for that purpose as well. There were later failed attempts to establish mulberry trees for silk production, including by the Raw Silk Company in around 1720. It planted 2,000 trees in the area of Chelsea Park, complete with a silk worm nursery. That came to nothing, but Morus Londinium tells us there are still plenty of mulberries around. It has recorded 135 sites so far and is still counting.

One surviving link with Jacobean times is the so-called King James mulberry, which was grown during the 17th century in what became the Chelsea Physic Garden. It was destroyed during the Second World War, but not before cuttings were taken, which have generated many descendants around London.

There is something special about sitting under a mulberry tree. There are two fine specimens on the terrace of the café in Hyde Park opposite the Duke of Wellington's abode, and there is a clump of them in St James's Park south of the blue bridge. The most newsworthy one is what is claimed to be the oldest mulberry in the East End, on the site of the former London Chest Hospital. It is threatened by a housing development by Crest Nicholson & Circle Homes. The tree may well have been planted as part of James's ill-fated scheme. For that reason alone, it should unquestionably be preserved.

113: THE LITERARY HISTORY OF ST JOHN'S GATE

If you walk through this medieval gateway with your imagination on high alert it will be like treading through an amazing repository of English religious, political and literary history. Only St John's Gate and a restored church the other side of Clerkenwell Road remain above ground to remind us of the Clerkenwell Priory, which was established in the 1140s as the English base of the Knights of the Order of St John, known as the Knights Hospitaller, the crusading military monks who cared for and protected pilgrims of all faiths who journeyed to the Holy Land. The St John Ambulance charity, whose offices are to the right of the gateway, is descendant from them.

The original St John's Gate was built in 1504 as an entrance to the priory's inner precinct. Henry VIII's dissolution of the monasteries in the 1540s also saw the dissolution of the Hospitaller order, and its property passed first to Henry's daughter Mary Tudor and later to a succession of aristocratic owners, including the dreadful Protector Somerset who blew up the nave to provide stone for his palatial residence Somerset House between the Strand and the Thames. He died before it was completed. The Hospitallers were briefly brought back under Henry's Catholic daughter Queen Mary, then dissolved again by her half-sister Elizabeth I. The Order of St John was re-established under Victoria. The Gate was greatly restored during the 19th century. Before that, the building it formed an entrance to was put to a great array of uses.

As you walk through its archway you will be beneath rooms Shakespeare would have frequently visited, because it housed the offices of Edmund Tilney, Master of the Revels to Elizabeth and King James, to whom Shakespeare would have presented most of the 30 plays of his that were registered here. On the right as you come out of the archway was a coffee house run by Richard Hogarth, father of the great artist William Hogarth, where customers were invited to speak in Latin. An advertisement stated that "there will meet daily some learned gentleman who speak Latin readily where any gentleman who is either schooled in that language or desirous to perfect himself in speaking thereoff will be welcome".

This building was where the Gentleman's Magazine, a hugely influential journal, was founded in 1731 by Edward Cave. He was a friend of Benjamin Franklin, some of whose books he printed there, and, in 1752, he erected a lightning conductor of the kind invented by Franklin.

This was where Dr Johnson, a contributor to the magazine, worked in a garret and wrote some of his books. In 1749, Johnson's friend David Garrick gave what is believed to have been his first public performance in Henry Fielding's The Mock Doctor. Oliver Goldsmith was a frequent visitor.

The eastern side of the gateway also hosted the old Jerusalem Tavern for many years. The gatehouse and associated room is now the St John Ambulance's headquarters. Once through the Gate you can sense the ghost of a palace that is no longer there. Hollar's engraving is the only memory of what it once looked like, though if you cross Clerkenwell Road, which runs straight across the original site, you come to St John Square with the reconstructed church with a 1950s facade on the right. The circle of cobblestones on the square in front follows the line of the circular nave of the 12th century church. The very impressive crypt dating back to the 1140s can be viewed during official visits and is one of the very few Norman buildings in London.

114: THE HORRIBLE HOCKLEY-IN-THE-HOLE

The Coach at the bottom end of Ray Street, off Farringdon Road, is a delightful gastropub. It is a great improvement on its predecessor, the Coach and Horses, which once served employees of the Guardian when the newspaper occupied a nearby building. Yet the Coach and Horses itself was a huge improvement on what used to be there.

In the late 17th and 18th century, the spot was known as Hockley-in-the-Hole, the site of a notorious bear and dog baiting arena, which also featured bare knuckle fights. What took place there is well described by an advert for events of April 27, 1700, described as "being a general day of sport by all the old gamesters and a great mad bull to be turned loose in the game place with fireworks all over him and two or three cats tied to his tail and dogs after them".

It was regarded as the lowest of low entertainment, yet attracted an unusual mixture of high and low life, including Alexander Pope and Jonathan Swift, author of Gulliver's Travels. John Gay, also a customer, mentions it in The Beggar's Opera, when Mrs Peachum says to Filch: "You must go to Hockley-in-the-Hole and Marylebone, child, to learn valour".

In Oliver Twist, Charles Dickens has the Artful Dodger, after a pickpocketing foray, moving "across the classic ground which once bore the name of Hockley-in-the-Hole; then into Little Saffron Hill; and so into Saffron Hill the Great, along which the Dodger scudded at a rapid pace, directing Oliver to follow close at his heels".

All the evidence of bear baiting and the like has long since gone, yet the Fleet River, which used to flow near to it, has not gone away. It is merely covered up. If you check there is no traffic coming, step a yard or two into the road outside The Coach and put your ear near the drain, you can hear the flow of the Fleet at the point before it joins the main sewer en route to Farringdon Road and the Thames.

115: GEORGE TRAIN'S VICTORIA STREET TRAM

If ever a man was destined to run a transport system it was the aptly named George Train. This flamboyant American entrepreneur gave London its first trams, a means of travelling round the capital that would last for over a century. At their peak 2,500 tramcars carried over seven million passengers a year round London, and when the last one of the first generation made its swan song journey from Westminster to Woolwich in July 1952, thousands turned out to give it a good sendoff.

Train was responsible for one of the very first tram services in the UK, a horse-drawn one started in 1860 which ran the length of Victoria Street, from the station to Parliament Square. It was a success with passengers, though not with other road users because the rails on which the trams were pulled protruded over a foot above the ground. Goodness knows how the horses pulling the trams coped with those, let alone all the other horse-drawn traffic that crowded Victoria Street at that time.

In 1861, Train was arrested for the unusual crime of "breaking and injuring" a London street – the Uxbridge Road where, presumably he intended to expand his business. But trams were catching on, and several new lines were started following an 1870 Act of Parliament, which required rails to be recessed into the carriageway.

Trams had advantages for their owners because the use of steel rails reduced friction, which meant fewer horses were needed for pulling heavier passenger loads, which boosted profits. It has been estimated that 50,000 horses were needed to keep the public transport system running in Victorian times. They were reckoned to eat the equivalent of a quarter of a million acres of food a year and deposited huge amounts of dung on the roads. A team of 12 horses was needed to keep a tram operating for 12 hours a day, each one working for three to four hours. Small wonder that the electrification of trams and the coming of motorised transport triggered the decline of the horse on London streets.

"Citizen Train", as he called himself, followed many other paths. He became a ship owner, a busy writer, a presidential candidate and a friend of French revolutionaries. In 1870 he embarked on a trip around the world and claimed to have completed it in 80 days. This was probably true, as long as you discount a month involved in revolutionary tactics in Paris. Two years later, Jules Verne published Around The World in Eighty Days, probably inspired by this much-publicised achievement. For Phileas Fogg read George Train.

116: EROTIC ABANDON AT RANELAGH GARDENS

The Chinese House, the Rotunda & the Company in Masquerade in RENELAGH GARDENS.   *La Maison Chinoise la Rotonde et les Masques en Masque dans les IARDINS de RENELAG.*

If you were looking for pleasure in late 18th century London there was only one place to go: Ranelagh Gardens. It was the Tinder and Spotify of its day, providing dating opportunities with seductive music. Edward Gibbon, author of the Decline and Fall of the Roman Empire, described it as "the most convenient place for courtships of every kind – the best market we have in England."

The Gardens were situated at what is now the Thames-side end of Christopher Wren's Royal Hospital in Chelsea. There is still a park there on the site called Ranelagh Gardens (pictured below), though all the buildings – including a huge Rotunda (pictured above) at which a nine-year old Mozart performed in 1765 – have long since gone. It opened in 1742, a time when Vauxhall Gardens over the river was in decline having entertained Londoners for almost 200 years.

Vauxhall also had a reputation as a pick up joint, but Ranelagh had a certain social cachet. It was twice as expensive as Vauxhall yet, interestingly, became a place where different social classes – well, upper and middle-classes at least – could meet and even date. Class distinction was preserved by five different levels of pricing. There was even a separate place built for servants, who needed to be nearby in case called upon by their masters. But these devices could not prevent the classes mingling, even though it was against the wishes of the proprietors. Horace Walpole commented: "It has totally beat Vauxhall. You can't set your foot without treading on a prince, or Duke of Cumberland."

Berta Joncus describes it thus in the London Journal: "Through its music, Ranelagh Gardens became a soundscape as well as a landscape. Characteristic of the vocal music performed at its Rotunda, Europe's first purpose-built concert space, was the projection – through words, orchestration, and pairings of singers – of the pastoral myth that the Gardens laboured to evoke." Visitors were offered, "the chance to enact, as well as witness, an Arcadia-themed erotic abandonment."

The Gardens were so named because they sat on the site of Ranelagh House, constructed in 1688–89 by The Earl of Ranelagh, treasurer of the adjacent Chelsea Hospital. It was so successful that it spawned lookalike gardens with the same name in Paris and New York. But a decline began at the turn of the century. The rotunda was closed in 1803 and pulled down two years later. We don't know if the bricks were recycled elsewhere, but it is known that the organ – which Mozart may have played – went to All Saints Church in Evesham until the Victorians replaced it.

Little known fact: Fulham Football Club played on the site from 1886-8, when it was known as the Ranelagh Ground.

117: SHAKESPEARE IN PALL MALL

Walk down Pall Mall today and you are denied entry to almost every building on its south side, unless you are a member of one of the posh private clubs there. It is difficult to believe that in the late 18th century this street was a hive of public artistic activity, mainly revolving around Shakespeare.

This was triggered by the artrepreneur James Boydell, who opened the Shakespeare Gallery, designed by George Dance the Younger, in 1789 at Number 52 Pall Mall. It soon contained 180 specially commissioned paintings depicting scenes from Shakespeare plays, many by established artists such as James Fuseli, Joshua Reynolds and George Romney.

In those days Pall Mall was a mixture of high-class residences, bookshops and bourgeois brothels. A statue by Thomas Banks showed Shakespeare between representations of the Dramatic Muse and the Genius of Painting. Underneath was an inscription from Hamlet: "He was a Man, take him for all in all, I shall not look upon his like again".

The statue was removed in 1869, when the building – by then occupied by the British Institution for Promoting the Fine Arts in the United Kingdom – was demolished. It was re-erected at the far end of Shakespeare's garden at New Place in Stratford-upon-Avon, where it still resides (pictured).

Entry to the Shakespeare Gallery was free and its intention was to direct British art in a more classical direction, choosing rich literary themes instead of portraits. Boydell also had a business plan. Like Hogarth earlier in the century, he sold engravings of the paintings here and on the continent with great success until the Napoleonic wars broke out, cutting off the continental market. This led to his bankruptcy and a fire sale of all his artworks in a lottery.

On January 28, 1805, William Tassie, a London gem engraver, struck lucky. His three guinea ticket to the lottery won him the gallery's entire contents. Tassie refused an offer from Boydell's nephew Joshua to buy them back for £10,000 and they were later sold at Christie's for just over £6,000, way below their cost price.

As a result, the Boydell collection, which in its day challenged the artistic supremacy of the Royal Academy – which had itself been located in Pall Mall until 1780, when it moved to Somerset House – bit the dust. Many of the paintings disappeared for ever. But some have been retained in galleries and private collections.

The Boydell gallery was but the biggest of a mini explosion of artistic galleries in Pall Mall, often featuring Shakespeare. In 1788, the year before the Boydell gallery was founded, Thomas Macklin's Poets' Gallery, which showcased over 50 British poets including Shakespeare, opened to an enthusiastic response.

In 1794, James Woodmason moved his New Shakespeare Galley from Dublin to Schomberg House at 88 Pall Mall, across the road from Boydell's initiative, which he copied by using illustrations and text employing some of Boydell's artists. Among the works Woodmason commisioned were Matthew Peter's Death of Juliet as she prepared for suicide, dagger in hand, and Fuseli's depiction of Titania falling in love with Bottom from A Midsummer Night's Dream.

The Shakespeare galleries in Pall Mall must have left something in the air, because in the 1840s, some years after their closure, the great engineer Isambard Kingdom Brunel, who was living in nearby Duke Street, commissioned paintings of Shakespeare scenes from some of the top artists of the day, including Edwin Landseer and Charles West Cope. They were hung in his spacious dining room, which came to be known as "the Shakespeare Room".

There were other kinds of gallery in Pall Mall too. Henry Fuseli opened a Milton Gallery in the late 1790s; Christies had their showroom there; Schomberg House, the facade of which still exists today (complete with statues made of artificial Coade stone), was host to the studio of Thomas Gainsborough.

There were also the exhibition rooms of the Polygraphic Society, which aimed to make multiple copies of oil paintings available for people who couldn't afford the originals. At the eastern end, at Spring Gardens, the Society of Artists had its main exhibition venue, while on King Street, off St James's Square, there was another gallery, the Imperial Museum, (later the European Gallery) which showcased British and Continental paintings.

There are still lots of paintings in Pall Mall, but they are all behind the closed doors of the clubs. There is nothing, apart from the Schomberg facade to remind us of the street's former glories.

118: THE LINCOLN'S INN FIELDS THEATRE

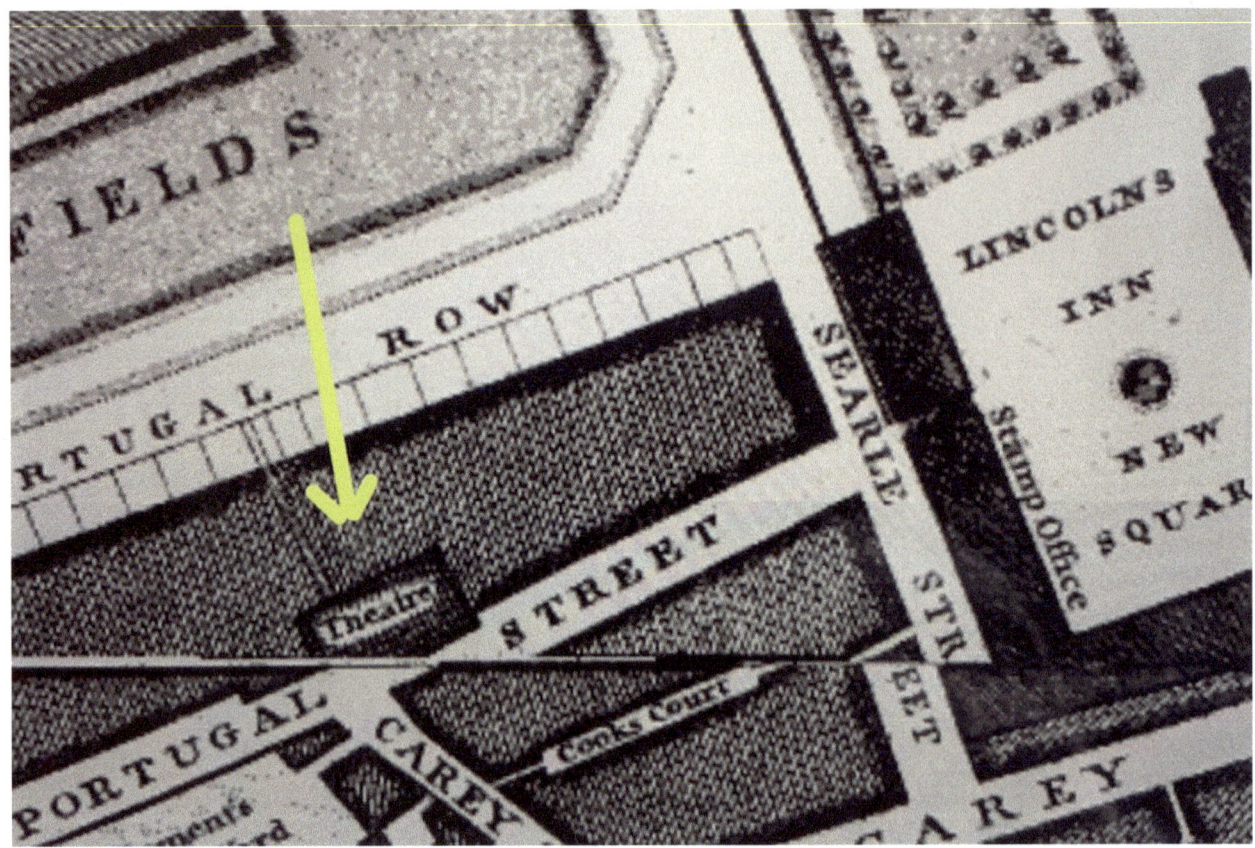

Behind an unimposing wall between Portugal Street and Lincoln's Inn Fields lies a long lost theatre where the modern musical was born.

It was in 1738 that a reluctant impresario, John Rich, put on a new kind of performance that mixed words with popular ballads laced with satirical references to contemporary politicians and events. The Beggar's Opera ran for 62 consecutive performances at the Lincoln's Inn Fields Theatre, an England all-comers record. It made the reluctant Mr Rich so rich he had enough money to build a swanky new theatre in Covent Garden that eventually became the Royal Opera House.

Rich was no beggar, but the play he put on was unusual in depicting ordinary folk backed by familiar tunes which the audience could hum to. Written by poet and dramatist John Gay, it was a multi-layered satire on politics (one of the characters, Bob Booty, was based on the Prime Minister Sir Robert Walpole), inequalities of wealth and even fashionable upper class Italian operas.

Gay got the idea by way of Jonathan Swift, author of Gulliver's Travels, who had written to Alexander Pope suggesting "a Newgate pastoral among the thieves and whores there". Gay decided a satire would be more appealing and his targets included well known criminals such as Jonathan Wild, heart throb highwayman Claude Duval, and Jack Sheppard, a master jail-breaker. This might have seemed a risky thing to do, but they probably wallowed in the publicity. Gay also wrote a sequel, called Polly. This was even more satirical and was banned after Walpole complained to the Lord Chamberlain, with the result that the work was not performed for over 50 years.

The Lincoln's Inn Fields Theatre had originally been Lisle's "real tennis" court, but was easily converted into a small theatre. It was the first in London to use movable backgrounds and scenery. Samuel Pepys described it as "the finest playhouse that ever was in England".

The popularity of The Beggar's Opera is attributed to it being about ordinary people with whom the audience could identify and its use of existing songs, including works from Handel. It has proved popular ever since and in these times of growing wealth inequalities and political intrigue, its message is as relevant as ever.

119: GEORGE WILKINS — BROTHEL-KEEPER, PLAYWRIGHT, THUG

Turnmill Street in Clerkenwell was the most notorious road in Tudor and Stuart London, a place where violence, drunkenness and prostitution were rife. There was a brothel, thinly disguised as a pub, around its junction with Cowcross Street (pictured). It was run by a highly discreditable fellow called George Wilkins, a violent man who was regularly in and out of prison for a variety of offences, including kicking a pregnant woman and stamping on others.

He and his pub would be of no interest at all, except for one thing: he wrote a play with William Shakespeare.

The play in question was Pericles, first performed in 1608. Wilkins is thought to have written most of the first two acts, and the brothel scenes would reflect much of his first-hand experience. It was not his first play. He wrote The Miseries of Enforced Marriage, based on a real-life murder trial, which was performed with some success at the Globe Theatre in 1606, and he briefly collaborated with some other minor Jacobean playwrights.

Theatres at that time had a close link with prostitutes, who frequently plied their trade both outside them and inside. Given this, it is not surprising that Shakespeare became acquainted with Wilkins, who also had links with the Mountjoy family, whose house in Silver Street, Cripplegate, Shakespeare lodged in for a couple of years. Both Shakespeare and Wilkins were witnesses in the legal case Belott v Mountjoy in 1612.

Wilkins died in 1618, two years after Shakespeare, an unlamented rogue with a talent he never fulfilled.

120: FLEET STREET'S DAILY COURANT

Britain's first daily newspaper was published in London on 11 March 1702 in somewhat unusual circumstances: it was produced by a man who turned out to be a woman; it carried no news about England, only from abroad; and it didn't offer any opinions, leaving its readers to make up their own minds.

The paper was called the Daily Courant and was produced at a house near the King's Arms inn near Fleet Bridge by Elizabeth Mallet, who found it a good career move to pretend it was all done by a man. Women weren't supposed to do that sort of thing in those days, although, curiously, the only paper which also claimed, less successfully, to be Britain's

first – the Norwich Post – was also run for a while by a woman called Elizabeth – Elizabeth Burges.

Elizabeth Mallet's journal consisted of two pages, with foreign news on the front and advertisements on the back. It is not clear why she chose to report only foreign news, but it may have been that it was considerably cheaper than paying for home news. She was way ahead of her time in presuming that her readers had "sense enough to make reflections for themselves". Not many papers today would follow that approach.

Mallet sold the Daily Courant to Samuel Buckley after only 40 days. He moved it to premises around Little Britain "at the sign of the Dolphin". Buckley eventually became publisher of the Spectator. The Courant itself lasted until 1735, before being merged with the Daily Gazetteer.

There is a plaque by the side of the Leon café at Ludgate Circus marking the spot near the King's Arms pub (or maybe in a lane behind) where the paper was first put together. It marks the birthplace of Fleet Street as the home of British newspapers.

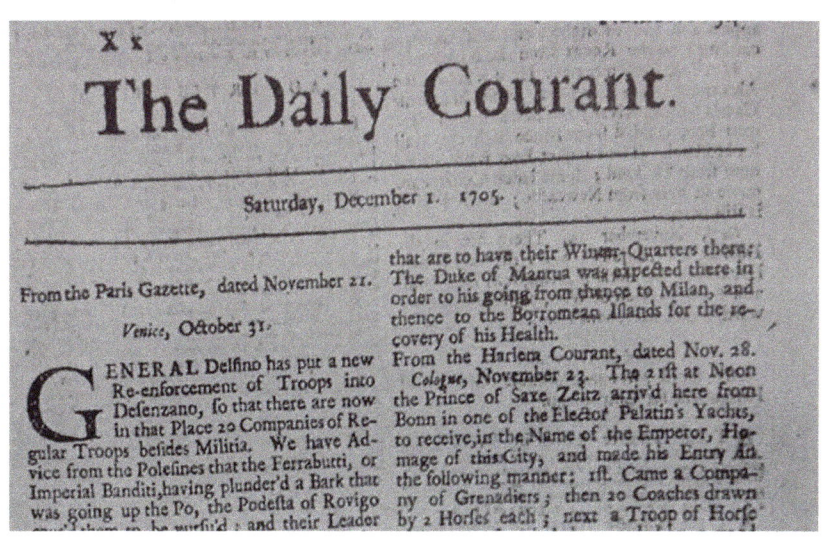

121: ELEPHANT & CASTLE'S LEISURE SPECTACULARS

It is difficult to believe that this spot in Walworth in the shadow of the Elephant and Castle was once the site of two spectacular leisure experiments.

In 1831, Edward Cross started the Surrey Zoological Gardens here, years before London Zoo was opened to the public. London Zoo is the oldest scientific zoo in the world, dating back to April 1828, but it didn't open its doors to the public until 1847. Cross had owned a menagerie at the Exeter Exchange building on the Strand. The building was demolished in 1829, but many of the animals were eventually moved to this new home within the Royal Surrey Gardens.

They were kept in a large domed glass conservatory, 100 yards in circumference with 6000 square feet of glass, housing cages for animals that included the first giraffe to come to Britain, tigers, lions, and even a rhinoceros. The Gardens, planted with exotic trees and plants, formed the background for large-scale entertainment spectaculars, such as re-enactments of The Eruption of Mount Vesuvius and the Great Fire of London.

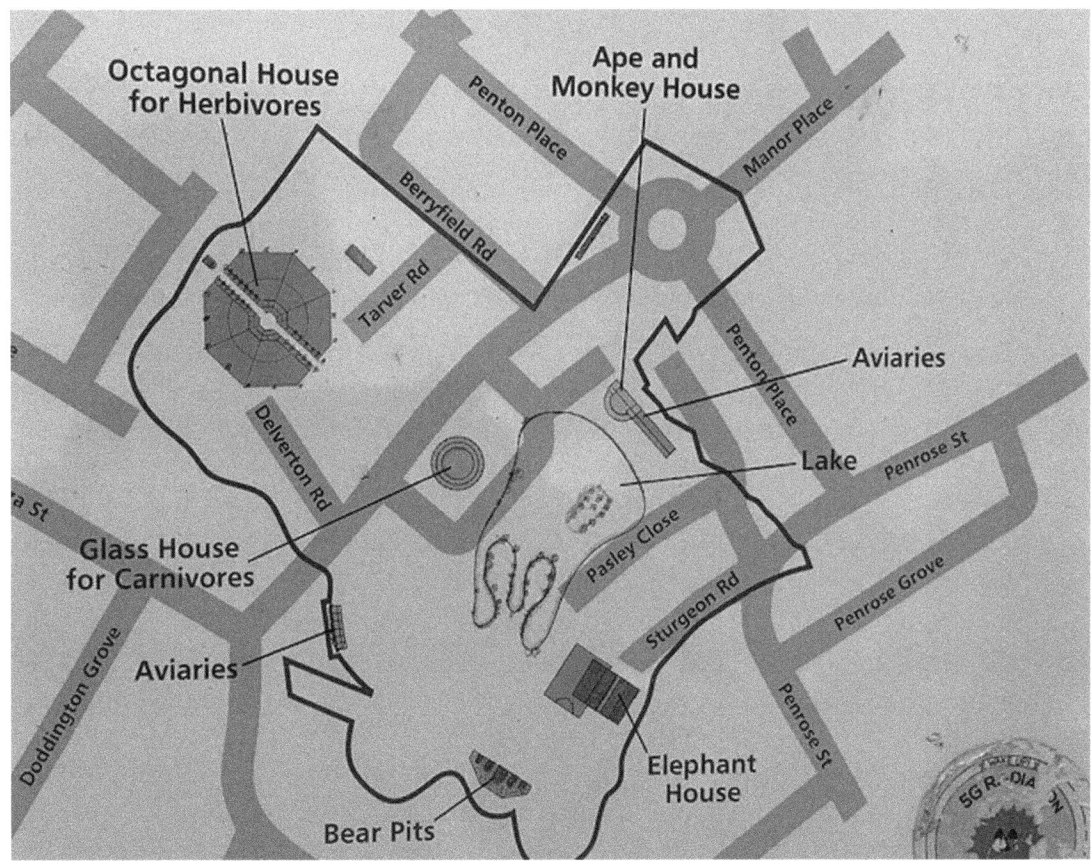

Octagonal House for Herbivores · **Ape and Monkey House** · Penton Place · Manor Place · Berryfield Rd · Tarver Rd · Penton Place · **Aviaries** · Delverton Rd · **Lake** · Penrose St · a St · **Glass House for Carnivores** · Pasley Close · Penrose Grove · Sturgeon Rd · Doddington Grove · **Aviaries** · Penrose St · **Elephant House** · **Bear Pits**

In 1856, following Cross's death, the Gardens and the animals were sold and the new owners built the second of the ambitious projects on the site, the Surrey Music Hall. This occupied 15 acres east of Kennington Road, of which three comprised a lake. The hall could seat 12,000 spectators in an iron and glass emporium that was clearly influenced by the Crystal Palace in its original home in Hyde Park.

Among the entertainments was a four-day military festival held in 1857 to honour and raise funds for Mary Seacole, the extraordinary nursing heroine of the Crimean War. It was also used for promenade concerts and revivalist meetings, including some by a charismatic Baptist preacher Charles Spurgeon, whose services in the music hall at weekends attracted huge audiences. The first one, held in October 1856, was reported to have drawn an audience of 10,000 people, with many more outside unable to get in.

The Gardens were sold for the development of residential buildings in 1877, but a much smaller public park opened there in the 1980s. It is now called Pasley Park. Some of the local roads reflect the site's history, such as Sturgeon Road, named after the evangelist, and Manor Place which references the original Walworth Manor on which the Gardens were built. Otherwise, nothing is left but grass. And memories.

122: PALMER'S VILLAGE — WESTMINSTER'S PIECE OF MERRIE ENGLAND

This needs an act of the imagination. If you stand in front of Westminster Council's City Hall in Victoria Street and look across the road at the House of Fraser store (formerly The Army and Navy) you will be seeing what used to be called Palmer's Village, a two-acre survival of Merrie England.

No one has described it better than Charles Manby Smith, who chronicled the rise and decline of Palmer's Village with aching nostalgia. To the north of the Village, towards Westminster Abbey, was a conglomeration of the most squalid buildings in London, where the police feared to tread. To the south and west was the wild and swampy terrain of Tothill Fields, stretching down to the Thames. Manby Smith wrote of "the great Babylon, where, though hemmed in all around by crowded streets, dark narrow lanes and fetid courts, it (Palmer's Village) yet retained many of the rural charms of its primal condition. It had yet a village green... and on the green, every first of May, up rose, reared by invisible hands in the night, the village May-pole, round which we have seen the lads and lasses dancing to the music of their own laughter."

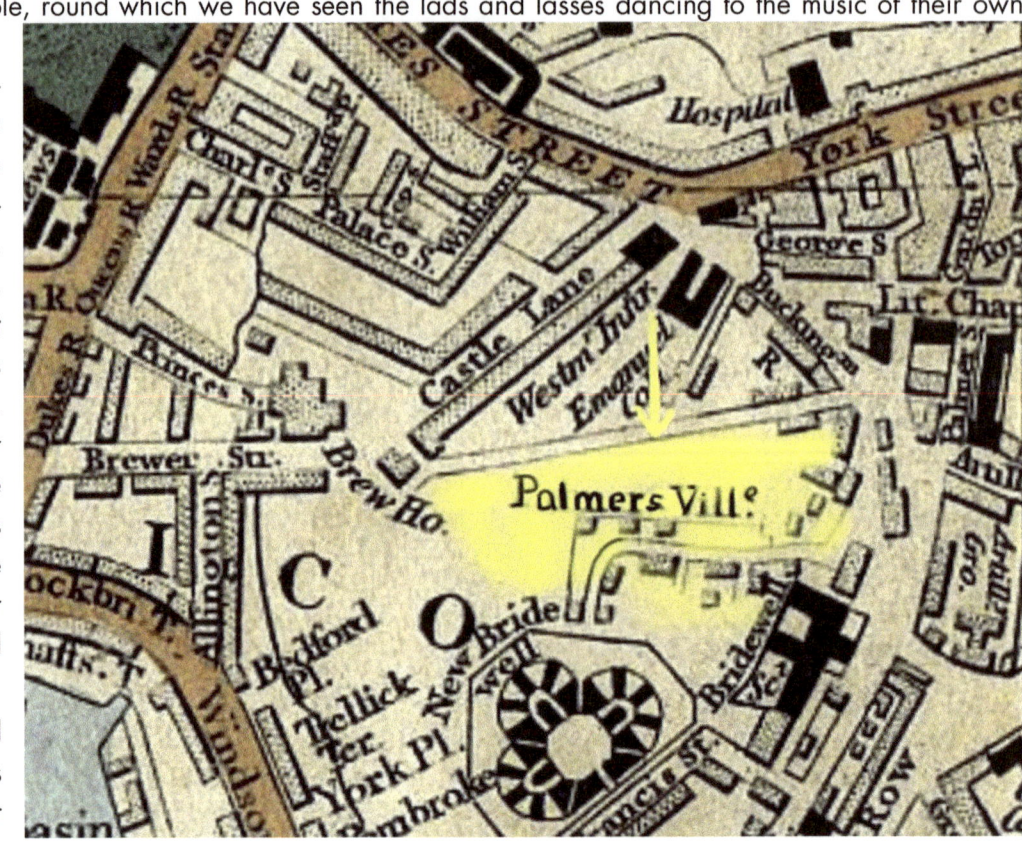

He added: "It had an old-fashioned way-side inn, the Prince of Orange; well we remember it, and its merry-faced and active little landlord, Wiggins, who never would be, still, and never could be sad, but with a perennial laugh on his lips and a joke on his tongue, welcomed the weary traveller to cheap and wholesome refreshment. Then there was Mrs Wiggins who lived in the bar, and of whom nobody ever saw more than the head and shoulders".

Palmer's Village was demolished as recently as the late 1840s as part of the Westminster

"improvement" scheme which gave us today's Victoria Street. However, decline had already set in according to Manby Smith, who blamed it on the horse-drawn cab, the owners of which made bad use of open spaces in the village with stables being erected and flowers replaced by dung heaps. And with the cabbies, he says, came "late hours and midnight riot, gin-drinking and squabbling."

Existing buildings were acquired by compulsory purchase orders and the new Victoria Street was built as much as seven feet above existing ground levels to improve drainage and use up the huge amount of rubbish left after demolition. When you walk along Victoria Street you are treading on submerged history. In keeping with the spirit of the time, no provision was made to re-house those displaced by the "improvements", so progress led to a worsening of poverty.

Palmers Village was set up in 1654 by the Reverend James Palmer, Vicar of St Bride's in Fleet Street, in order to finance almshouses for 12 poor people and a school for 20 boys he had built at the side of St Margaret's burial-ground in Christchurch Gardens (next door to today's Albert pub). It was called the Black-Coat School which eventually morphed into today's Westminster City (comprehensive) School. Palmer's name is kept alive by Palmer Street, which runs along the line of the old almshouses from Victoria Street next to the Albert pub to Caxton Street.

Those almshouses are long since demolished. The outside walls of properties of the Westminster Almshouse Foundation in Rochester Row have busts of Palmer and another benefactor, Emery Hill preserved from the original housing. Hill's name too is remembered in a road name, the adjoining Emery Hill Street. Both men are commemorated with plaques in St Margaret's church, next to Westminster Abbey.

123: CLERKENWELL HOUSE OF DETENTION

There must have been some symbiotic reason – maybe to do with sin and redemption – why Clerkenwell was once so dominated by monasteries and prisons. They included the Priory of St John adjacent to St Mary's Nunnery (both early 12th century) with Charterhouse (14th century) nearby and Blackfriars monastery a short walk away.

The road up from the Thames included the original Bridewell prison on the left or western side, then, after crossing Fleet Street, the Fleet Debtors prison was on the right. After that came the Clerkenwell House of Detention which was close by Cold Bath prison. The curious thing is that remnants of nearly all of them are still extant, though you may have to explore underground to find them.

None are more underground than the House of Detention, a dank and allegedly haunted prison, recently restored and rebranded as the Clerkenwell Catacombs. It was rebuilt in 1818 and later in 1847 on the site of two earlier prisons and achieved notoriety on December 13, 1867 when Fenians blew up part of it in an attempt to release Richard Burke, one of their arms suppliers.

Twelve bystanders were killed and over 100 wounded in a tragedy known as the "Clerkenwell outrage". Some of the participants were executed, including Michael Barrett, the ringleader. He was the last person to be publicly executed at Newgate prison. When the House of Detention was demolished above ground in 1890, the much lauded Hugh Middleton school was built, before being converted into apartments in the 1960s.

The extensive cells and the vaults beneath, however, were retained and are well worth visiting on the occasions when they are open to the public. They are mainly used now for film locations and product launches but there are open days. The address is Sans Walk EC1.

124: VICTORIAN TEA SHOP, STRAND

A faded shop sign above a Tesco Express where the Strand meets Fleet Street is the last trace of the curiously named Aerated Bread Company. It was the Pret a Manger of its day, in fierce competition with another catering giant, J Lyons. Both of them have completely disappeared from the High Street, except for a few ghostly reminders like this one. Pret, beware!

The Aerated Food Company started in 1862, making bread using a revolutionary new method that saved costs by avoiding expensive fermentation. It diversified two years later into a chain of tea shops. At the height of its success in 1923 the company – by then called ABC – had 150 branches and 250 teashops in London.

Lyons flooded London and elsewhere with a rival chain of teashops 30 years after the start of Aerated. Both companies employed smartly- uniformed women as waitresses, creating an atmosphere in which, for the first time, Victorian women could eat in safety together or even alone. The company went on went on to huge success in Britain and around the world.

By the early twentieth century, as company biographer Thomas Harding recalls, it was the undisputed king of British catering. It opened hotels like the Regent Palace and more tea shops than ABC. It has some claim to have produced the first programmable business computer in the world and, during the Second World War, even ran the Royal Ordnance Factory at Elstow in Bedfordshire. It is estimated that one seventh of all explosives dropped on Germany were made there.

Lyons reached its peak with the opening of its celebrated Corner Houses, some of which had multiple restaurants, stayed open all night and employed as many as 400 people. It was at the forefront of foodie trends, but not in its treatment of women. It emerged later that as early as 1873 the company had secretly set up The Fund, a benevolent provision for members of families it employed, but only if they were men.

The last of the Corner Houses closed soon after Lyons was bought by Allied Breweries in 1978 and closure of the tea shops followed not long after. The likes of ABC and Lyons were criticised by George Orwell as the "sinister strand in English catering, the relentless industrialisation that was overtaking it... everything comes out of a carton or a tin".

But ABC was lauded by others, including George Bernard Shaw, and its tea shops appeared in numerous novels by Graham Greene, Agatha Christie, Somerset Maugham and many others. T S Eliot even wrote these lines which could have – but didn't – come from The Waste Land:

"Over buttered scones and crumpets
Weeping, weeping multitudes
Drop in a hundred A.B.Cs"

But drop out they eventually did, as changing fashions and new ways of making bread emerged. The Aerated Bread Company was taken over by Garfield Weston's Canadian Allied Bakeries, which already owned Fortnum and Mason. London's high streets were never the same again.

125: THE DEVIL TAVERN

What have Oliver Cromwell, Charles II, Nell Gwyn and Samuel Pepys got in common? Answer: they all banked with a firm called Child & Co, based at the grandly named Number One Fleet Street, adjoining Temple Bar, which straddled the road.

What have Samuel Pepys, Dr Johnson, Jonathan Swift, Alexander Pope, Ben Jonson and a whole crowd of literary giants, maybe even including William Shakespeare, got in common? Answer: they all caroused at the Apollo Club or Devil Tavern at Number Two Fleet Street next door, usually with Jonson presiding.

Oh, to have been a fly on the wall to hear some of the literary – and not so literary – banter that must have taken place. Tradition has it that Gwyn was a great depositor of savings in the bank, while Charles was frequently overdrawn. I wonder if there was any connection...

Later, stuff happened. In 1787, the owner of Number One Fleet Street purchased Number Two in order to expand its banking activities, and the Devil Tavern was closed down. Today, it is reduced to a blue plaque on the wall, while Child and Co is still flourishing there today as a brand of the Royal Bank of Scotland.

It has a good claim to be Britain's oldest financial institution, having been trading at the Fleet Street site since 1673 and previously been based in the Strand. It did business under a "Marygold" sign (with its gold centre!). Its current logo, a sun and flower motif adopted in 1988, is based on the original.

The building didn't completely lose its literary associations when the bank expanded. It re-emerged as the model for Tellson's Bank in Charles Dickens' Tale of Two Cities. The author described it as, "an old fashioned, boastful, small, dark and ugly place with musty odour".

In the novel, it became such a magnet for French bankers visiting London to hear the latest gossip that Tellsons sometimes wrote the latest news and posted it in its window. Maybe this was the true beginning of Fleet Street, albeit in the form of fake news.

126: THE BLACKFRIARS ROTUNDA

On March 23, 1786 James Parkinson struck it lucky. He won the entire contents of a large London museum in a lottery for which he had paid a little over £2 for two of the 8,000 tickets sold. Sales were considerably lower than the 36,000 target hoped for. It must be the cheapest museum ever sold.

The collection – including lots of specimens collected by Captain James Cook on his voyages – had been painstakingly built up by Sir Ashton Lever, first in Manchester and later in Leicester House, the former royal dwelling that dominated Leicester Square. He rather ambitiously gave it the Greek name Holophusicon after a word meaning "whole of nature". John Quincy Adams, the future President of the United States, wrote home in the 1780s during a sightseeing visit to London full of praise for it.

Lever obtained an Act of Parliament to sell all of it by lottery after failing to get the British Museum or Catherine the Great of Russia to purchase the collection. This enabled him "to dispose of his Museum, as now exhibited at Leicester House, by Way of Chance." It by then included 26,662 specimens.

At first, lottery winner Parkinson kept the collection at Leicester Square. But after a few years he moved it to a new building on the southern side of Blackfriars Bridge at No 3 Blackfriars in Albion Street (as that end of Blackfriars Bridge was then known) and renamed it the Lever Museum, though it became known as the Blackfriars Rotunda because of its circular core. It would have occupied much of the space now dominated by the huge "carbuncle" skyscraper there.

After a while, Parkinson, like Sir Ashton, also tried to dispose of the contents including another attempt to sell it to the government which, on this occasion, was stymied by the distinguished naturalist Joseph Banks.

Instead Parkinson decided to sell the contents in an extraordinary auction (not to be confused with the lottery in which he won it in the first place). It commenced on May 5, 1806 and didn't terminate until the end of July. The official part of it finished on the 57th day after the 6,800th item had been sold. But after that there was an Appendix which took up another five days. Among the thousands of smaller items sold were two fighting cocks "trimmed down for fighting", a small crocodile, a Southsea snake, Siberian Jaspar and a gilt frame with skins of North American snakes. The catalogue has been put online, but you may need to take a short holiday to get through it all.

The contents ended up all over the country and abroad – maybe Britian's first distributed museum – but the building itself continued with multiple uses, including as a music hall and a pub – the Royal Albion – until it was eventually demolished in 1958. Whether the skyscraper that now dominates the site marks a cultural improvement can only be left to the imagination.

127: HOLLAND'S LEAGUER, THE LUXURY THAMESIDE HOUSE OF ILL REPUTE

As brothels go, Holland's Leaguer must have been in a class of its own, even for Shakespeare's time. It was located in the notorious Paris Garden, in a "liberty" free from the rule of the county of Surrey and the City of London opposite, situated on the southern side of the Thames, at the point where Blackfriars Bridge lands today.

You couldn't miss the brothel, which was named after its proprietor Elizabeth "Bess" Holland. It was located in a former manor house once owned by Henry VIII's third wife, Jane Seymour. It had its own moat and drawbridge (see engraving) which could be pulled up to keep out undesirables, such as apprentices on their annual Shrove Tuesday rampages, and sometimes the police as well.

It was sited close to the Swan Theatre, which was the biggest of its day, seating – or standing – 3,000 punters, not all of them there just for the show.

The brothel was said to be based on "The Lovely Little Maiden" in Brussels, offering luxurious ambience, fine food and clean linen. All of this would have come in handy when Charles I tried to close it in December 1631.

When his soldiers arrived, Holland apparently raised the drawbridge over the moat, causing soldiers to fall into the water. The brothel was besieged for a month, until it was finally closed in January 1632 causing Ms Holland to pursue her business elsewhere. How her customers reacted to being locked in a brothel for a month can only be guessed at.

This brothel was also unusual in that it had a play written about it called Holland's Leaguer, written by the improbably named Shackerley Marmion. It was staged in 1631 at the Salisbury Court Theatre near St Bride's Church

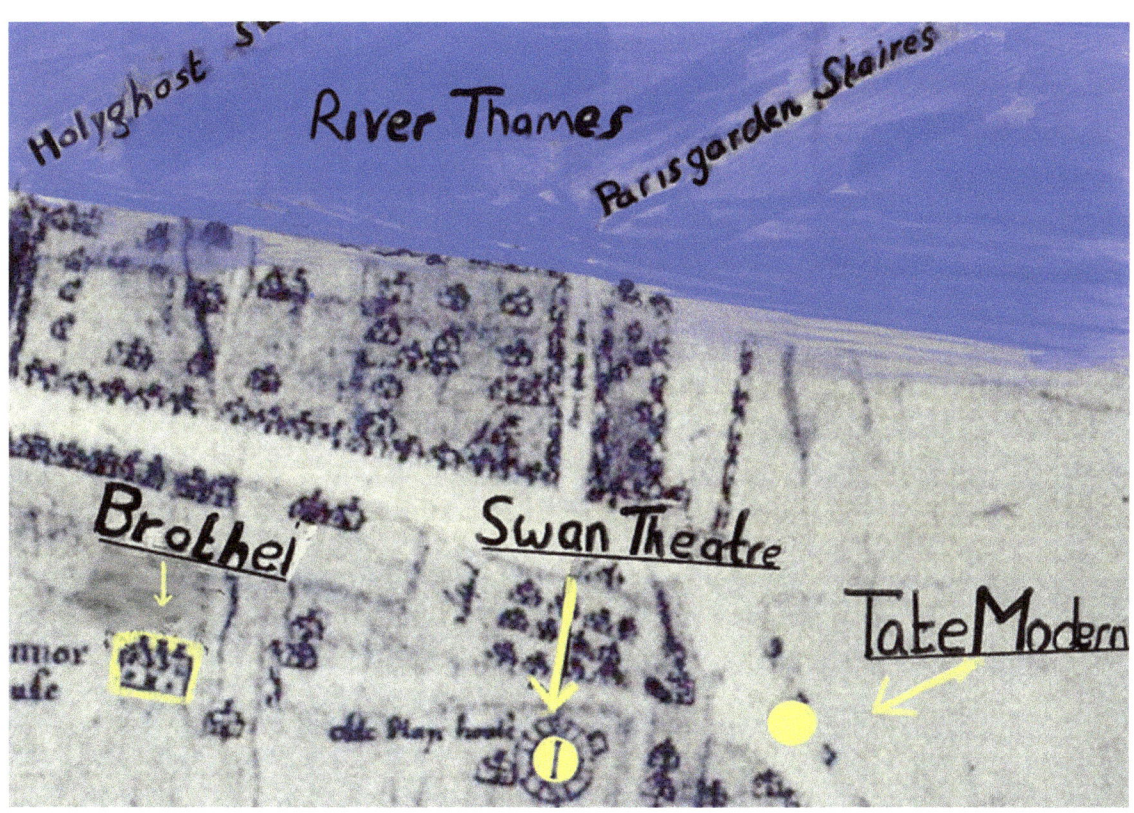

off Fleet Street and ran for six consecutive performances, making it one of the most successful plays of its time.

A contemporary court case shows that Shakespeare lived around Paris Garden for a couple of years after moving from north of the Thames in 1596, possibly in the area known today as Upper Ground. The case, in which William Wayte brought a restraining order against Shakespeare and others because he was in fear of his life, does not show Shakespeare in a favourable light.

If you stand on the streps of Tate Modern, the Swan Theatre would have been about 100 yards in front of you, where a new office block is under construction and the Holland Leaguer would have been a short walk behind. It's name is preserved today in Holland Street.

128: THE REMAINS OF COLONEL BLOOD

On August 24, 1680, a man died and was buried in the graveyard of New Chapel, an overspill cemetery of St Margaret's Church – almost next door to today's Albert pub in Victoria Street – where his body still resides. Soon after, he was dug up again because a lot of people refused to believe he was dead.

And with good reason. This was Colonel Thomas Blood, the Irishman described as "the greatest rascal in British history" and said to have shed more innocent blood than any other adventurer of his day. Blood's impersonation skills were so formidable and his ability to leave the scene of a crime undetected – such as when he tried to murder the Duke of Ormond – so seemingly miraculous that many would not accept that it was his body that had been buried, not least because Blood had just been ordered to pay £10,000, which he did not have, to the Duke of Buckingham following a court case and had good cause to, so to speak, lie low.

Christchurch Gardens where Blood is buried, before the recent construction

His greatest feat of escapology was stealing the Crown Jewels – at least for a brief period – and instead of being executed, as would have happened had he stolen a sheep, he was reprieved by Charles II in person in Westminster Hall and given back his estate in Ireland plus a £500 a year pension. Talk about the wages of sin!

Why Charles granted this extraordinary act of clemency is still a bit of a mystery. Blood's actual words to the king were: "If his Majesty would spare the lives of my friends and myself it would save His Majesty and his minister further harm, and His Majesty would make his enemies his friends." Did Charles genuinely feared that if he executed Blood his associates might kill him? There were a lot of plots around. Or was it because Charles thought it was all a bit of a joke or, maybe more likely, that Blood's value as a spy outweighed other considerations?

When Blood's body was dug up, the coroner summoned a jury and called upon his relatives to identify the remains. The only way they could do this was by recognising the abnormal size of his thumbs, whereupon he was reinterred and left to rot in what used to be called Tothill Fields, where he still resides under the last bit of greenery left in Victoria Street. A local resident at that time, he had a house on the corner of Great Peter Street and Tufton Street (image above).

129: BRUNEL THE ELDER'S WONDROUS TUNNEL

If you take the Tube between Rotherhithe and Wapping stations you will be travelling through the eighth wonder of the world which, in its time, was also the most successful tourist attraction on the planet.

That is what it became when it opened in 1843 as the world's first underwater tunnel. Built by the redoubtable Anglo-Frenchman Sir Marc Brunel – helped by his son Isambard – it was originally designed to convey horse-driven cargo under the Thames. The aim was to avoid the hassle of having to cross the surface of the river, with thousands of ships sailing along it in both directions each day.

Digging started in 1825 on the Rotherhithe side of the river, but soon ran into horrendous problems of fire, flooding, subsidence and foul air and was closed for seven years. Work started again in 1834 with the help of a loan from the Treasury. Five and a half years later, hugely over budget, it reached the other side of the Thames but it was not opened to the public until 1843.

The tunnel wasn't wide enough to accommodate vehicles and the builders couldn't afford the money for the ramps needed for lifting cargo onto trucks, so it began as a tunnel for pedestrians only.

Then came the surprise – an amazing 1.4 million people came to see the eighth wonder of the world in its first four months

and two million in the first year, making it the most successful tourist attraction on the planet. Visitors came from around the world to see the first tunnel of its kind, even though the curmudgeonly Victorian essayist Augustus J Hare described it as "this long useless passage under the river".

The tunnel was built with innovative building techniques involving a slowly advancing rectangular cage, the principle of which has continued to guide the construction of underground tunnels across the world, including the Channel Tunnel and Crossrail.

Miners would dig inside a protective frame, leaving bricklayers to construct a retaining wall as they moved very slowly

The Victorian Tunnels

forward. Incredibly, Marc Brunel based the design on how the shipworm Toredo Navalis bores into ships' timbers by excreting the bored wood and using it to re-inforce the tunnel as it moves along – a marvellous example of engineering mirroring nature.

The project was not without tragic consequences. The tunnel flooded five times. Six men died during the construction and Brunel Junior narrowly escaped with his own life during one of the floods.

In 1865 the East London railway company purchased it, and four years later trains started to run through the tunnel. In those days, the trains were steam-driven with no ventilation shafts, so it cannot have been a relaxing journey.

The tunnel is still there, more or less as it was, and you can journey through it on the train. If you start from the Wapping side of the river you can see the twin Victorian shafts at the end of the platform (pictured).

If you go to the nearby Brunel Museum – a must for anyone with an interest in Britain's industrial history and the genius of the Brunels – you can tread on the floor of the large tunnel entrance shaft, where father and son were often to be seen.

This was another Marc Brunel first. He built a large brick tower and allowed it to sink under its own weight, avoiding the need to dig a big hole and line it with bricks. On a side wall there is the original pipe which Thames water was pumped up to prevent the tunnel from flooding. It is still doing the same job today.

The museum is planning a major reconstruction, but it is absolutely worth a visit as it is now in order to get immersed in one of the amazing achievements of the Industrial Revolution. If you have time, walk a little way eastwards along the other side of the Thames and you will see the remains of the launching pad of Isambard's Great Eastern, which was the largest ship in the world at the time and held that record for 40 years. This part of the river should be renamed Brunel-on-Thames.

The Sunken Brick Tower

130: THE ABBEY UNDER THE MINT

In recent years, the government of China purchased the second most fortified building in London as the future new home for its embassy. The Royal Mint Court site stands opposite the Tower of London – the most fortified London building of all – on a site which, for hundreds of years, housed the Royal Mint, where most of the country's coins were manufactured, hence the fortifications. And underneath it lie the extensive remains of London's least known abbey.

It was dedicated to St Mary Graces, and used to be known as Eastminster to distinguish it from Westminster Abbey in the west. It was founded for the Cistercian order in 1350 by Edward III on the site of a notorious plague pit and fulfilled a vow Edward made to God and the Blessed Virgin Mary of Graces after his life had apparently been spared at sea.

If you walk around the block, starting at East Smithfield, turning left along Cartwright Street and left again along Royal Mint Street, you are walking around the space where the abbey was. Today, it is a case of "hunt the remains". Excavations on the old Royal Mint site involving 150 people started in the 1980s. These revealed walls stretching to 76 metres surrounding a hospital, a dining hall, chapel, chapter house (where abbey business was discussed), a refectory and other buildings.

To see the preserved remains today you need to seek permission from the building's owner – which now seems unlikely to be granted, given who the new owners are – or make do with fuzzy glimpses from the pedestrian walkway (see photo).

Some of the hidden remains

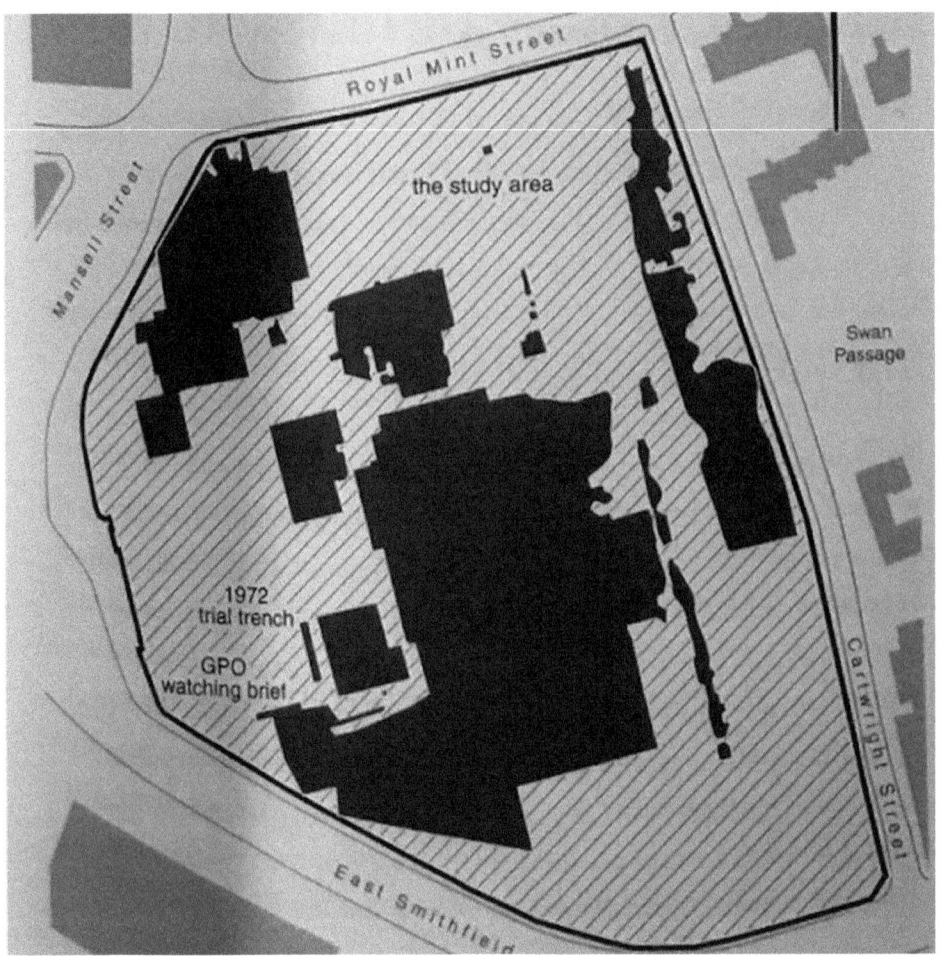

The Museum of London says, rather sadly, in its book about the excavations: "Those lucky enough to see the remains... are unlikely to be able to identify them without prior knowledge. They are not signposted and do not feature in tourist guide books for either London or abbeys and monasteries." It is a great shame that so many remains are hidden underneath new buildings in London, but at least they have been recorded and, in many cases, not destroyed.

For those interested in monasteries, this was an unusual one for the Cistercians, whose rules normally required their abbeys to be "far from the concourse of men" rather than on the edge of a city. It was the last Cistercian abbey built in Britain, but never attracted enough monks to make it a big success.

After the dissolution of the monasteries in the late 1530s, the abbey passed into the hands of a knight who completely rebuilt it, as was the habit for those who profited from Henry VIII's sequestrations.

131: SHAKESPEARE'S UNDERGROUND LODGINGS

The green space between Noble Street and London Wall in the City of London – where land values are astronomical – is unusual. It has been empty for over 350 years. St Olave's, the 12th century church which once stood there, was destroyed by the Great Fire in 1666 and, as consecrated ground, has been left vacant ever since. You can see it from a window in the Museum of London, which stands opposite. This would not merit any further comment except for one thing – it was the local church of William Shakespeare when he lodged quite literally across the road in Silver Street at its junction with Monkwell Street.

Shakespeare stayed with a French Huguenot family called the Mountjoys for a period between 1603 and 1605. It is the only place we know for certain that he lived, yet it is buried, plaque-less, in the underground car park on the other side of London Wall, whose construction destroyed the two streets. The house itself was another of the Great Fire's victims.

Shakespeare's time there has been known about for over 100 years, thanks to diligent American researchers Charles and Hulda Wallace. They came across a vital law case in the Public Records office in which Shakespeare was called as

Shakespeare's home was somewhere along here

a witness in a dispute over a dowry with the Mountjoys. James Joyce even mentioned it in Ulysses: "Shakespeare has left the Huguenot's house in Silver Street and walks by the swanmews along the river bank". Yet it wasn't until less than four years ago that a small tablet was put up in St Olave's churchyard saying Shakespeare lived "near here". Until then there was no indication that Britain's greatest writer had been a local resident. Only in England…

The plaque was probably a consequence of the publication of Charles Nicholl's marvellous book The Lodger, which filled in a lot of fascinating background, including that some of the goings-on inside Shakespeare's dwelling found their way into some of his plays. Nicholl points out that there is even a French herald called Mountjoy in Henry V, Act III. Professor James Shapiro, author of 1599 and 1606, two major books about Shakespeare, comments: "After finishing The Lodger it will be impossible to read Measure for Measure, All's Well, and especially Pericles as before".

Although the buildings and the roads have disappeared, it is still possible to sit in the abandoned churchyard of St Olave's and stare across the busy thoroughfare of London Wall and wonder what might have been. The buildings may have gone, but the scenes from plays that were written here live on and eerily conjure up what life was like inside.

132: WATER TROUGHS OF A HORSE-DRAWN PAST

This is a rare example of a horse trough in Central London, situated at Smithfield in front of St Bartholomew's hospital. There used to be hundreds of them and, boy, were they needed. At the beginning of the 20th century, London had a population of well over 50,000 horses which needed to drink to survive. It apparently took 12 horses a day just to pull a horse-drawn bus, and there were also 11,000 horse-driven Hansom Cabs.

All of which produced an enormous amount of manure. So much of it accumulated that in 1894 the Times predicted that 50 years hence every street in London would be buried under nine feet of it. This was dubbed the "The Great Horse Manure Crisis of 1894". It didn't happen because of the invention of an affordable mass-produced motor car. Thank you, Henry Ford.

We have to thank the Metropolitan Drinking Fountain and Cattle Trough Association, based at 111 Victoria Street, for the proliferation of drinking fountains and horse troughs in London. It was set up in 1859 by two philanthropists, Samuel Gurney MP and barrister Edward Thomas Wakefield, to provide free drinking water for Londoners. In 1885, it extended its remit to providing troughs for horses, and for Smithfield cattle as well.

There are still horse troughs scattered around London, which can be found with the help of the website waymarking.com.

Occasionally, they are stolen. But as the granite of which they are made contains unique constituent parts – a kind of DNA – they can be easily traced. No new horse troughs are being provided these days, but drinking fountains are making a comeback in order to reduce the considerable carbon footprint caused by the production of bottled water.

To close, a little-known fact. The very first drinking fountain, paid for by Gurney, can still be seen at the end of the church of Saint Sepulchre near the Old Bailey.

133: THE FIRST CURRY HOUSE IN TOWN

The green plaque at 102 George Street in Marylebone must be the least conspicuous commemoration in the whole of London. I passed by it twice without realising it was there. That is because it is fixed to a wall behind a window in an office block to which there is no public access. When I took a photo through the window I ended up with this image – a weird reflection rather than the real thing – which, I suppose, is rather appropriate.

This is the site of what is claimed to be the first Indian restaurant in London, and it doesn't take us back, as you might imagine, to the 1960s but to 1810, over 200 years ago. The restaurant was owned by Sake Dean Mahomed, an employee of the East India Company from Bengal, who was, among other things, a surgeon, a shampoo specialist, a traveller, a writer and an entrepreneur described by Wikipedia as "one of the most notable early non-European immigrants to the Western World".

Mahomed didn't introduce curry to Londoners, which had been savoured for centuries in private homes by discerning palates. Hannah Glasse's 1774 international best seller The Art of Cookery – buyers included Benjamin Franklin and Abraham Lincoln – contained recipes for curries. There is evidence that some restaurants also sold individual curry dishes but, at the very least, 102 George Street (or 34 as it was then numbered) was the first dedicated curry house run by an Indian. Authentic.

The restaurant, near Portman Square, was called the Hindoostane Coffee House. Its menu modestly included "Indian dishes...allowed by the greatest epicures to be unequalled to any curries ever made in England". By all accounts it would also deliver food to your home – the first Indian take-away. Alas, despite such grandiose claims, the restaurant was not a success and had to close after barely a year. Mahomed was ahead of his times. London was not yet ready for what would eventually become one of the city's favourite foods.

But Mahomed the entrepreneur was undaunted. In 1814, he and his wife moved to Brighton, where they had lived before, and opened England's first commercial shampooing vapour masseur bath (not to be confused with shampooing your hair) where the Queens Hotel is today. It was an immediate success and Mahomed became known as "Dr Brighton" eventually becoming shampooing surgeon to King George IV and William IV. He was also the first Indian to publish a book in English. He is buried at Brighton's St Nicholas Church.

134: GREAT GARAGES OF MAYFAIR AND ST JAMES'S

This is a tale of two garages. One was in Mayfair, and modestly described itself as the world's greatest. The other was on the other side of Green Park and has an amazing history unknown to nearly all nearby residents.

Let's start with the second. In June 1881, a panorama of the Battle of Waterloo, covering an astonishing 20,000 square feet of canvas, was unveiled at the Westminster Panorama, a venue that specialised in showing such works close by St James's Park station, which had opened 13 years earlier. The panorama was claimed to be the largest in the country, and seeing it must have been an impressive experience in the days before cinema and television. Seven or so years later, by then renamed the National Panorama, the same venue exhibited a new "wonderfully realistic" panorama of the Niagara Falls. This was over 130 yards long and seen by 667,000 visitors in the year to March 1889. The building became known as Niagara Hall.

But that was only the beginning of its many lives. It was situated next to the notorious Queen Anne's Mansions at the end of today's Ministry of Justice building in Petty France, then called York Street. In 1895 it was converted into an ice rink, complete with a new version of the Niagara Falls work. It soon became a hip venue for fashionable Londoners, hosting carnivals, competitions and exhibitions, reaching a peak in 1902 when it staged the World Figure Skating Championships. The first indoor ice hockey tournament in England took place there too. Yes, all right next to St James's Park Tube.

But soon afterwards this "skaters' paradise" came to an abrupt end. The pioneering Niagara Falls canvas was flogged off cheaply when the Niagara Hall building was purchased by the City and Suburban Electric Carriage Company to become one of the biggest garages in London, and almost certainly the most architecturally inspiring, as it retained the original circular theatre-like interior (see photo).

The Niagara Garage, as it was named, was in liquidation by 1903, despite a client list that included the king and queen. But soon after another phoenix arose from its ashes, when it became the London office and garage of Wolseley, which was, for a while, the biggest

The Niagara ice rink/garage

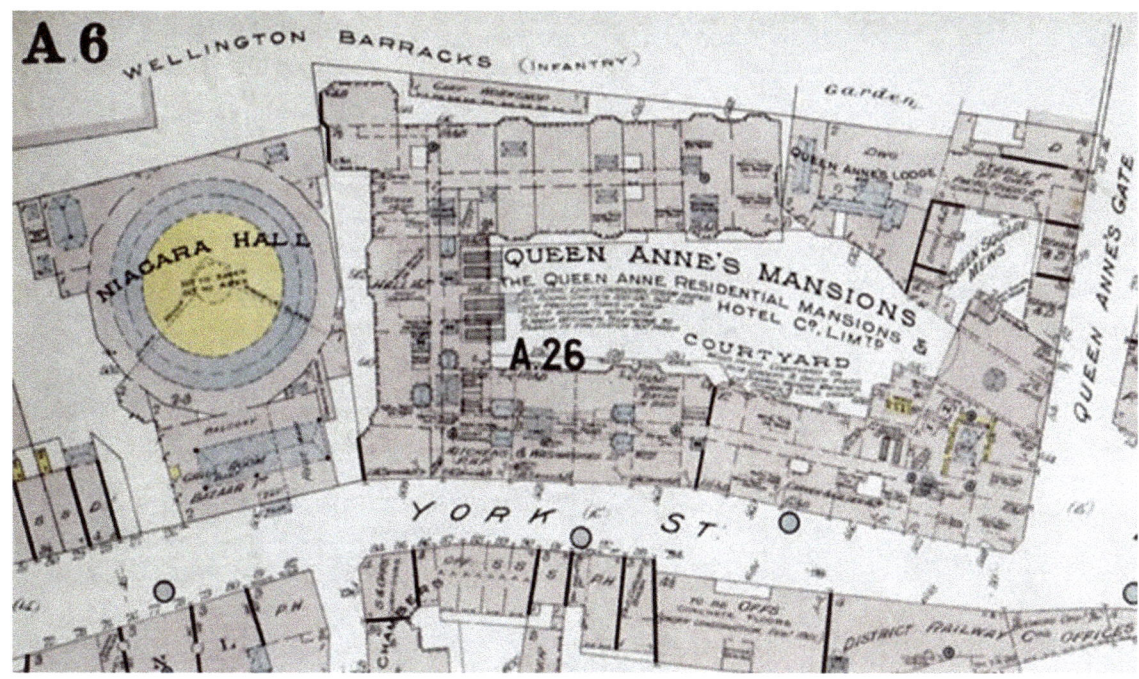

car manufacturer in the UK, housing 69 cars with another 50 in the gallery – accessed by an electric car lift – not to mention 22 in lock-up cubicles.

The other garage in this story is the Electromobile Garage, now masquerading as an NCP car park among the opulent buildings of Mayfair's Carrington Street. It has a secure place in motoring history. You don't have to believe its boast of being "the world's greatest garage" to acknowledge its important innovations. Electric-powered vehicles – which were rented out to town travellers – were its principal business. Customers could pop in, leave their batteries with the garage for recharging, and install another one for immediate use (Elon Musk, apostle of electric cars, please note!).

The garage was on three levels and had its exit and entrance on the same approach road. Cars could be edged sideways onto a platform running on rails. According to buildingourpast.com, these "transversers or trolley ways", were used for parking vehicles on the ground and first floors. It adds: "This could be seen as a semi-mechanised parking system. Cars were moved between floors by three hydraulic lifts. One of these went up to the flat roof, where cars could be washed."

The Electromobile was undoubtedly the more innovative and efficient of the two garages, but I know where I would have preferred to park my car. What a tragedy that the Westminster Panorama turned Niagara Garage was demolished. Today it would have been listed.

135: THE ORIGINAL HUNGERFORD FOOTBRIDGE

Hungerford Bridge, which carries trains across the Thames between Charing Cross and the South Bank, is not the first known by that name at that location. The original Hungerford Bridge was a suspension footbridge, built by Isambard Kingdom Brunel and opened in 1845. It took its name from Hungerford Market, which occupied a site where Charing Cross station now is.

Brunel's was the first pedestrian bridge to span the Thames. The noted Bradshaw guide book, called it "a marvel of modern mechanical ingenuity" But it wasn't there for very long. In 1864, it was replaced by the railway bridge designed by Sir John Hackshaw that has been there ever since. The official name of Hackshaw's bridge, as used by its current owner, Network Rail, is Charing Cross Bridge, though the name of Brunel's has long adhered to it. And the name isn't the only part of the original footbridge to stick around.

The two huge wrought iron chains from which it was suspended were recycled to create the Clifton suspension bridge in Bristol which looks uncannily like Brunel's footbridge. That is not surprising as its engineers built it as a tribute to Brunel based on his London design. And very substantial parts of the original bridge are still in situ supporting the current Hungerford Bridge.

Two large red brick towers helped support Brunel's bridge, built directly on the river bed without using piles. You can still easily see the remains of these masonry buttresses either side of the Thames.

One of the parts of the original Brunel Bridge that can be seen today

Brunel's Original Hungerford Bridge

On the South Bank side, the original pier with a door to stairs which led down to a docking place for steamboats survives. The one on the north side is now closer to the river bank than when it was built due to construction of the Victoria Embankment in 1870.

Today, most Londoners are familiar with the Golden Jubilee Bridges, the pair of modern footbridges, designed by Lifschutz Davidson Sandilands, which have flanked the Hungerford (or Charing Cross) Bridge since 2002. These are successors to various walkways that were appended to the rail bridge to make up for the loss of Brunel's, and they too unofficially bear the name of their lost forerunner, being often referred to as one or other "Hungerford footbridge".

The original suspension footbridge was not Brunel's only contribution to the history of the Thames. He helped his father, Marc, build the world's first underwater tunnel at Rotherhithe a few miles downstream, which is still used as part of the underground system. A little further east he built the Great Eastern steamship in 1858, which was by far the biggest ship in the world at the time and continued to be so for over 40 years. London owes him a big debt.

136: THE WALLACE COLLECTION

The Wallace Collection is not lost, but it is a bit out of the way for such a jewel of a place. I doubt anywhere else could boast of such a huge concentration of cultural wealth in so small a space. Except, of course, the Wallace Collection never boasts...

There are so many pictures in the gallery, many of them masterpieces, they have to be tiered along the walls. The collection includes 22 Canalettos and French 18th century classics, plus works by Titian, Velasquez, Rubens, Gainsborough, Reynolds and some amazing Rembrandts. It feels as if a multibillionaire – a rare one with good taste – has run amok with his chequebook. I like it a bit more every time I visit, not least for its intimacy. It doesn't even have lines forbidding you to go near the exhibits.

The Conservatory Restaurant

And that's only the paintings. There is also a very large collection of furniture, including more Marie Antoinette treasures than Versailles, numerous miniatures and the biggest collection of armour in the land etc etc. A unique factor is that in order to see the Wallace's treasures you have to go to the gallery itself, as it is a condition of their bequest to the nation by the widow of Sir Richard Wallace (illegitimate son of the fourth Marquess) that nothing is ever loaned out or, perish the thought, sold.

One of my favourite paintings is Frans Hal's The Laughing Cavalier (even though its subject is neither laughing nor a Cavalier). It was acquired at an auction in Paris in 1865, when it was called Portrait of a Man. Two of the richest people in the world, James de Rothschild and the fourth Marquis of Hertford, engaged in a fierce battle to buy it, which was won by the latter for a price six times the painting's pre-sale estimate.

The Wallace Collection is at Hertford House, Manchester Square, London W1U 3BN. Sadly, at the time of writing it was temporarily closed due to the coronavirus outbreak. In normal times, entrance to the gallery is free and you can salve your conscience by making a contribution or having a glass of wine and a snack in the glorious Norman Foster-designed atrium restaurant (see photo).

To end, a little known fact: Sir Richard, who was a francophile, built 50 drinking fountains scattered around Paris, which to this day are known as "Wallaces".

137: THE EXPLODING TEMPLE OF GREEN PARK

It is the sparsest of the Royal Parks, boasting no buildings apart from a few memorials. St James's Park is a destination, but The Green Park, though lovely – especially when a million daffodils pop up in spring – is mainly somewhere you pass through, just as the Tyburn river flows underneath it.

It was not always so. There have been numerous edifices there in the past, including two ice houses (to cool Charles II's drinks, of course), a ranger's house, lodges, a basin or pool, the Queen's Library (for Queen Caroline, wife of George II) and a fountain (pictured) designed by Edward Smirke, the brother of Sir Robert Smirke, architect of the British Museum. All are now gone.

But the most spectacular of all by a distance was a very large Temple of Peace erected in 1749 to celebrate the Treaty of Aix-la-Chapelle, which ended the War of the Austrian Succession embracing Britain's War with France in the Americas. Under its terms, Britain gain Canada while France – which didn't want the expense of maintaining Canada – opted for the sugar-based riches of Guadeloupe, exploited by the slave trade.

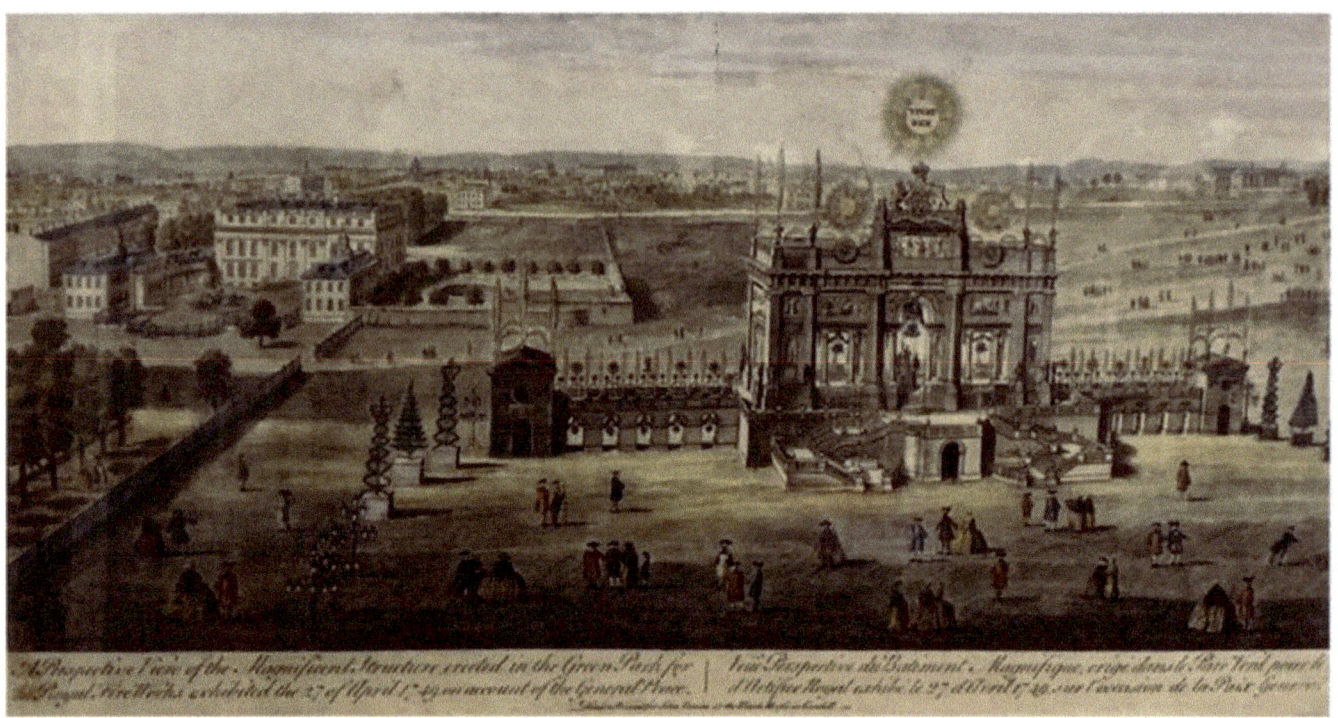

The Temple of Peace

Smirke's Fountain

The peace may have been a success, at least temporarily, but, alas, The Temple of Peace was not. In 1749, during a grand firework display accompanying a specially-commission work by Handel – entitled Music for the Royal Fireworks – it was hit by a stray rocket. Ten thousand fireworks were being stored there. The temple exploded, killing three people and injuring many more. Nothing is left of it now, nor of the event, except for Handel's music.

Green Park was mostly open fields until Charles II acquired the land, between St James's Park and Hyde Park, and put a wall around it so he could walk freely between the two parks through what he called Upper St James's Park. It was opened to the general public in 1826, during the reign of Queen Victoria, when the Queen's Basin was filled in and all the buildings were demolished.

The reason The Green Park doesn't have any flowers, apart from the daffodils, is attributed to the day when Charles II's wife saw him collecting flowers for his mistress and ordered that all the flower beds should be taken up and no new ones planted. That would learn him.

138: THE ORIGINAL WATERLOO BRIDGE

A contemporary engineer said it was "perhaps the finest large masonry bridge ever built in this or any other country". Antonio Canova, the Italian sculptor of The Three Graces, called it "the noblest bridge in the world" and said it was worth going to England just to see it. Painters such as Monet and Constable loved it.

They were talking about Waterloo Bridge. Not the present one, handsome though that is, but the previous one, built in the early 19th century. This first Waterloo Bridge was designed by the great Scottish engineer John Rennie, complete with dramatic Doric columns. Inspired by the look of a previous Rennie bridge, the Kelso Bridge that spans the River Tweed in Roxburghshire, it was originally to be called Strand Bridge, but success at the Battle of Waterloo in 1815 led to a clamour for a change to commemorate that military triumph.

When the bridge opened in 1817 it again followed Kelso Bridge in being a toll bridge. This had made a fistful of money for investors in the Scottish project, but it wasn't the case with Waterloo Bridge because it was always possible to cross the Thames using instead Blackfriars or Westminster bridges, which were free. This particular Waterloo battle was finally lost in 1878, when the bridge was nationalised under the auspices of the Metropolitan Board of Works and the tolls were removed.

Rennie's Waterloo Bridge lasted for over 100 years until it was unintentionally killed by its own architect. A subsequent new London Bridge, replacing the historic multi-arched one with all the houses on top, was also designed by Rennie. What he failed to foresee was that the smaller number of arches this latest London Bridge possessed compared with its predecessor meant the flow of Thames water increased.

In 1884 it was discovered that this had resulted in increased scour – the displacement of sand and gravel – around the foundations of the Waterloo Bridge piers, resulting in their erosion. By the 1920s, the problems were severe, with "a visible dip" appearing at the Strand end. In 1924 the bridge was closed completely, and though some temporary reinforcements enabled it to re-open, in 1930 the London County Council decided it should be demolished.

It was a rare example of a thriving bridge being killed off by the competition, an outcome for psycho-geographers to salivate over. The replacement Waterloo Bridge, the one we have today, was designed by Sir Giles Gilbert Scott, officially opened in 1942 and fully completed in 1945. Many of those who did the work were women.

All was not lost for the old bridge. As so often happens with bridges, some of the foundations were still so strong that they were retained for its replacement. If you look at the northern (Somerset House) end, you can see some remnants of Rennie's work. There is even a plaque there to explain everything. There are remains on the southern side too.

And that's not all. Bridges made of stone are often recycled. Some of the old Waterloo Bridge also found its way into the new one in the form of facading or infill, while many of its granite blocks were offered as gifts to Commonwealth countries in a kind of diplomatic bridge-building exercise.

These can still be seen as monuments in parts of Australia and New Zealand. Some of the stone balustrades even found their way to a house in the former Rhodesia (now Zimbabwe) owned by the author Dornford Yates. Matt Brown of Londonist has written a fascinating piece about where bits of the old Waterloo Bridge are now.

Finally, a little known fact: Waterloo Bridge was the only bridge in London to be hit by a bomb during the last war.

139: THE GREAT ROYAL JEWELS HEIST OF 1303

We hear a lot about the Great Train Robbery of 1963, but hardly anything about its more daring predecessor, which took place 700 years earlier – Great Royal Jewels Heist of 6 June, 1303, which saw most of the Crown's treasures stolen from the supposedly impregnable Pyx Chamber off the east cloister of Westminster Abbey.

The robbery was obviously an inside job, so Edward I did what a king had to do. He arrested the Abbey's abbot, its 48 monks and 32 servants, as they were the ones with access to the Pyx. All were imprisoned in the Tower of London.

The Chamber, which still exists, dates from about 1070. There, gold and silver were measured in little round containers called pyxes. With its 13-foot thick walls, it had long been considered the most secure room in the whole of the kingdom. It had two heavy oak doors, one behind the other, each with three locks, meaning six keys were required to gain admittance.

And so it had been until the arrival of Richard de Podnecott, a "gentleman" from Oxfordshire, who is believed to have had a grudge against the king dating back a few years to when he was imprisoned in Flanders as a guarantor for the monarch's spiralling debts.

Podnecott shadowed the Abbey for months while Edward ("Longshanks") was at war with William Wallace (he of Braveheart fame) in West Lothian, Scotland. Then, almost certainly with the connivance of some monks, he entered the Chamber on the night of St Mark and stayed hidden there for most of the day before making off with the bounty.

He was later arrested with over £2,000 worth of booty on him, after some of the stolen property started turning up in nearby brothels and pawn shops. By that time, the monks had been released from the Tower, but Podnecott was hanged along with a few who were suspected of helping him.

The Pyx Chamber can be viewed by the public, and, unlike the main Abbey interior, there is no entrance charge. You can get to it via Dean's Yard. One curious fact is that there clearly used to be an altar there, where mass would have been celebrated in Catholic times, but was not destroyed during the Reformation, probably because it was disguised by the royal treasures.

The theft from the Pyx was only the most serious in a series of robberies from the Abbey during that period, and it is still puzzling that the king continued to use it and a crypt in the Chapter House next to it as main storehouses for his treasures when they were clearly so vulnerable.

Afterwards, the royal treasures were removed to the Tower, but only until the undercrofts at the Abbey had been reinforced. They were then brought back to their historic resting place. Maybe the thinking was that God would still be their best guardian.

The Pyx chamber today

140: THE GOTHIC FOREIGN OFFICE THAT NEVER WAS

In 1858 the great architect George Gilbert Scott was awarded the contract to build the new Foreign Office building in Horse Guards Road. It was a dream come true. Here was his chance to create a masterpiece in his favourite Gothic Revival style to mirror the elegance of the Houses of Parliament, designed by his friend and rival Charles Barry, on the other side of Parliament Square.

All was going swimmingly until he met an immovable object in the form of the new Prime Minister, Lord Palmerston, an unabashed classicist who feared that, left to himself, Scott would "gothicise" the whole of London.

In a desperate attempt to get his plans confirmed by the new government before Palmerston interfered, Scott submitted over 100 drawings to the House of Commons library and had the plans featured in the leading building magazines. He even had a competitive tender for the construction of the building submitted, which delighted the then chancellor, William Gladstone, who was able to include the agreed figure in his budget.

But Gladstone was not Palmerston, whose implacable distaste for all things Gothic proved an obstacle too far. He summoned Scott and told him bluntly that he would have nothing to do with his ghastly plan, but would be happy for Scott to retain his commission as long as he did something in "the Italian style". Scott agreed, but only after writing a final 20-page detailed case in a forlorn hope that the PM would change his mind. He duly built an admirable neo-classical building, which still stands proudly facing St James's Park.

However, if you want to know what the Gothic version might have looked like, take a trip to St Pancras to see what was originally called the Midland Grand Hotel, another Scott design. Now the St Pancras Renaissance Hotel, it bears a bizarre resemblance to what Scott would have designed for Horse Guards Road had he been allowed.

The tower has been repositioned and implanted with a clock, but the stylistic similarities are unmistakeable. The building was saved from demolition in the 1960s by a campaign led by Sir John Betjeman. And so Scott's dream continues to be fulfilled, despite the fact that his fantasy building contains no diplomats, only overnight guests.

141: THE 'HIDEOUS' MORLEY'S HOTEL

Augustus J C Hare, a curmudgeonly Victorian essayist, was not a fan of Trafalgar Square. Writing in 1896 he saw a "dreary expanse of granite" with the "miserable buildings" of the National Gallery. Nelson's Column, he said, was "a very poor work", flanked by a "hideous hotel and a frightful club".

That "hideous" hotel was called Morley's, and it ran the whole width of the square on the site of today's South Africa House. It did not generate many plaudits. British History Online holds its breath enough to say that it "possessed a certain charm". Its guests included Sir Arthur Conan Doyle, who wrote much of The Hound of the Baskervilles there. The Northumberland hotel mentioned in the book is almost certainly based on Morley's. But Conan Doyle soon got bored with it, writing to his mother in 1900 that he was "somewhat sick" of Morley's and intended to try the nearby Golden Cross instead.

The hotel cannot have been that bad because it was eventually purchased in 1920 by the Old Colony Club of New York, which was having difficulty booking places in London for its burgeoning membership of US businessmen, who travelled to Europe in their thousands for business and pleasure. The deal was done by club president Albert J Norton, who, after signing it, flew to Paris and bought the prestigious Hotel du Rhin as well. Both deals were, apparently concluded in a single day, a record at the time.

Among other people who stayed in the hotel were "Buffalo Bill" Cody, the US showman, and James Gordon Bennett, the newspaper magnate whose son, Gordon Jnr's controversial behaviour spawned the phrase "Gordon Bennett" as an expression of incredulity and surprise.

Morley's was demolished in 1936, but the name Morley has left its mark on London history. Its owner Atkinson Morley gave a handsome donation to help found the Atkinson Morley hospital in Wimbledon, which became one of the most advanced centres for brain surgery in the world. The hospital was closely involved with the innovative British company EMI in developing the CT brain scanner, which won Nobel Prizes for its inventors, Sir Godfrey Hounsfield and Dr Jamie Ambrose.

The Atkinson Morley hospital has since been absorbed into St George's Hospital, Tooting, obscuring the fact that one of the great medical inventions can be traced back to the money made from a hotel in Trafalgar Square.

142: VICTORIA'S SHORT-LIVED TURKISH BATHS

The rather magnificent building in the illustration here is what you would have seen in 1862 if you had visited the site of Victoria Station. It was not Victoria Station, but housed Oriental or Turkish baths. It was constructed barely three years before the decision to build the station was made, so it had to come down again.

This was, in fact, a pleasant surprise for the bath's developers who feared they had built it in the wrong part of town because it wasn't doing very well financially. Ironically, the arrival of the station might have made the location of the baths very convenient. But they didn't fit into the plans of the Metropolitan Railway Company, which purchased the land.

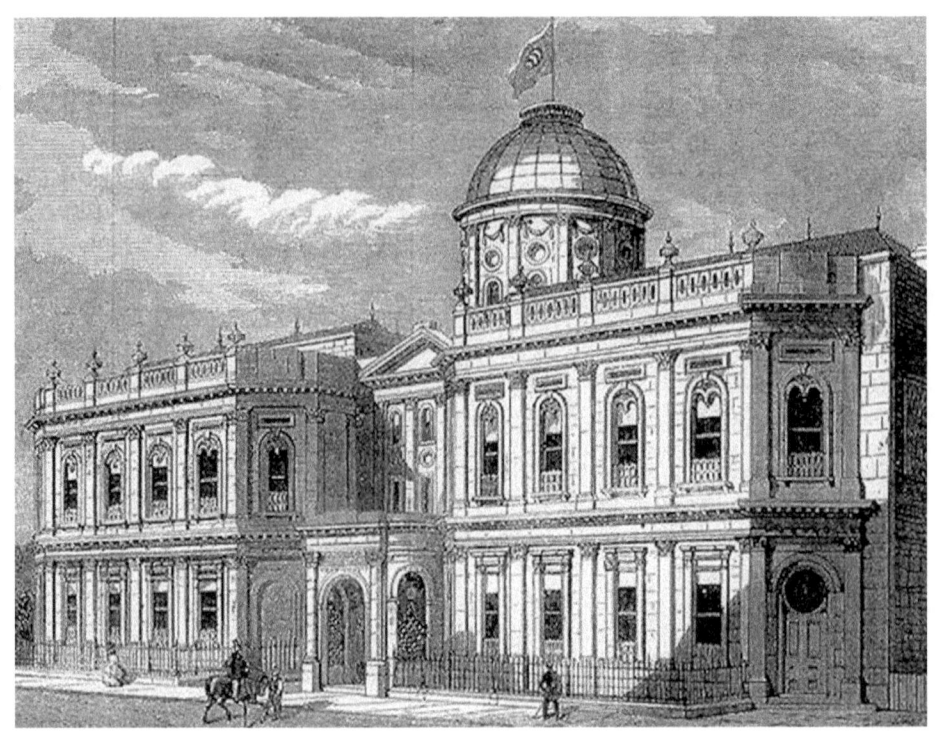

The facility was rather grand. It even had baths for horses, which may have been related to the fact that the Metropolitan Drinking Fountain and Cattle Trough Association had been established up the road at 111 Victoria Street three years earlier.

The baths were built by an Irish company led by Dr Richard Barter, who had constructed a "hydropathic establishment" in County Cork, Ireland, claiming it to be the first of its kind since the Roman occupation. They didn't catch on in England, but proved more popular on the continent, where Turkish baths are to this day known as Irish-Roman baths.

They didn't generate a new genre of literature either, though they do get a mention in James Joyce's Ulysses when Leopold Bloom savours their delights in Dublin: "Nice smell these soaps have. Time to get a bath around the corner. Hammam. Turkish. Massage. Dirt gets rolled up in your navel. Nicer if a nice girl did it. … Feel fresh then all day."

Maybe it is just as well the baths were closed. Commuters might have started arriving for work even later.

143: THE GRAND EXTRAVAGANCE OF CARLTON HOUSE

Imagine you are walking from Trafalgar Square towards Buckingham Palace in the late 18th century. There was no Mall or Admiralty Arch in those days, and the whole space from where the Institute of Contemporary Arts (ICA) is today right down to Marlborough House on the far right was taken up by Carlton House which, together with its gardens, spilled over the land occupied by The Mall today to the edge of St James's Park. Its frontage spanned much of Pall Mall.

It was an extravaganza building in an age of extravagances, which gained notoriety from 1783 when it was occupied by George, Prince of Wales (later Prince Regent) until he was crowned George IV in 1820. A house, it was not – more like a mini-Versailles. George enlarged and embellished it, spending vast sums of money he hadn't got in order to make it worthy of his name. He famously fell out badly with his father George III, and Carlton House became the centre of a glittering rival royal court to the one down the road. The prince even sketched out what his future administration would look like when his father died, packing it mainly with his aristocratic cronies.

In May 1784, to celebrate the return to parliament of a controversial friend, the Whig politician Charles Fox, George had nine large marquees erected in the garden. Guests, mainly others Whigs, were entertained by four bands and plentiful wine, timed for when his father was proceeding in state along St James's Park to open the new Parliament. Only the walls of Carlton House separated them – hardly the action of a future king trying to keep his distance from party politics. Later that year, when he secretly married Maria Fitzherbert, re-construction of the house was halted because George's debts had reached an astronomic £250,000 in the currency of the day.

Carlton House Interior, London's Versaille

Carlton House has been described as "the most important house of its time" in Britain, but this was a political rather than aesthetic judgement. Robert Smirke, who designed the British Museum, thought it "overdone with finery" while Antonio Canova, the distinguished Italian sculptor who had extolled the praises of Waterloo Bridge, dismissed Carlton House as "an ugly barn". That was just the outside. Inside was something else: room after room of opulent decoration and sculptures. In 1816, an inventory of the house revealed there were over 450 pictures in the state rooms and other parts of the house.

FRONT OF CARLTON HOUSE, 1820.

Carlton House: The front entrance in Pall Mall

In fact, the Prince Regent never really liked Carlton House, not least because the entrance in Pall Mall was, how shall we put it, a bit too near his subjects. On his accession as king he dropped it to concentrate his overdraft on improving Buckingham Palace.

In 1828, Carlton House was pulled down to pave the way for the opening of John Nash's Waterloo Place, complete with the Duke of York's column, providing an entrance to Nash's Regent Street. As with so many other London mansions, a lot of its stonework and contents were recycled. Most of the furniture, carpets and works of art found their way to Buckingham Palace and other royal residences. The portico of Carlton House was reused in the new National Gallery in Trafalgar Square – against the wishes of the architect William Wilkins – where the columns can still be seen.

Carlton House, originally erected by Lord Carlton in 1709, was rebuilt by Nash as Carlton House Terrace. Today, the north side of where it stood is an array of very handsome Georgian houses. If you view the same complex in the Mall from the ICA, looking towards the Palace, you will find that behind the mock columns, extending for over 100 yards, is a car park. How the mighty have fallen.

144: THE UNMARKED HOME OF 'REAL TENNIS'

Nothing remains of what the interesting street pictured used to look like in olden days, except for the tiny plaque high up on a wall highlighted in the photo, which looks as though it might have been hit up there with a tennis racket. Maybe it was. The building it is mounted on, which stands on a site formerly occupied by the Duke of Monmouth's stables, used to be home to a fashionable royal tennis – or "real tennis" court – and for well over 50 years from 1780 was actually the headquarters of English tennis.

The plaque says James Street 1673, though today we know it as Orange Street, which stretches from the Haymarket to north of the National Gallery. As can be seen in this 1850 painting by T H Shepherd (courtesy of the British Museum), the game of billiards was on offer on the same premises, which was next door to a coach manufacturing works.

The "real tennis" court, which also doubled occasionally as a theatre, was later pulled down and an office block now fills the spot, beyond which on the far left of the road is a Byron burger restaurant. Opposite it on the right is a covered market occupying what used to be a Burberry store. There is nothing in the street to indicate its role in the history of tennis.

England may have invented lawn tennis, but it was based on royal tennis, an import from France. Lawn tennis has become a global success story – sadly jettisoning the lawn in many venues – but real tennis has not gone away. The oldest and most famous example of a surviving court is at Hampton Court, where Henry VIII played. It is still in use, as are two other very old courts at Merton College, Oxford and Falkland Palace at Fife in Scotland. There are other active real tennis courts in London, including at Queen's Club and Lord's.

The capital's real tennis tradition also includes the remains of the Tudor courts in Whitehall, though you will have difficulty finding them as they are not open to the public. Simon Inglis points out in his magisterial book Played in London that there have been nearly 50 real tennis courts in the area that now forms modern London, including three in Southwark – one of which is memorialised by Tennis Street, off Newcomen Street – and others at Essex House off the Strand, Blackfriars, Somerset House and Southampton House, where the legacy of the game used to be marked by an alley called Tennis Court. The only visible reminder of the game's former headquarters in what is now called Orange Street is that unreadable James Street plaque. Shame.

145: THE HOUSE OF JUDGE JEFFREYS

The Treasury building in London stretches from Whitehall to Horseguards Road on the edge of St James's Park. Unknown to many of the civil servants who work there, it was built on the home of one of Britain's most notorious characters. Not in this case a former Chancellor of the Exchequer but a judge – the notorious Judge Jeffreys (1645-1689), the original "hanging judge".

His most infamous act was to preside over the "Bloody Assizes" that followed the failure of Monmouth Rebellion in July 1685, when James Scott, the first and last Duke of Monmouth and illegitimate son of Charles II, rose up against the government of Charles's brother and successor James II. It is reckoned that up to 320 people were hanged and over 800 transported to the West Indies in addition to others imprisoned, fined or flogged.

The curious thing was that although Jeffreys has been accused of lots of things, from drunkenness to corruption, there was no technical irregularity in the brutal sentences he and his team doled out. The Monmouth rebels, whether you approved of them or not, were trying to overthrow a legitimate government. This was a treasonable offence, which carried with it the death penalty. Indeed, capital punishment for treasonable offences was only finally erased from the statute book at the end of the 1990s.

Defenders of Jeffreys – and they exist – argue that blame should be heaped not on the judge himself, who was merely carrying out the law, albeit in a very cruel way, but on James, who had the power to grant clemency but declined to do so. Take your choice.

Another curious fact is that Jeffreys was a Protestant and the rebels whom he executed were also Protestants, protesting against Monmouth's Catholic uncle.

Jeffrey's first major trial, three months earlier in May 1685, was that of Titus Oates, who was accused of having fabricated the existence of a "Popish plot" plot against Charles (who had died in February, converting to Catholicism just before he met his end).

The trial was characterised by so many insults exchanged between Oates and Jeffreys that it threatened the continuance of the proceedings. At one stage, Jeffreys said Oates was a "shame to mankind", conveniently ignoring the fact that he had previously helped to condemn innocent people of being involved on the plot on the basis of Oates' now perjured evidence.

Jeffreys couldn't order Oates to be executed because perjury was not a capital offence. Instead, he imposed punishments so brutal that it has been suggested that the aim was to kill Oates by ill-treatment.

When James fled the country during the "Glorious Revolution" of 1688, Jeffreys tried to follow him abroad but was captured in a public house in Wapping called The Town of Ramsgate, apparently disguised as a sailor and recognised by one of his surviving victims. He later died in the Tower of London, probably from a kidney disease.

His remains were later taken to St Mary Aldermanbury (named after one Alderman Bury), a church on the edge of the city.

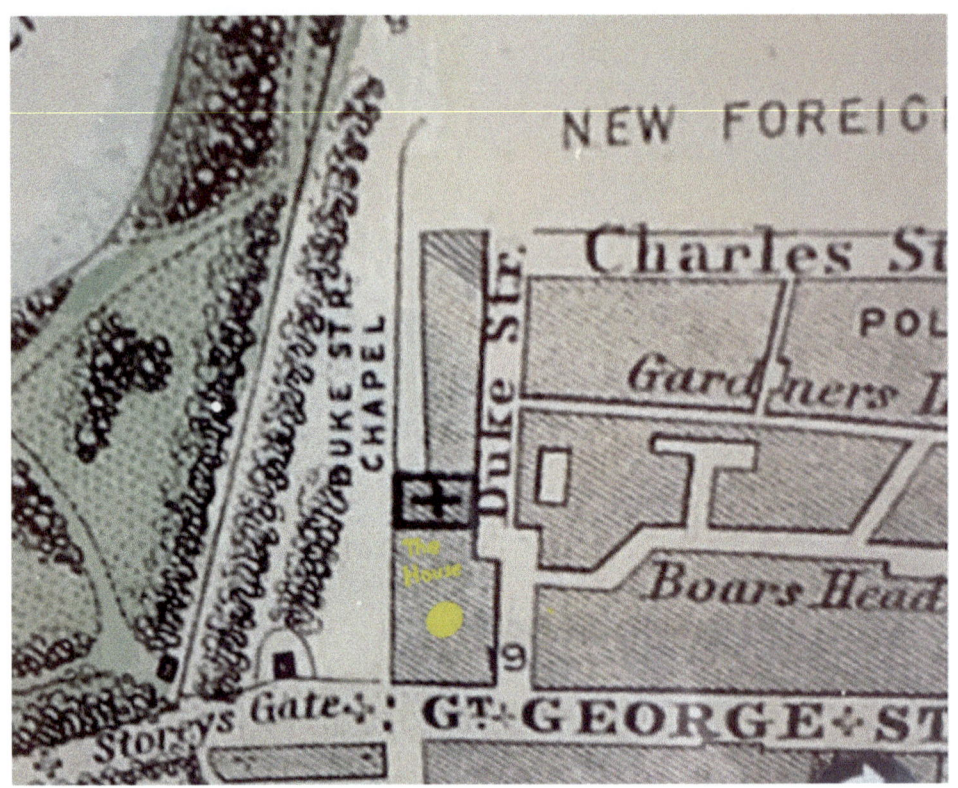

The church was bombed during the last war, and Jeffreys' tomb was destroyed. The remains of the church were transported to the United States in 1966, to be reassembled at Fulton in Missouri as a memorial to Winston Churchill. It is just possible to imagine that some molecules of the notorious judge survive in that church.

By fair means and foul, Jeffreys, who was made 1st Baron Wem, owned a house at Wem in Shropshire and a mansion at Bulstrode Park near Gerrard's Cross in Buckinghamshire as well his London abode. That dwelling was in Delahay Street, which was later absorbed into Duke Street and then redeveloped for government offices. His house is easily identified on old maps as Number 9 Duke Street, next door to a chapel (see above). It was the only house in the street with its own entry to St James's Park.

146: FORGOTTEN FACADES OF BUCKINGHAM PALACE

Buckingham Palace is beautifully situated near St James's Park and the Green Park, looking along a magnificent boulevard leading to Trafalgar Square. It seems like the least lost building in the whole of London. But appearances can be deceptive.

What you see today is a Portland stone facade constructed as recently as 1930. It replaced an earlier facade by Edward Blore, a fashionable architect of his time, and the Blore front had itself replaced an even earlier one by the great Georgian architect John Nash, who had risen from a humble background in Lambeth to become the man who most changed the face of Central London.

The Prince Regent, later George IV, had commissioned Nash to build Regent Street, Trafalgar Square and Carlton Gardens, all of which were great successes at the time. Nash remodelled the state rooms of the Palace – which still survive – but his most dramatic change was the construction of much larger north and south wings, with a triumphal arch in the middle to commemorate the victories of Nelson at Trafalgar and Wellington at Waterloo (see picture).

The arch was a mistake as it looked a bit out of place and was too narrow for some royal carriages to get through. Queen Victoria had it removed and re-located at the north east part of Hyde Park, where we know it and the neighbourhood to which it gave its name as Marble Arch.

Nash's Buckingham Palace looked quite dramatic compared with the bland facade we see today, and there were mixed reactions at the time. Many regarded it as a masterpiece. However, in the words of the 1869 Ordnance Survey map: "Nash's one great failure was Buckingham Palace, where many windows and doors would not open or shut properly, where the drains were a disgrace. The front of the palace, too, became a laughing stock and was rebuilt by Edward Bore" (we think the OS may have meant Blore but we are not completely sure).

Nash's extravagance cost him his job, and when William IV – George IV's younger brother – succeeded him in 1830 he got Bore, sorry, Blore, to finish the job, though the king never actually moved in. When Parliament burned down in 1834 he offered the palace as an alternative home for it. No one seems to have mentioned reviving the option as a way of avoiding spending billions on temporary accommodation while today's Parliament buildings are being restored.

For all the money spent on the palace by previous sovereigns, Queen Victoria was the first monarch to actually live there (from July 1837) and it had to be expanded yet again – including a fourth wing – to accommodate guest rooms and nurseries for the many children. George IV's Royal Pavilion at Brighton was sold to help pay for the extensions.

By the start of the 20th century London's pollution – soot and smog – was eroding Blore's facade and Sir Ashton Webb was commissioned in 1913 to reface it with Portland stone, which is hardier and largely self-cleaning.

Buckingham Palace has at last enjoyed a long period of stability after a series of different ownerships. It started off as Goring House (the nearby Goring Hotel recalls this memory) before becoming Arlington House (after the Earl of Arlington). In around 1703 it was rebuilt by the Duke of Buckingham, whose name it still bears.

147: THE ADMIRALTY'S HIDDEN CITADEL

In any competition for the most brutalist building in the country, the Admiralty Citadel on the edge of St James's Park and Horse Guards Parade must have a chance of winning first prize. Ever since Winston Churchill dismissed it as "a vast monstrosity", ministers and civil servants have been free to castigate it. The only solution so far has been to cover it with Virginia creeper in the hope that nobody will notice it.

It was never meant to be pretty, just functional. Built at the beginning of World War II as our bomb-proof last defence against a German invasion, it was the equivalent of Hitler's bunker. When all else failed, this is where what remained of our defensive forces would repel the German army as they marched up The Mall through the gun turrets that still exist. True grit.

According to rear Admiral R K Dickson DSO, chief of naval information overseas service, speaking in 1945, the Citadel could withstand a siege. He said: "If you went down there at this moment, you'd find 80 girls working teleprinters to all the naval headquarters in Britain and the continent…That citadel is just a maze of machinery and conveyor belts. One week last year in secret messages alone, the Admiralty handles over 1.3 million groups of naval cipher."

In October 1955, John Tilney (Liverpool, Wavertree) made a not untypical comment about the Citadel in the House of Commons: "Considerable sums have been spent on the nearby Carlton House Terrace, yet immediately opposite, standing between the Mall and Horse Guards Parade, the Citadel seems to be resigned to being the ugliest building in London. Up to now the Ministry of Works has seemed not to care for this most valuable site, built out of keeping with the splendid facade of John Nash or even of the more modern building of the Admiralty to which, despite a splash of common brick due to the Blitz of the last war, is not an unsightly building. The granite of the Citadel is hideous enough and an offence to the architecture of London."

This plea fell on deaf ears and the Citadel is now brutalism's last stand, as no one wants to take a decision to pull down its nine metres-deep foundations and 6.1 metres thick concrete roof. If they did, they would unveil an attractive hidden section of the Admiralty building behind it. The roof of the Citadel, judging by aerial photos, is liberally endowed with soil beds, presumably to camouflage the site from enemy planes.

Among suggestions for improvement are to face the outside of the structure in Portland stone with statues at strategic places. Better still would be to transform it into a living garden with dozens of perfumed plants, such as Jasmine or Philadelphus. With a bit of luck it might even become a tourist attraction as the Hanging Gardens of London with a swimming pool on top. Dream on.

148: THE STAR & GARTER'S SPORTING PAST

It is well known that Pall Mall, the heart of London's clubland, was named after the French game of Pell Mell. But it could equally have been called Cricket Mall. Many of the rules of cricket were devised in 1774 by "a committee of noblemen and gentlemen" at the Star and Garter tavern, which was sandwiched in the space between the Reform and RAC clubs where the bland office block pictured below now resides.

Rules devised included the first for LBW (leg before wicket), when the ball hits a batsman's pad rather than his bat. A cricket club existed here long before the establishment of the Marylebone Cricket Club (MCC) which later took over responsibility for rule-making.

Cricket was not the only sport to be spawned at the inn. In 1750, a different bunch of "noblemen and gentlemen" – this time those of the Jockey Club – laid down the rules for horse racing before moving their operation to Newmarket. The Club was the public face of the sport even though, this being class-conscious England, jockeys themselves were not allowed to join it.

Not content with helping to create two major sports, the site of the Star and Garter was also the foundation of one of Britain's major industries. British Gas can trace its origins directly back to 1806 when Frederick Winsor started experiments with producing gas from coal here, and set up the Gas Light and Coke company. It was the world's first public gas distributor and the first public utility in the world.

On June 4, 1807, its carbonising furnace dispatched gas along small pipes to illuminate gas lights in the nearby Carlton House home of the Prince Regent.

It is ironic that at a time when there is so much controversy about foreigners taking over our utilities that Winsor was a German, born Friedrich Winzer and used disputed French patents to found the British gas industry. The gas lights in this part of Pall Mall were recently removed as part of an "improvements" policy, but there are still thousands of working in Central London, including in St James's Park – a testament to Winsor's pioneering endeavours.

149: THE GREEN-FINGERED TRADESCANTS OF LAMBETH

Look at the less than imposing shops on London's busy South Lambeth Road pictured below and let your imagination roam. Think of the sight and aroma of michaelmas daisies, poppies, scented stock, Virginia creepers, columbine, phlox and white jasmine – just a sample of the plants brought into this country for the first time by the inhabitants of a large house that was built on this site nearly 400 hundred years ago.

Meet the super-gardeners of 17th century England – John Tradescant and his son, also called John, who lived in that house (pictured opposite) and who voyaged around the world to change the face of horticulture in England. They also brought some of our best loved trees to England, including horse chestnut, tulip trees, magnolias, yuca and the bald cypress. Some experts credit them with introducing London plane trees and even the growing of pineapples. And, of course, the wandering plant tradescantia, which takes its name from them.

John Tradescant senior was head gardener to Robert Cecil – chief of staff to Elzabeth I and James I – at Hatfield House, who kindled his enthusiasm by sending him to the Low Countries in 1610 in search of fruit trees. In 1618 he was off to Arctic Russia then to the Levant, Algiers and Paris in search of plants, trees, seeds and also any rare or unusual objects. These "curiosities" were kept in the grounds of his house in what was called The Ark or Musaeum Tradescantianum, for which there was access for a small charge, making it the first public museum in the country and quite possibly the world.

John junior followed in his father's footsteps by inheriting the job of head gardener to Charles I and made several trips to the new colony of Virginia, bringing back curiosities, trees and plants including magnolias and the tulip tree. He bequeathed the contents of the museum to his neighbour Elias Ashmole who, after a contretemps with John's widow, donated them to the University of Oxford. They were the foundation of what became the Ashmolean – not the Tradescantian – Museum.

There is no plaque to mark where the Tradescant's house was, but the boundaries of the estate are circumscribed by South Lambeth Road, Tradescant Road and Walberswick Street. Both John Tradescants are buried and commemorated in the churchyard of St Mary's Lambeth next door to Lambeth Palace. The deconsecrated church is now the Garden Museum – claimed to be the first of its kind in the world – which includes a small Ark containing some curiosities that have returned home from the Ashmolean. There could not be a more fitting resting place for the fathers of English gardening.

150: THE AMAZING ST MARGARET'S

St Margaret's Church is lost in plain sight. It has a perfect position on Parliament Square but it is hardly noticed by the hundreds of thousands of visitors, almost entirely from abroad, who in normal times visit nearby Westminster Abbey each year. It is as if a changeling child has been abandoned outside the Abbey for protection. Yet were it not for the existence of the Abbey – literally a few yards away – it would be a major destination for visitors in its own right.

The church was founded in the 12th century by the Abbey's Benedictine monks ostensibly to give local people a church of their own. A more cynical view was that it was to keep the lowlife, which included lots of criminals seeking legally protected sanctuary in the vicinity of the Abbey, from disturbing their activities (the image below includes the church in medieval times, surrounded by hovels).

Some famous people are buried there, such as Sir Walter Raleigh (who was executed around the corner in Old Palace Yard), the printer William Caxton, and Wenceslas Hollar, the great illustrator of London. So are over a dozen "regicides" who signed Charles I's death warrant. They were originally interred as heroes in the Abbey on Oliver Cromwell's instructions, but disinterred on the orders of Charles II, Charles I's son, and laid to a more permanent rest in the churchyard.

The only burial with a gravestone above ground is that of Alexander Davies, whose daughter Mary aged 12, married Sir Thomas Grosvenor, aged 21, a little-known baronet from the north of England in 1677. Mary brought with her a large acreage

of land in London thought to be useless at the time but which later became Mayfair and Belgravia. It has been in the Grosvenor family ever since.

The church has had its fair share of fashionable marriages, from those of Samuel Pepys and John Milton in the 17th century to Winston Churchill's and Harold Macmillan's in the 20th. But the real interest of St Margaret's is inside it. You won't get a more dramatic contrast in stained-glass windows than that between John Piper's deliberately soft toned modernist windows on the right as you go in and the amazing east window, which is a history lesson in itself.

It was constructed around 1526 at Gouda in Holland and intended as a gift to celebrate the marriage of Catherine of Aragon to Henry VIII, both of whom are featured in the stained glass. However, in the five years it took to make the window, circumstances changed. Henry ditched Catherine for Ann Boleyn, so the window embarked on a prolonged ecclesiastical version of pass the parcel. It was hidden in as many as ten churches and private homes in Essex. At one stage it was kept buried by George Monck, a Roundhead general, to conceal it from the destructive eyes of the Puritans. It was eventually re-purchased by the churchwardens of St Margaret's in 1758, only to have its installation blocked for several years by the Dean and Chapter of the Abbey because it was too "popish" or high church.

In the 1540s, the church was nearly destroyed – not by the Reformation or riots but by the outrageous actions of one man, the rapacious Lord Protector of England, Edward Seymour, the first Duke of Somerset. In order to build a palace on the Strand to match his ego he set about destroying other buildings, such as the monastery of St John in Clerkenwell and the charnel house at St Paul's in order to steal the stone. But when he tried to pull St Margaret's down he met fierce resistance from armed parishioners and gave up. Justice took its own revenge – Seymour died before Somerset House was completed.

St Margaret's is also linked with the extraordinary success of two black men who emerged from a background of slavery at a time of widespread illiteracy to become eminent men of letters in the latter part of the 18th century. Olaudah Equiano, who wrote a best seller about his experiences as a slave, is commemorated by a plaque inside the church where he was baptised. Ignatius Sancho, who was married in St Margaret's, is buried in its burial ground in Christchurch Gardens, Victoria Street. His letters, published posthumously, were subscribed to by a dizzy list of aristocrats, led by the Prime Minister Lord North – a fascinating case of Black Lives mattering over 250 years ago.

151: THE OTHER GREAT EXHIBITION

Everyone knows that the Great Exhibition of 1851 in Hyde Park, held in the Crystal Palace, was an outstanding, and hugely profitable, international success. But hardly anyone has heard about its successor, the International Exhibition held eleven years later in 1862 in Cromwell Road, where the Natural History Museum and the Science Museum now stand.

It was much bigger than the 1851 version, stretching an astonishing 384 yards along Cromwell Road, and sporting two domes, each 87 yards high, claimed to be the biggest in the world. It attracted 29,000 exhibitors from 37 countries and more visitors (marginally) than its illustrious predecessor. It achieved all this despite low participation from America because of the civil war going on there at the time.

So why has it sunk into oblivion? It is partly because the building itself looked, well, glum compared with the innovative glass cathedral designed by Sir Joseph Paxton for the 1851 extravaganza. It was partly because the entrepreneurial dynamism of Prince Albert, who died in 1861 before it was completed, was missing. His death plunged the country and the Queen, who did not attend the opening, into a state of mourning.

But there was a deeper reason too. In retrospect, it is clear that 1851 marked the high tide of Britain's industrial might and self-confidence. We had dared to create a huge exhibition space, not just for British products but for anyone in the world to come and dare to compete. It was the apex of the movement for "free trade" before government regulation stepped in.

Some critics said there was a democratic deficit compared with 1851 because of the lack of direct public engagement.

In the run-up to 1851, hundreds of local committees had been formed, partly to raise money but also to give people the chance to choose what products they would like to see.

There was also a really stupid mistake, which was repeated later with the Millennium Dome in 2000. The organisers predicted the 2000 Dome would attract 12 million customers, and when it only achieved half that rate (not bad in itself) it was deemed a failure. Exactly the same happened in 1862. The organisers predicted 11 million and when the figure turned out only to be 6.1 million. This gave the impression of

failure, even though six million in those days when the national population was, at 29 million, less than half of what it is now, was no mean achievement. Some visitors to the exhibition complained it was too big, while some exhibitors claimed it was too small. It couldn't win.

To add insult to injury, Parliament vetoed the government's plan to purchase the building as a permanent venue. Instead it was pulled down and the materials sold for the construction of Alexandra Palace. Part of the glumness of the building was because it was intended to be permanent and was constructed in a deliberately plain style so it could be added to later when more money became available. It was constructed fairly simply of cast iron frames with brick facades.

Yet the exhibition was not without its attractions. In spite of its external plainness, it could be very ornate within. Picture galleries occupied a large part of the south side of the site – a reminder that sponsorship was provided by The Royal Society of, Arts, Manufactures and Trade.

Among the exhibits were Charles Babbage's Analytical Engine, arguably the world's first computer; demonstrations of the electric telegraph, submarine cables, cotton mills, maritime engines and an early refrigerator (which apparently caused a sensation); and work by William Morris's decorative arts firm. Some 350 stereo views of the exhibition were made for the London Stereoscopic Company, providing a three-dimensional record of the exhibition. There was plenty of classical music, including work by Verdi and even an international chess tournament.

In retrospect the exhibition did not deserve some of the reactions it got at the time. Its fault was that couldn't live up to the surprise and charisma of its 1851 parent. On its own terms it was a remarkable success.

152: THE 10TH CENTURY ORIGINS OF SCOTLAND YARD

If you look at cartographer John Rocque's famous map of London you will see an area in Whitehall below Trafalgar Square called "Scotland" whose provenance reaches back to the latter part of the 10th century. That was when King Edgar of England gave King Kenneth II of Scotland "a piece of ground" as his place of residence when he came to London to be involved with making new laws. Kenneth is reported to have built a house there on what became, in effect, part of Scotland itself.

This arrangement ceased under Henry II's rule (1154-1189) when England and Scotland were at war, but the three interlinked yards in London carrying Scotland's name continued to do so. The Metropolitan Police occupied part of the space from 1850 until 1890, which explains why the name "Scotland Yard" is known today all over the English-speaking world, though its earliest mention as a location was in 1603.

Much of the site is now occupied by a Hyatt hotel within an Edwardian building that has been so carefully restored that it is difficult to detect. A link with the past has been preserved, thanks to a base for the Met's mounted branch being next door.

In 1890, the Met moved to the Victoria Embankment for another encounter with history. Its new offices, designed by the renowned architect Norman Shaw, were built on a site where the grandest opera house in the whole of Europe had been partly constructed. Five million bricks were laid, but the project was abandoned at the point when the roof was to be added because the money ran out.

When the incomplete structure was demolished, its foundations were found to be so strong they were retained. And so New Scotland Yard was built on the basement of a grand opera house. Rooms designed for the use of divas would now house criminals instead.

The Met stayed put for almost 80 years until 1967, when it again had to change its beat, this time to a new building in Victoria Street at the junction with Broadway. It was based there until 2013, when, needing to fill a gaping budget gap, it sold the freehold for £370 million – it had cost it £123 million – and moved back to Victoria Embankment into what was then known as the Curtis Green Building, an annexe to the Shaw offices which the Met had retained in its portfolio.

Meanwhile, the the Abu Dhabi Financial Group, which purchased the Victoria Street site, has been building a series of residential and office blocks up to 20 storeys high that have interfered with the skyline for miles around and set an unhealthy precedent for future developments.

How all of this was allowed to happen would not, of course, be an appropriate subject for a Met investigation. But if someone doesn't call a halt to the spiralling heights of developments in Central London, future generations will find it difficult to forgive us.

153: THE COWS OF ST JAMES'S PARK

If you felt like a glass of milk in the 1700s, Georgian London had the answer: go to St James's Park and get it straight from a cow. The royal park had a thriving milk industry in those days, which actually survived until the early 1900s (see photo below).

Although no-one worried about air miles in those days, customers contributed to keeping transportation impacts low by buying milk straight from the udder from obliging milk maids, rather than it being conveyed in lorries from farmer to wholesaler and on to retailer. There was also less need to cut the park's grass, as it was all done by the grazing cows. The country had come to town.

It must have been a bucolic scene, of which there is no trace today apart from Milkmaids Passage, an alleyway leading from the Green Park to St James Palace (currently closed because it runs along the wall of Lancaster House).

But as is so often the case, it wasn't quite as idyllic as it might seem to us today. The milkmaids didn't own the cows. They were hired from those who did – almost invariably men – who kept the cows in nearby stables. The milkmaids were paid low wages, the equivalent of the forgotten poor today who have fallen beneath the social safety nets. There wasn't a minimum wage in those days, and milkmaids were ripe for exploitation.

Henry Mayhew, the chronicler of London's poor, pointed out that there was no security in the job: "As the sellers of milk in the park are merely the servants of cow- keepers and attend to the sale as part of their business, no length of notice is required." He explained that the milk sellers obtained leave from the Home Secretary to ply their trade in the park. In the summer there were stands and numerous cows, but in the winter, cows only. On wet day, scarcely any milk would be sold.

Mayhew quotes one girl as an example: "It's not at all a lively sort of life, selling milk from the cows, though some thinks it's a gay time in the Park! I've often been dull enough, and could see nothing to interest one, sitting alongside a cow. People drink new milk for their health. They're mostly young women…The greatest fools I've sold milk to is servant-gals out for the day. Some must have a day, or half a day, in the month. Their mistresses ought to keep them at home, I say, and not let them out to spend their money, and get into nobody knows what company for a holiday; mistresses is too easy that way. It's such gals as makes fools of themselves in liking a soldier to run after them."

Sellers were not above diluting the milk with water often from unhygienic sources In order to increase their profits. Some things never change.

154: THE ORIGINAL WESTMINSTER BRIDGE

On 31 March, 1736, Parliament voted by 117 votes to 12 to remedy a situation that had resisted reform for 600 years. It was to provide the great city of London with a second bridge across the Thames to complement the original, iconic, London Bridge, on which houses had been built. Looking back it still seems extraordinary that vested interests could have succeeded in preserving the dominion of just one bridge over the river for so long.

It was a formidable cartel, backed by an unholy alliance of Mammon in the form of the City of London (which collected lucrative tolls from people and goods crossing London Bridge), God, in the form of the Archbishop of Canterbury (who received tolls from the Horseferry at Lambeth), and the thousands of watermen who earned their living by conveying people across the Thames in boats. It was one of the most successful monopolies ever.

Opponents of the new bridge warned that it would be to "the great prejudice of the navigation of the river" and would "endanger the lives of the practitioners and the loss of goods or merchandise by them carried". The General Evening Post predicted with great confidence that, "It will enrich the inhabitants of Westminster, and impoverish the citizens of London... In short, it will make Westminster a fine city and London a desert". Even the Thames itself seemed to object. During the first debate, the river rose almost to the doors of Parliament and left lawyers in Westminster Hall a foot deep in water.

But built it was, and by an innovative engineer from Switzerland, Charles Labelye (1705-1762), there being no English engineer capable of taking on the task, apparently. He pioneered the use of caissons (retaining structures) to support the bridge, rather than the traditional coffer dams, providing a watertight fence of wood or steel. Labelye

modestly claimed that his bridge contained twice as much stone as St Paul's Cathedral and was "unquestionably the greatest and most difficult work that has ever been attempted in this country".

The bridge was funded by a combination of money voted by Parliament and the proceeds of several then fashionable lotteries, which enabled it to be constructed without the necessity of imposing tolls. It was greeted at home and abroad as a magnificent achievement, not least for the citizens of Westminster, who at last gained the infrastructure suitable for a the newly fashionable area it had become. There was, though, one unforeseen design flaw. Labelye built cubbyholes on each side of the bridge so pedestrians could take a rest. Unfortunately, they became an easy target for thieves, vagabonds and ladies of the night, who would accost unsuspecting visitors.

There is a sad ending to the story. When a new London Bridge was built, its arches were of a different size to those of the old one. These had served as a kind of breakwater, and the change meant that water poured through at greater speed. Over time, this caused "scouring" of the foundations of both Westminster Bridge and Waterloo Bridge (built in 1817).

Both bridges developed subsidence and had to be replaced as a result. It was almost as if the ghost of the old monopolistic London Bridge had cast a spell over Johnny-come-lately rivals.

The Westminster Bridge we enjoy today was built in 1862 by Thomas Page. It is coloured green to match the seats of the House of Commons. It is the oldest bridge existing bridge in Central London and has so far escaped the revenge of the old London Bridge. Time is a great healer.

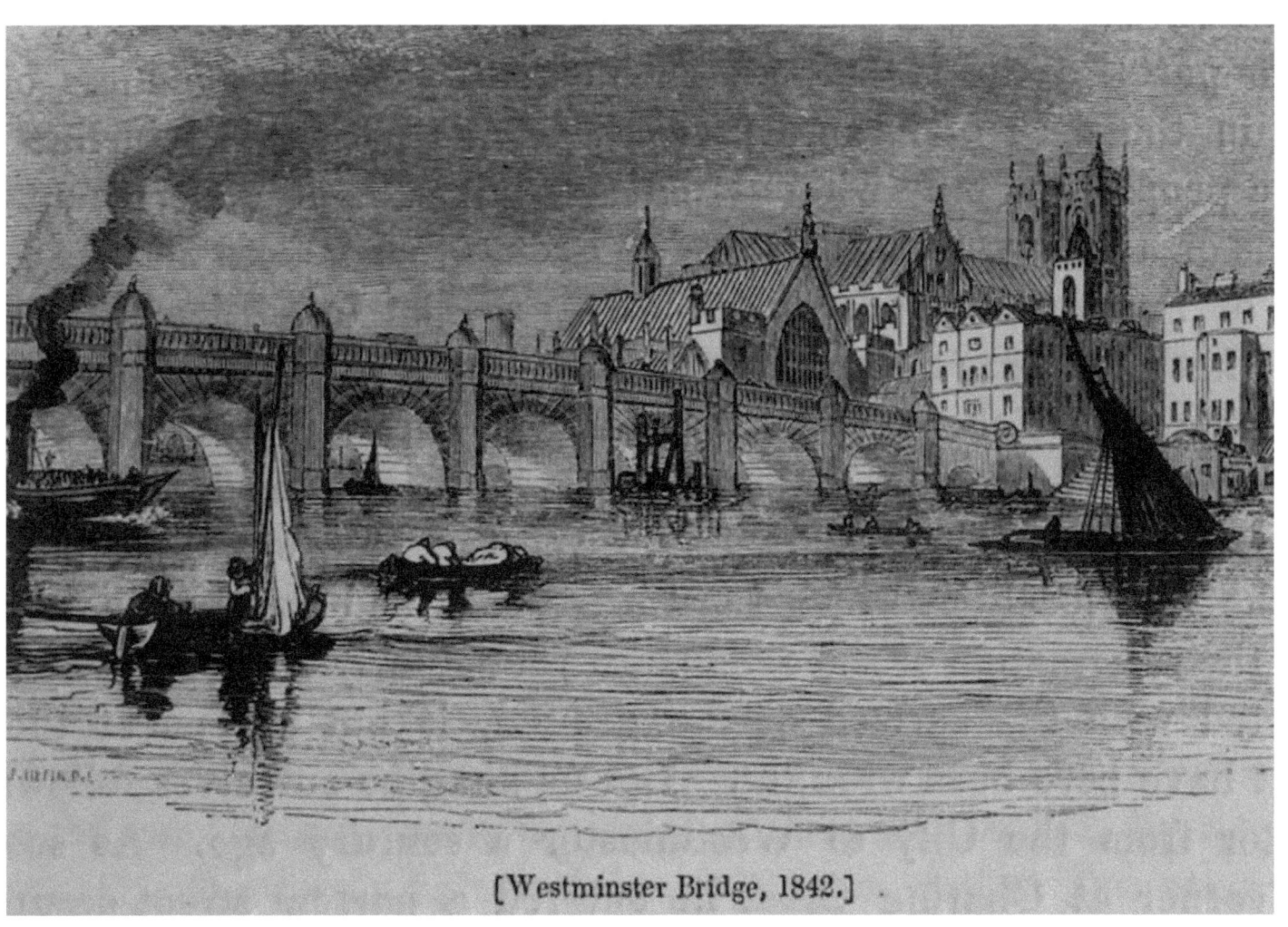

[Westminster Bridge, 1842.]

155: PALACES OF THE STRAND

In medieval times, if you looked across the Thames from near where the London Eye now stands, you would have seen an extraordinary sight: an unbroken battalion of overpowering buildings, palaces in all but name, stretching over three quarters of a mile from what is now Trafalgar Square to the site of today's Temple Station. They were occupied first by bishops, then by aristocrats.

Each one would need a book to do it justice. On the west, where Whitehall began, was Cardinal Wolsey's York House. Next to it was Suffolk House – later known as Northumberland House – followed by Durham House (home to Sir Walter Raleigh among others) Salisbury House, Worcester House, Savoy Palace, Somerset House and Arundel House.

Their gardens occupied the whole of the southern section of the Strand down to the river (which was nearer in those days, before the Embankment was built). Today, only Somerset House still stands, and that is a later re-construction, not the original. It does, though, give you an idea of the scale of these mansions. They were brazen displays of ostentatious wealth, often only yards away from some of the most deprived slums in the city.

There are few other remains, but they are impressive. The most fascinating is Cardinal Wolsey's wine cellar at York House, later appropriated by Henry VIII, which is buried in almost pristine condition in the bowels of the Ministry of Defence and is not open to the public (though I did once blag a visit). The only visible remnant of York House today is the Watergate, from which the Earl of Essex departed to be executed after his abortive attempt to foment a rebellion against Elizabeth I's government. It can be seen in all its glory in Embankment Gardens, by Embankment station.

Northumberland House was the last of the grand houses to be demolished, a necessary sacrifice to Joseph Bazalgette's sewer improvements. There's nothing left of it on site, but the famous lion that stood on top of the edifice still graces Syon House in Brentford, another family property. William Kent's gates can be seen at Bromley Health Centre, and part of one of the magnificent rooms is now in the Victoria and Albert museum.

Further along the Strand was the vast Savoy Palace, named after Peter, Count of Savoy, who was given it in 1246. It achieved notoriety when occupied by John of Gaunt, the younger son of Edward III, the richest man in England. His Palace lasted until the Peasants Revolt of 1381, when it was destroyed. A hospital was later built on the site, taking its name from the Savoy. This was demolished in the 19th century, and all that is left of it is its chapel – now

called the Queen's Chapel – whose medieval walls are still intact. They form the largest remains of the Strand palaces above ground. Some of the stones rescued from the hospital's demolition were recycled into the Royal Coburg Theatre (today's Old Vic), where they can still be seen.

Next along is Somerset House, where remnants of a late 17th century wall can be found at a side entrance to King's College, which occupies part of the site. That is the only free standing survival from the old palace, but even older ones lie under a glass floor in the archaeological department. They include a Tudor wall and a rubbish tip dating from when Saxons established the trading port of Lundenwic along the Strand.

Finally, Arundel House, which was granted in 1232 to the bishops of Bath and Wells, covered almost five acres, the largest site of all the Strand palaces, with a river frontage of an astonishing 150 metres. A modern day Arundel House reminds us of the extensive ruins excavated nearby.

The original was purchased in 1549 by the Earl of Arundel after the execution of its previous owner Thomas Seymour, brother of Lord Protector Seymour, who built Somerset House before he too was executed, prior its completion. There can be a downside to being very rich. Archaeologists uncovered extensive remains. A wall with stairs was found very close to Somerset House next door.

All of these houses have been lost, but numerous street names – from York Buildings to Arundel Street – preserve their memory.

156: MONTAGU HOUSE — ORIGINAL HOME OF THE BRITISH MUSEUM

The picture is of the British Museum. Not the one we know today, but its pioneering predecessor, Montagu House, which, for nearly 100 years, housed the amazing collections which three benefactors – Sir Hans Sloane, Sir Robert Cotton and the Earl of Oxford – gathered from around the world, creating a history of the planet in thousands of artefacts.

From its inception in 1753 the British Museum was dedicated to providing free access "to all studious and curious", though as late as 1836 the principal librarian defended closure of the museum at weekends "to keep out the more vulgar class, such as sailors from the dockyards and girls whom they might bring with them".

By a distance the grandest mansion in London of its time, Montagu House was sold by the second Duke of Montagu after he had moved to Whitehall. It was built on the site of an earlier Montagu House designed in 1675 by the polymath Robert Hooke who, when he wasn't arguing with Isaac Newton about the inverse square law, was mainly responsible for the design of the Monument and the Bedlam mental hospital.

Opened to the public in 1759, it was situated along Great Russell Street in exactly the same place as today's British Museum, only a few hundred yards from the house of Sloane, the most important of the three benefactors. His house was already a museum, albeit not open to the public, showcasing most of his collection of 70,000 books and manuscripts, not to mention an even bigger number of objects and plants from his herbarium. The other two founding benefactions came from Cotton's priceless medieval manuscripts (including the only copy of Beowulf), plus tens of thousands of books and manuscripts owned by the Earl.

The directors of the museum, meeting at the former Cockpit in Whitehall in the year the museum opened, turned down a number of alternative venues. These included what is now Buckingham Palace – too expensive at £30,000 and, would you believe it, considered to be in an inconvenient location – in favour of what was then a little-known mansion in Bloomsbury.

Neither the government nor the king, George II, was keen on the idea of such a museum. It only happened because Parliament – and all credit to it – took the matter into its own hands and passed a law in order to create it, which the reluctant George assented to. The museum quickly outgrew its original home. It was augmented with new buildings, and by 1845 the Montagu House part had been completely demolished. But the museum went on to become one of the wonders of the modern world, attracting over six million visitors a year to make it one of the top five museums on the planet in terms of visitors.

One of its lesser known features is that it actually contains remains of the original seven wonders of the world, including impressive parts of the Mausoleum at

Halicarnassus, the Temple of Artemis and a tiny bit of the Pyramids. If you believe recent research that the Hanging Gardens of Babylon were actually at Nineveh, that makes a fourth.

The origins of the British Museum also have a dark side, one that is slowly coming to light as Britain starts to come to terms with the consequences of the hideous slave trade. Sir Hans Sloane himself had first hand knowledge of slavery. In 1687 he sailed for Jamaica as physician to the colony's new Governor, the Duke of Albemarle and acted as surgeon in the plantations.

In 1695 he married Elizabeth Rose, widow of slave owner Fulke Rose, whose plantations brought substantial wealth, which greatly helped to finance Sloane's acquisitions. That is a different avenue of Lost London that we will be hearing a lot more about in future.

157: THE HERO AND THE VILLAIN OF KING CHARLES STREET

The effigy of the frightful Robert Clive at the end of King Charles Street, facing St James's Park, is a prime candidate for removal when Sadiq Khan's review of London's statues is completed. Clive's presence also provides one of three "names" in a street that is otherwise devoid of anything to distract from an unending vista of Whitehall stone. The second is that of the street itself, christened in honour of Charles II, who was the monarch when it was built in 1682. The third, unlike the other two, is easily missed.

It appears on a plaque above most people's line of sight on the wall of the Foreign Office. Similar in colour to the stone, it is so slight that it looks as though it might slip down at any moment. It refers to Ignatius Sancho, who escaped from a background of slavery to become a distinguished man of letters in 18th century England. Unlike Clive, he actually lived in the street. And there couldn't be anyone less like him.

At a time of mass illiteracy, Sancho educated himself to compose music and to write to an exceptional standard. He was the first black person to vote, thanks to his ownership of a shop in the street (its position is marked by the small yellow circle is in the photo). When his letters were published after his death – including an exchange with Laurence Stern, author of the hugely influential Tristram Shandy – they became best selling, attracting a distinguished list of subscribers, which included leading dukes, earls and duchesses, the Prime Minister, Lord North, and historian Edward Gibbon, author of the Decline and Fall of the Roman Empire. If such success had happened to a white working-class lad, it would have been extraordinary. For it to happen to a black slave at a time when Britain was still the leading slave-trading nation is almost unbelievable.

More than 250 years before Black Lives Matter, Sancho was feted as an example of what black people were capable of if only they were given a chance. He was one of a number of slaves who did well in Georgian London. Another was Oludah Equiano, who for a time lived locally and was baptised in nearby St Margaret's Church, where Sancho was married and where his children were baptised. Equiano wrote a riveting page-turner of a book about his experiences as a slave. It too became a best seller, read by the Prince Regent among others on a distinguished list of subscribers. Equiano, who had another name, Gustavus Vassa, given to him by a slave owner, soon became a leading light in the anti-slavery movement.

Sancho and his family lived above his shop thanks partly to a legacy given to him by the Duke of Montagu's family, which had encouraged his education. He sold groceries – including, ironically, products of the slave trade like sugar, tea and tobacco – and received distinguished visitors, such as Whig politician Charles Fox, who would stop by for a gossip. It is even possible that Clive visited, as he was often in the area. Sancho's neighbours were a motley collection of lower middle-class folk including victualers, bricklayers, sadlers, schoolmasters, bricklayers, surveyors and a "gentleman" or two.

The conclusion of all this is obvious. If the powers that be are looking for a new statue to replace that of Clive, what could be more appropriate than one of Sancho, who was actually a resident of King Charles Street. Or it could be of Sancho sitting back to back with Equiano. It is not known for certain if they actually met, though it would be curious if they hadn't, as they both attended local churches and were among the initiators of a movement which, over 250 years later, has yet to reach its goal.

158: THE HOUSE WHERE WILLIAM BLAKE LIVED

In 1918, number 13 Hercules Buildings in Lambeth was demolished. This was the house in which William Blake lived with his wife during what is regarded as his most productive period in the 1790s. It was here that he wrote works such as Visions of the Daughters of Albion, Songs of Innocence and of Experience and poems like The Tyger, and produced his famous prints, including of Isaac Newton and Nebuchadnezzar.

It appears he had his vision of the measuring compass – now memorialised in Eduardo Paolozzi's giant statue outside the British Library – on the stairs of his home. And it was here where, in his words, "We builded Jerusalem as a City & a Temple; from Lambeth We began our Foundations; lovely Lambeth!"

It was a clean house with about nine rooms, which housed Blake's printing press and working areas. People visiting in later years found the front door of the house nailed up and, after achieving entrance to its garden through the next door neighbour's passage, found it was overgrown with the vine and fig tree Blake often wrote about.

In those days, stepping out of the front door would have presented a semi-rural outlook. Today, there are dark railway arches resurrected with lovely mosaics of Blake's works. (see one superimposed on the old photo of the house opposite). Together, they create the sort of derelict atmosphere that Blake, a compulsive night walker, wrote about in one of his most famous poems:

I wander thro' each charter'd street,
Near where the charter'd Thames does flow.
And mark in every face I meet
Marks of weakness marks of woe.

It was at about the same time as Blake was in Lambeth that another poet called William – William Wordsworth – was rhapsodising about the view from Westminster Bridge. If he had turned the other way to face Lambeth Bridge the view would not have been so romantic. But then, unlike Blake, Wordsworth was not a Londoner.

Near Blake's house was a small road leading to the home of Philip Astley who ran a famous circus – claimed to be the world's first modern circus – on the southern side of Westminster Bridge. Apparently, Hercules Road was named after one of its long-lasting performers.

Also not far away, at the southern end of Blackfriars Bridge, was Albion Mills, built by the great engineer Matthew Bolton between 1783 and 1786 and powered by steam engines which physician Erasmus Darwin called "the most powerful machines in the world". Albion Mills was almost certainly the inspiration for Blake's "dark satanic mills". The mills caught fire in 1791, a spectacle that Blake would almost certainly have seen.

It is tragic that Blake's house was demolished at a time when conservation was not in vogue. But Blake himself would have been pleased that his poems – through the mosaics – still haunt the place that inspired them.

159: THE MEDIEVAL CITY OF VINEYARDS

If you could time travel back to medieval London you would be struck by three things then commonly seen in the centre of the city, but which have long since disappeared: monasteries, prisons and, especially, vineyards. London was awash with vineyards at that time. You could find them in Southwark, Westminster, Saint Giles, Bermondsey, East Smithfield, Holborn, Piccadilly (the Vine Street on Monopoly boards), St James's Park, the Tower of London and almost anywhere with a road containing the word "vine".

They were mainly owned by aristocrats, royalty and the church. The two most prominent were in Westminster and Holborn. Monasteries needed wine for communion and for the monks' pleasure, so it is no surprise that Westminster Abbey had one south of Tothill Street, near where the almonry was located – commemorated in the Peabody building in Abbey Orchard Street, as the photo shows – and another south of Great Peter Street between Horseferry Road and the Thames. There, eight acres of the Abbey vine garden were situated near another Vine Street, the old name of today's Romney Street. The St James's Park vineyard too was possibly owned by the Abbey.

How much wine was produced in those days and beyond? An awful lot if you believe the writer Thomas Pennant (1726-1798). He describes Lambeth as remarkable for the manufacture of English wines: "The genial banks of the Thames opposite to our capital yield almost every species of white wine; and by a wondrous magic, Messrs. Beaufoy here pour forth the materials for the rich Frontignac, destined to the more elegant tables, the Madeira, the Calcavella, and the

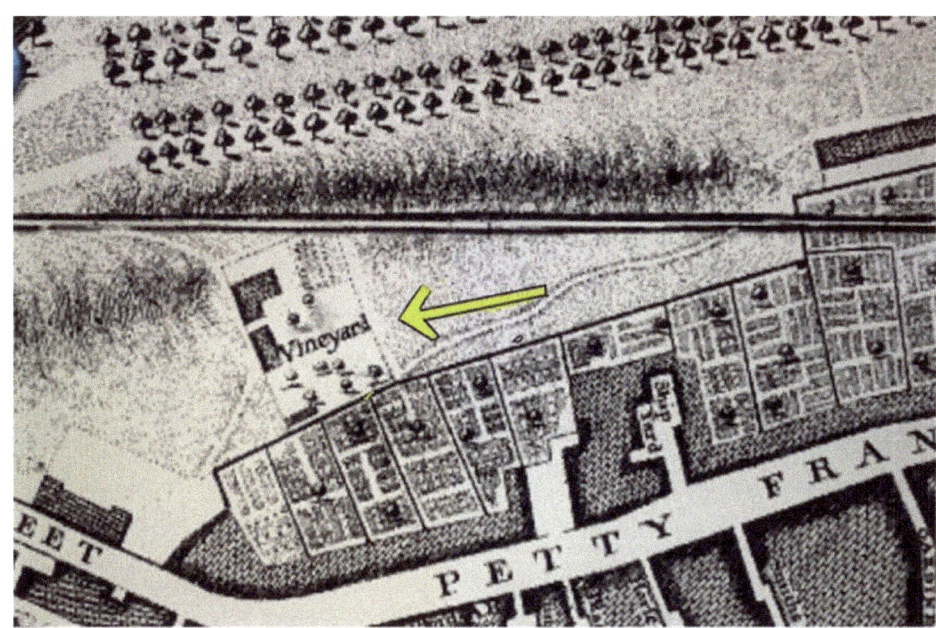

Lisbon, into every part of the kingdom." Pennant said that one of the "conservatories" contained 58,109 gallons of sweet wine, and added this astonishing claim: "It has been estimated that half of the port and five sixths of the white wines consumed in our capital, have been the produce of our home wine presses."

Holborn's main vineyard (there were several) was on land taken over from the Bishop of Ely by Sir Christopher Hatton (of Hatton Garden), one of Elizabeth I's favourites. It was reported to extend to seven acres. The first Blackfriars monastery (close by today's Holborn Viaduct) had a vineyard, as did St Mary's nunnery further up Farringdon Road by today's Vineyard Walk.

There was also a thriving bottling industry, which reached a high point in the 1660s when polymath Christopher Merrett, a member of the Royal Society – until he was kicked out for not paying his dues – recorded that London vintners were inducing a secondary fermentation in white wine bottles, thereby inventing what today we call the méthode champenoise. Yes, Londoners invented what we today call champagne decades before the French because their bottles, made from wood-fired rather than coal-fired furnaces, were so fragile they would explode under secondary fermentation.

The current boom in English sparkling wine is thus merely reviving a lost industry. London no longer has plentiful vineyards and probably won't ever again, despite the boost from global warming, if property prices remain high. However, there is one successful new vineyard in a London postal area. Forty Hall in Enfield has made the first sparkling wine from London grapes for centuries. The fruit has been turned into wine by a distinguished winery outside London (Davenports). But last year, Forty Hall sold some of its Bacchus grapes to Blackbook Winery in Battersea, one of four brand new London wineries, to produce the first totally London wine for a very long time. Few things in London are ever truly lost – they just return in different forms.

160: THE MONUMENTAL LEGACY OF ELEANOR COADE

A national conversation is brewing about who should be commemorated with statues other than white males with dubious military histories. In London, there is one rather special candidate with a unique qualification. Eleanor Coade was an extremely successful business person in the late 18th and early 19th centuries, when female entrepreneurs were extremely rare. Her products, 250 years on, can still be seen all over the capital and elsewhere in England and indeed around the world in almost pristine condition.

Coade made artificial stone for statues and artefacts to what was then a secret formula. Among her clients were the great architects of the day, Sir John Soane, Robert Adam, Sir William Chambers, Sir John Nash and James Wyatt. Once you see a few and get used to their appearance (clue: they last much better and longer than real stone) you come across them all over London. So what better memorial for Eleanor Coade than a statue of her made from her own Coade stone?

There is only one place where it should be erected: the Royal Festival Hall. It was on this very site that the Coade "manufactory" was located (map opposite), a timely reminder of how London's manufacturing base has been significantly replaced by the creative industries, now in deep trouble because of the Covid-19 virus.

Until a few years ago, one of the original stone mill wheels of the Coade factory (see photo) was given pride of place on the terrace outside the Festival Hall, but was removed. I suggested to them that they put it back, but nothing was done.

If you want to see a Coade statue, there is one only a few hundred yards from the original factory site – the huge lion standing on the south side of Westminster Bridge. It was made for the Lion brewery, which was situated between Westminster Bridge and the Coade works. Observe how well-preserved it is. Another lion made for the brewery is now at Twickenham rugby football ground.

Recently, a lot more interest has been shown in Coade stone, not least by the National Trust and English Heritage. It is amazing how so many of her artworks – many fashioned by the distinguished sculptor of the day John Bacon – have survived two-and-a-half centuries of inclement weather, including one of the biggest, a statue of Rowland Hill, who served under the Duke of Wellington. He stands 17 feet high on top of a column in Shrewsbury that is even higher and wider than that of Lord Nelson in Trafalgar Square.

The Landmark Trust has compiled a list of some of the more notable examples of Coade stone works, but there are plenty to be seen just by strolling through the streets of Georgian London. The most dramatic product of the manufactory was a very impressive ceramic relief of Nelson, measuring 40 feet long and ten feet high, for the Royal Naval Hospital at Greenwich, designed by Benjamin West, President of the Royal Academy (see photograph).

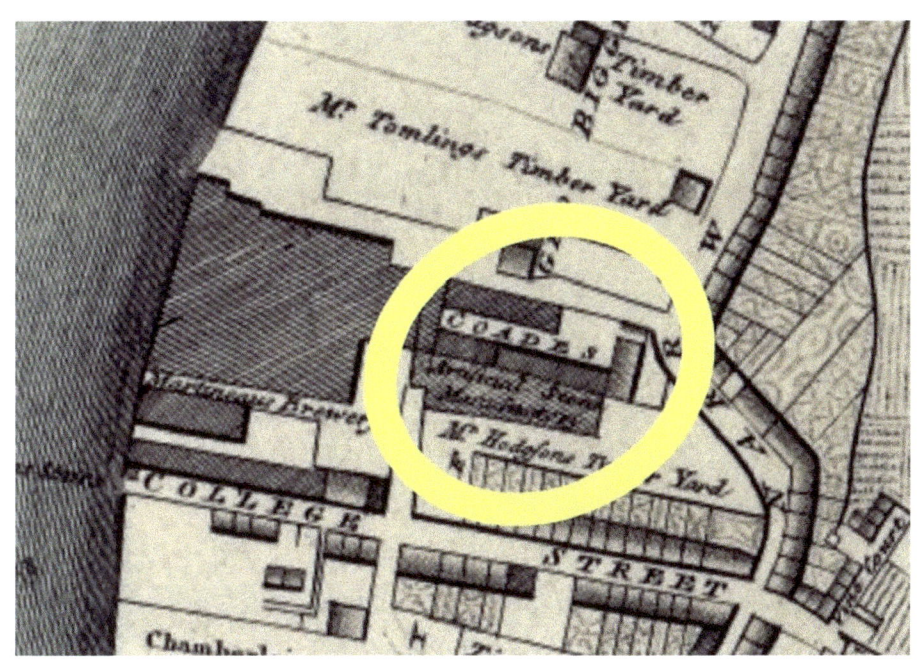

Eleanor Coade died in 1821 aged 88 (and was succeeded by her daughter, also called Eleanor). She is buried in an unknown grave in Bunhill Fields with no Coade stone to memorialise her. However, she is not far from her heritage. John Wesley, the preacher, who lived opposite, chose Coade stone in preference to Portland stone for a frieze above his door, running the width of the house.

ABOUT THE AUTHOR

Victor Keegan spent 40 years on The Guardian editing and writing about economics or consumer technology. He now mainly pens poems and explores the hidden history of London's buildings for his weekly column Lost London on the website OnLondon.co.uk from which this book is compiled.

He splits his time between relaxing in Herefordshire and tramping the streets of London looking for hidden stories to write about armed with his mobile phone for photographs. Victor has written six and a half poetry books and he is married to Rosie with two sons Dan and Chris.

Lightning Source UK Ltd.
Milton Keynes UK
UKHW051142280721
387854UK00002B/63

9 780954 076276